Wellington's Lieutenants

Duke of Wellington

Wellington's Lieutenants
The Campaigns & Battles
of 8 British Generals
During the Napoleonic Wars

Alexander Innes Shand

Wellington's Lieutenants
The Campaigns & Battles of 8 British Generals
During the Napoleonic Wars
by Alexander Innes Shand

First published under the title
Wellington's Lieutenants

Leonaur is an imprint of Oakpast Ltd

Copyright in this form © 2010 Oakpast Ltd

ISBN: 978-0-85706-397-7 (hardcover)
ISBN: 978-0-85706-398-4 (softcover)

http://www.leonaur.com

Publisher's Notes

The opinions of the authors represent a view of events in which he was a participant related from his own perspective, as such the text is relevant as an historical document.

The views expressed in this book are not necessarily those of the publisher.

Contents

Lord Hill	7
General Craufurd	69
Sir Thomas Picton	123
Marshal Beresford	160
Lord Lynedoch	195
The Earl of Hopetoun	226
The Marquis of Anglesey	245
Lord Combermere	259
Maps	287

Lord Hill

1

Among his lieutenants in the Peninsula there was none in whom Wellington reposed more absolute confidence than Rowland, Lord Viscount Hill. He was assured of his cool judgment, his imperturbable self-possession, his intuitive grasp of his superior's far-reaching plans, and of a self-abnegation altogether untainted by personal ambitions. In strong contrast to Craufurd, who was all fire and passionate impulse, though he could dare much on occasion he was never betrayed into imprudence; and unlike Picton and other warriors of a hard-swearing generation, he was so temperate of speech that a single occasion is recorded as noteworthy, when he was tempted to an ejaculation resembling an oath. Perhaps there was little merit in curbing a temper so absolutely under command.

With his squire-like seat on horseback and his phlegmatic face, he was familiarly known by the *sobriquet* of "Farmer Hill"; but the soldiers, who appreciated his kindly care for their comforts, affectionately translated "Farmer" into "Father." Wellington said, indeed, in the conversation with Lord Stanhope, that, like all his lieutenants, Hill shrank from responsibility, but when he said so, he must have forgotten Arroyos Molinos and Almarez. Hill was the only one of his generals to whom be confided independent and most important commands; undoubtedly, of all his comrades-in-arms, Hill was the man to whom he was most tenderly attached; and he gave proofs of his firm faith in his capacity and organising power, when he handed over to him the command of the army, with the title of General-Commander-in-Chief.

Rowland was the second son in a prolific household of sixteen. He was the scion of an ancient family, and his father was heir-presumptive to the Shropshire baronetcy, to which he succeeded. Those Hawkstone Hills were a martial race, and when England had caught fire at the French conflagration, five of the brothers went into the army. Moreover, there was variety of talent in the family, for his uncle and namesake was the Whitefield and famous field preacher of the Anglican Communion. Young Rowland gave no indication of the manner of the distinction he was to attain. He is said to have been a gentle, good-humoured, and almost stupid boy, who, like the "old madman" in *Tom Brown*, amused himself with hedge botany and the study of eccentric animals. As he shirked cricket and other boyish pursuits, it was only that good-nature of his which saved him from being sent to Coventry.

Certainly no one could have suspected that soldiering was his vocation. A girl playmate said that his sensibility was almost feminine. He shrank from the very sight of blood, and once fainted over a companion's cut finger. The incident was recalled to his recollection when he had come home after one of the bloodiest battles in the Peninsula, and was asked how he could support the sight of such horrible carnage. The answer was eminently suggestive of the man. "I have still," he replied, "the same feelings; but in the excitement of battle all individual sensation is lost sight of." It was a surprise to his parents, who had intended him for the law, when he insisted on following his elder brother into the army.

In 1790, at the age of eighteen, he was gazetted to the 38th Regiment. In those days the French were our acknowledged masters in everything military. Generations of discredit and decadence had gone by since the victories of Malplaquet and Blenheim. As Wellington studied the art of war at Brienne, Rowland obtained leave to study at Strasburg. A year afterwards, on his return, he was promoted to a lieutenancy in the 53rd, joining his new regiment, like Waverley, with a dozen stalwart recruits, enlisted on the ancestral estates. He had found his vocation, unlikely as it had seemed, and was set upon the determination of achieving success. Getting leave again, he went back to Strasburg, but this time his sojourn was cut short by storm-warnings. In the beginning of 1792 it became clear that Europe was verging towards a cataclysm.

But, though Hill was to play so conspicuous a part in the impending war, for years he was condemned to comparative inactivity; yet, reading between the lines of his life, we can see the evidences of latent ambition. When the war broke out in 1793, the young lieutenant had raised an independent company, and was rewarded with his captain's commission. His company, when handed over to the authorities at Chatham, was ordered to Cork, whence it was marched to Belfast, to be embodied in the 38th Regiment. He used to recall one amusing incident of his short stay in Ireland. He had gone on a visit to a brilliant literary man, distinguished for originality and eccentricity as for talent. Shown to his room, before dinner, he looked in vain for any washing apparatus. When his hand was on the bell, the floor opened, and a wash-hand stand, with everything from towels to hot water, rose into its place.

It was an adaptation of the *tables volantes* of the French *petites maisons*. He used to say he never was so much surprised, save when he saw an anticipation of the modern invention of a tramway bringing dishes from the kitchen to the dining-room. His stay in Ireland was short, for the ardent youth of deceptively apathetic aspect, had no mind to fritter away his opportunities in country quarters. He had made some mark at the Horse Guards, and, moreover, he had found a friend in Mr. Drake, who in July was appointed Minister-Plenipotentiary to the republic of Genoa, then trembling for its future between the French hammer and the Austrian anvil. Drake had instructions, besides, to accompany the English expedition to Toulon, and he nominated Hill his assistant secretary.

There is nothing more luridly dramatic in the annals of the long war than the tragedy of Toulon. For the horrors of the Moscow retreat fell in the way of professional work, on an army that had provoked ruthless reprisals. In the revolt of Southern France against the Terror, when the Girondists had fallen under the axes they had sharpened themselves, Toulon hoisted the white flag, and invited British protection. It was given in that grudging and inefficient fashion which marked every initiative of our operations. We had the chance of capturing the Mediterranean fleet of the French—thirty of their line-of-battle ships were lying in the harbour—and of seizing and holding their Mediterranean arsenal.

There were men of sense who saw that it was a golden opportunity, and there were experts who said that 40,000 or 50,000 men was the smallest strength with which Toulon could be defended. We landed a paltry force of 2000 Britons to stiffen foreign contingents, many of which were worthless. The admiral did all that could have been asked of his means, but matters were complicated further by the arrival of our Spanish allies, with their eternal *mañana* and their inflated pretensions.

Lord Hill

On land, among the British troops, all the talent was with the obscure subalterns, for among them were Hill and Beresford and the future Lord Lynedoch. Among the ships of the fleet was Nelson with the *Agamemnon*. But behind the French batteries, which were being pushed forward to the brows of the encircling heights, was the aspiring Corsican gunner, then barely twenty-five, who made the siege of Toulon his spring-board. Young Hill had his chances too, though poor in comparison, nor did he fail to make the most of them. He seems to have had no special interest, save the backing of the civilian Drake, and with the example of French Commissioners from the Convention before their eyes, civilians were regarded by our fighting men with somewhat contemptuous jealousy. But Hill acted as *aide-de-camp* successively to Lord Mulgrave, O'Hara, and Dundas. O'Hara was a brave and hot-headed Irishman, who had come from Gibraltar to assume command of the garrison.

On "the Rock" he has left his record behind him, in a grand reputation for hospitality, and a watch-tower which bore the name of "O'Hara's Folly." At Toulon, where skill and science had rare opportunities, his one idea was to repel force by force. Whenever the enemy broke ground he hurried forward to fight them, and to carry their advanced batteries by frontal attack. He was fast using up his gallant Britons, who, as Kinglake said of the Crimean *Zouaves*, were the sharpened point of his lance. These Britons never showed to more advantage than when they stormed the battery on the heights of the Arenas. They hunted the broken enemy before them in hot pursuit, to be involved in the laps of the rugged ground, and assailed on all sides by overwhelming numbers. Many were cut down, more were made prisoners, and among the rest O'Hara himself, who was, as always, well to the front.

His *aide-de-camp* was more fortunate, for he came out of the fray safe and with honour. It was owing to the coolness with which he conducted the retreat that he was selected to go home with despatches. In the sanguinary action he had a remarkable escape. He had climbed a tree to take observations of the enemy, when O'Hara called him down. Another *aide-de-camp*, who mounted to his place, was immediately killed. In after days, when the tide of naval and Peninsular victories had set in, the fortunate messenger from a Trafalgar or a Vittoria was the hero of the hour. He carried all the barriers of etiquette that guarded the convivial privacy of the Regent; his arrival was the signal for decorating London with flags and laurel, for kindling bonfires and letting off fireworks from Dover to Cape Wrath. He was sure of an immediate step, with fair prospects of future promotion. Hill's mission, though flattering, was a less agreeable one. His despatches announced that Toulon was untenable, and prepared the Government to break the news of an evacuation to the country.

The evacuation followed his departure in a few days, and he was spared those almost unexampled scenes of terror, in which the naval officers necessarily took the lead. The harbour of the port was the stage of an amphitheatre, which the French batteries were illuminating with incessant discharges from the surrounding heights. Shot, shell, and shrapnel tore through rigging and planks, lashing the surface of the harbour into showers of foam and spray. And all the time the miserable population, warned from their homes at a moment's notice, were very literally between the devil and the deep sea.

They had no mercy to expect from the Terrorists who superintended executions; their sole hope of refuge was the British fleet, and, in panic and desperation, women and children were scrambling for places in the overcrowded boats that were to convey them across the zone of fire. Nor were all the boats at their disposal by any means, for belated business had to be attended to. A naval contingent, under Sidney Smith, was doing its best to fire the French ships which should have strengthened the British navy, and the fall of blazing spars, with frequent explosions of magazines, added to the perils and horrors of the night.

At Toulon Captain Hill had attracted the notice of the future Lord Lynedoch, then simply known as the Laird of Balgowan, and serving as a volunteer—in the following year, 1794, "Colonel" Graham—who was raising his corps of Perthshire volunteers, afterwards the 90th Regiment. Graham, who was an excellent judge of soldierly qualities, remembered his Toulon acquaintance, and offered him the majority. It was gladly accepted, and three months afterwards Hill bought his step as lieutenant-colonel. Thus at three-and-twenty he was in command of a regiment; and of a regiment which, thanks to him, was destined to crown itself with glory in Egypt. Meantime, in common with other corps, it was the plaything of circumstances, and of a War Office that never knew its own mind from one month to another.

As our sailors made sure of victory, our soldiers expected to be baffled and were seldom disappointed. There were endless orders and counter-orders; marching and counter-marching; sailing away and sailing back. In the autumn of 1795 the 90th was with the expedition under General Doyle to Isle Dieu, off the coast of Poitou. The regiment remained in occupation of the island, when Hill, who was always devoted to field sports, and who used to supply Lord Lynedoch after his retirement with pointers from Shropshire, imported greyhounds for the use of the mess, and amused their leisure with coursing.

Brought back to Southampton, it was ordered to St. Domingo. Then it was counter-ordered to Gibraltar, where the colonel had warm welcome from his old chief O'Hara. For two years he was on garrison duty there, and with his regiment was at the descent on Minorca in 1798. From Minorca he obtained leave of absence, and while on leave, on New Year's Day, 1800, was gazetted brevet lieutenant-colonel At that time things were quiet in the West Mediterranean; he had left a capable substitute in command of the 90th, and, at the request of his old patron Drake, he applied for leave to accompany him on a diplomatic mission to Switzerland, intending to rejoin at Minorca after a tour in Italy.

Leave was readily granted, but he changed his plans when he heard that the regiment was to be sent on active service. He took passage on a troopship to Gibraltar, narrowly escaping a French fleet which had suddenly put to sea. Thence he sailed with a large convoy, sent in search of Sir Ralph Abercromby. The convoy missed Sir Ralph, who had gone over to Malta, but Hill found his regiment at Leghorn and returned with it to Minorca. He commanded it on the mismanaged descent on Cadiz, where neither the admiral nor the general, nor Moore, who was second in command, gained any credit by the ineffective demonstration. Hill, who was always of a weakly constitution, had a serious attack of illness, and when he returned to Gibraltar, was forbidden to eat anything but fresh meat. He complained afterwards that it was a costly regimen, for victualling the fleet for the Cadiz voyage had run up provisions to famine prices. Even in the memorable siege three guineas and a half for a turkey would have been considered extravagant. Fortunately he had the warm sympathy of his friend the Governor, whose habit was to keep open house for all comers.

These aimless expeditions and idle alarms were bad training for the troops. But the day was at hand when British soldiers were to be pitted in a fair field against the veteran French, and Abercromby's Egyptian campaign was to restore the *morale* of the army. The Government had entered on it with a light heart, but on the strength of information apparently reliable. The despatches of the French general had been intercepted; they had been written in the darkest pessimism, and if Kleber had intended to deceive he could not have done it more successfully. He described his forces as sick, disgusted, and demoralised, and he reduced their numbers by exactly a half. Abercromby had sailed with 16,000 men, expecting to deal with the same number of fever-stricken Frenchmen. He found himself confronting over 30,000 veterans, as fit to take the field as when Buonaparte deserted them, and holding the fortified harbours which forbade access to the interior.

How he effected his landing on the open beach, in face of a watchful foe and beneath a semicircle of armed batteries, is matter of history. Hill kept a diary which is brief as may be. The entry for 12th March 1801 is:

Attacked the French, defeated them and gained a glorious victory, was wounded and went on board the fleet.

As matter of fact, he and his regiment had the honours of the day. Abercromby was advancing on Alexandria and the French positions along a natural causeway—a mile and a half in breadth—between the sea and the lake. The 90th, in line, led the advance. General Brou with his *chasseurs-à-cheval* charged them furiously. There was no time to throw the regiment into square, and had it closed up to meet the cavalry shock, the passage would have been left open. Hill calmly halted his raw infantry, in the same thin red line that stemmed the Russian onset at Balaclava. Ordered to reserve their fire, they stood the impact like seasoned veterans. The *chasseurs* were met with a point-blank volley, which emptied saddles by the score, and the shattered ranks were received at the point of the bayonet.

The survivors of the crack corps rode back in dire confusion, and the 90th resumed its march. But their colonel saw no more of the fighting. Struck on the head by a ball—fortunately it did not come from a Lee-Metford carbine—he was partially saved by the peak of his helmet. He revived when borne back to the field-hospital, and there, a couple of days afterwards, he was cheered by a note from Lord Keith, dated from the flagship:—

Dear Hill,—I am happy to hear you are so well, and I think you will be more at ease here than where you are. . . . I will do all I can to make the ship comfortable to you.

Five days afterwards, as he lay in the *Foudroyant*, Abercromby was carried into the same cabin. There the old chief lingered for a week in agony, with intervals of delirium, knowing well that the end was near. Like Craufurd, he had a soldier's burial on the bastion of Fort St.

Elmo at Valetta.

While still confined to his berth Hill had a visit from the Capitan Pacha, who presented him with a sabre, a gold box, and a shawl, in recognition of the gallantry with which he had led his regiment. Very gratifying was the kind hospitality of the admiral, though Hill was used to friendly acts and kindly offices—perhaps there was a vein of undue gentleness in his martial temperament, for he is said seldom to have made an enemy, and never to have quarrelled with any man. But still more touching was the conduct of his servant whom he had left at Hawkstone. When the man heard his master was wounded, he insisted on starting for Egypt to join him, and at that time the Channel and Mediterranean were swarming with hostile cruisers and privateers.

The letters he brought from Hill's uncle and sisters are pleasantly suggestive. They are full of the little home-like details which the writers knew would cheer the invalid. There are messages from old servants, and mention of humble friends, and notably of the pheasants in the Hawkstone covers, and of the colonel's pet poultry. But long ere the letters had been delivered he was in the field again. In the middle of April 1802 he was in command of the camp at Hamed, and in the subsequent operations he played a conspicuous though subordinate part. Perhaps they have never received the attention they deserved, for they fired the martial spirit of the British linesman, depressed by a succession of disasters. The army had lost faith in its leaders, and it was the sullen determination of Hutchinson, supported by an iron will, which paved the way for the victories of Wellington.

He had succeeded to Abercromby; he had barely 11,000 soldiers at his disposal, supported by a horde of undisciplined Turks; there was no news of Baird, who was on his way from India; but what he knew was that the French in superior strength, with ample artillery, held the positions which were the keys of Lower Egypt. When he had left Coote with 6000 men to blockade Menou in Alexandria, he had only 5000 at his disposal for the advance upon Cairo, where Kleber with double that number had his headquarters. When the silent man, who had neither confidants on his staff nor friends among his officers, issued his orders for the march, there was something like a mutiny in the higher ranks.

It seemed to them as if a captain, either drunk or mad, was steering his ship upon reefs and breakers. For once British regimental officers signed a round robin, inviting the chief's lieutenants to assume the command. Happily Moore and Coote, whatever their private opinions, had sounder ideas of discipline, and Hill with the other generals of brigade lent them loyal support. The venture was rash, but the results, which were astounding, justified the general's self-confidence. There was a striking example of the unexpected in war, when 5000 French veterans were broken before the rush of the Turks. Cairo capitulated, Alexandria followed suit, and then was seen the inconceivable spectacle of 8000 Frenchmen, retaining their arms and followed by their batteries, marching in peaceful submission to the coast, under the escort of half their number of Britons.

The memory of those days of glory and triumph had far-reaching results. The regiment returned home and was ordered to Fort George to be disbanded. But with the *coup d'état* of Brumaire the hopes of an enduring peace were doomed to disappointment. With Buonaparte wearing the purple of the Consulate, it was no time to reduce our military strength, and the 90th, having replenished its ranks, was despatched to Ireland. Ireland was the object of immediate interest, alike to Buonaparte and to the British Cabinet. Three-fourths of the island was seething with disaffection, and the French believed that if they once established a footing there, a revolted province might be their base of operations against England.

French squadrons which had eluded our blockades were continually on the Irish seas, and our frigates were keeping a watchful guard to intimate the landing of some flying expedition. It was in these circumstances, and in August 1803, that Colonel Hill was appointed a Brigadier-General on the Staff. He parted from his comrades-in-arms with great mutual regret. The officers issued an address, saying that the renown so rapidly acquired in the brief regimental existence was entirely due to the discipline the colonel had established and maintained. They added that the discipline had been so tempered with mildness as to endear him to every individual in the regiment.

The Bay of Galway was as likely a place as the Bay of Bantry for a descent. The new brigadier-general was stationed at Loughrea, in command of some light infantry of the Irish militia, and with supervision of all the western coast. There was the same false economy which nearly proved fatal in Spain. Irish affairs were miserably mismanaged by the Horse Guards. The Galway volunteers broke into mutiny, simply because their pay was long in arrear. It was a reason with which Hill could sympathise, for he had the utmost difficulty in wringing money from headquarters, not only for his own pay and allowances, but for each extra piece of service which was ordered or urgent. He settled the matter with his characteristic blending of the mild with the firm.

He had the mutineers tried by a Court of Yeomanry Captains, who were instructed to investigate the justice of the complaints. In forwarding the report to Sir Eyre Coote, while acknowledging that the men had undeniable grievances, he said their conduct was none the less reprehensible, and added that though he believed in their penitence he hesitated to restore their arms. Sir Eyre took a merciful view of the case, and the ringleaders who had been in temporary confinement were released; but Hill had established his reputation as a disciplinarian. Shortly afterwards he was able to report that all the militiamen and volunteers under his command were animated by a loyal and soldierlike spirit.

He studied the possible *kriegspiel* from all the points of view of a general who might have to face an enemy landing anywhere. He visited all the places where a descent could be conceivably effected. He surveyed all the passes leading inland, decided on the positions where an advance could be most effectively opposed, and arranged for the prompt destruction of the bridges on the roads that were practicable for the passage of artillery in that wild country. With a disaffected peasantry an enemy might have landed and marched far into the bowels of the land, without intimation reaching Loughrea or any quarter of the British garrison.

Consequently he arranged a system of signalling which, as he wrote to Sir Eyre Coote, could communicate minute information with profound secrecy. Between Loughrea and Galway he established a line of semaphores, and no little trouble he had—strange as it may appear—in persuading the landowners to consent to the erection of those telegraphs. For the squires and even the "Shoneens" were Protestant for the most part and had no sympathy with the French. There is a curious letter of his to "Dick Martin" of Ballynahinch, who owned half Connemara. It shows that Hill had surveyed those unexplored wastes more carefully than any land surveyor, and gives the most detailed instructions as to what ought to be done in the event of a French column marching upon Oughterard.

During the first period of his Irish duties he was incessantly haunted by the reasonable expectation of invasion. During the second, he could dismiss that apprehension, for, though Austerlitz had been lost, Trafalgar had been won. In the interval came the interlude to which we have alluded, when in command of a brigade he sailed from Cork to take part in another of our luckless continental expeditions. The troops reached the Weser, only to re-embark when they heard that Buonaparte was carrying all before him. Luckless the expedition was from the first, for Hill wrote home, when he was keeping a cold Christmas, that when he reached the river the headquarters ship of each regiment attached to him was missing: "some were wrecked on the Dutch coast, and many souls perished on the Goodwin Sands." But that hopeless expedition was fortunate for him, for it was then he made the acquaintance and won the appreciation of Sir Arthur Wellesley. They had met first at Deal, when the Cork transports touched there: for Sir Arthur was in command of another of the brigades.

2

In June 1808 came a note from Sir Arthur:—

> My dear Hill,—I rejoice exceedingly at the prospect I have before me of serving again with you, and I hope we shall have more to do than we had on the last occasion on which we were together.

The hope was fulfilled. Ministers had at last decided to strike at Napoleon through Portugal, and Sir Arthur—he had scarcely sailed before he was superseded—was selected as the fitting man for command. But vacillation and the policy of penny-wisdom were still in the ascendant. The 30,000 men destined for the army of Portugal were scattered for the most part in camps on the Channel and in the eastern counties, or in fleets between Cherbourg and Cadiz. As Napier says, the only force available for immediate operations was the 9000 in Irish garrisons who mustered at Cork under Hill. Even at Cork there were delays which tried Sir Arthur's patience: but till his arrival Hill took the utmost care of his men, landing them regularly for service and supplying them with fresh provisions.

By the way, among the 9000 there were no fewer than 227 drummers, reminding us of Ayton's metrical romance of the Fairshon's feud with the M'Tavish. They sailed at last on July 12, but next day Sir Arthur quitted the convoy in a fast-sailing frigate for Corunna, whither he went to consult with the Asturian deputies, whose importunity had set our slow machinery in motion. General Hill reported good progress to Lord Castlereagh from the *Donegal* at sea; for a marvel, none of the transports were missing and the troops were in perfect health. When Sir Arthur came on board the *Donegal* at the appointed place of meeting, he had settled his plans. Junot held the south. Bessières was threatening the northern provinces; but he decided on disembarking at the mouth of the Mondego and marching straight upon Lisbon.

While off the river he had the unwelcome news of his being superseded: it only excited him to more strenuous effort, for it was everything to take the enemy by surprise. On August 1 he began landing his 9000, and on the 5th, before the disembarkation was completed, he was happily reinforced by General Spencer from Cadiz, bringing 3000 more. With these feeble means, with the Atlantic rollers behind, breaking on a rock-bound and harbourless coast, the first campaign in Portugal was begun.

In their first meeting with the French the British had the best, for though Junot had early information he had to concentrate his scattered troops. Yet his able lieutenant, Laborde, though inferior in strength by a third, had the advantage of formidable positions. On August 16 he occupied the lofty plateau which took its name from the village of Roliça, and commanded the steep and narrow valley through which the main road led to the south. He had covered the heights with detachments, and in case of reverse he had a second line of hills to fall back upon.

On the morning of the 19th he was assailed in three columns. Hill, supported by cavalry and covered by the spluttering fire of a cloud of skirmishers, led the attack to the right of the road and pushed it fiercely. Hard pressed at all points and with both his flanks menaced, Laborde extricated himself with admirable skill, and, covered by his cavalry, retired on his second position. That involved new dispositions on the part of the British. Generals Hill and Nightingale were ordered to a full frontal attack on those frowning heights of Zambugeera. It was a trying experience for entering young troops who had never before fired a shot in anger.

The only approaches to the precipitous faces were by foot tracks through rugged gullies. The columns, preceded by the skirmishers, involuntarily deployed, in inevitable disorder, as they worked their way through the tangled shrubbery that clothed the bottom of the rocks. Neither general spared himself: the defence was as obstinate as the assault was determined, but Laborde saw his left and centre forced back by irresistible pressure. Looking vainly for Loison, who should have been coming up from the east, he held tenaciously on to his right, till there too he was compelled to retreat. After an obstinate defence that did him as much honour as a victory, he left the road to Torres Vedras open, abandoning three of his guns. Rifleman Harris, from the private's point of view, gives a graphic account of the fierce fighting on the 17th, and of Hill's composure at the critical moment.

> The 29th Regiment received so terrible a fire that I saw the right wing almost annihilated, and the colonel (I think his name was Lennox) lay sprawling among the rest We had ourselves caught it pretty handsomely, for there was no cover for us and we were rather too near. The living skirmishers were lying beside heaps of their own dead, but still we held our own till the battalion regiments came up. 'Fire and retire!' is a very good sound, but the Rifles were not fond of such notes.... At the moment a little confusion appeared in the ranks, I thought. Lord Hill was near at hand and saw it, and I observed him come galloping up. He put himself at the head of the regiment and restored it to order in a moment. Pouring a regular and sharp fire upon the enemy, he galled them in return, and remaining with the 29th till he brought them to the charge, quickly sent the foe to the right about. It seemed to me that few men could have conducted the business with more coolness and quickness of manner under such a storm of balls as he was exposed to. Indeed I have never forgotten him from that day.

It was not his first meeting with the general. The day before the battle he says:—

> We were pelting along through the streets of a village, the name of which I do not think I ever knew. I was in the front and had just cleared the village when I recollect observing General Hill (afterwards Lord Hill) and another officer ride up to a house and give their horses to some of the soldiery to hold... I stood leaning upon my rifle, near the door, when the officer who had entered with Lord Hill came and called to me. 'Rifleman,' handing me a dollar, 'go and try if you can get some wine, for we are devilish thirsty here.

> Harris hurried off for the wine, and when he brought it, found General Hill loosening his sword belt "'Drink first, rifleman,' said he, and I took a good pull at the pipkin and held it to him again. He looked at it and told me I might drink it all, for it appeared rather greasy." Harris honestly handed back the dollar, for in his haste and the bustle he had not paid for the wine. "Keep the money, my man," said

Hill, giving a second dollar. "Go back and try if you cannot get me another draught." That was "Father Hill" all over, with the consideration, affability, and free-handedness that won the hearts of his men.

On the 19th the army fought again at Vimiero, but there Hill was merely a spectator. The village was in a valley, overlooked by a mountain dominating a little eminence to the south-east which was the key of the British defence. For it was Junot who took the initiative and advanced to the attack. Again it was a battlefield of wood and rock and of the vineyard enclosures surrounding Vimiero. The French assault was delivered in three columns. Hill's brigade remained on the slope of the mountain: in immediate support of the centre and a reserve for the whole army. It was never called into action. The central attack failed; the battle was over early in the afternoon, and Wellesley, when assured that the enemy had made his last effort, had all in readiness for changing defeat into disaster.

General Ferguson, having repelled a bold flanking movement on our right, was driving Solignac's broken column before him. Wellesley, who with half his forces had beaten Junot, meant to follow with that half in hot pursuit: while Hill, Fane, and Anstruther with the other, taking the road by the sea to Torres Vedras, were to turn the mountain ranges and cut the French retreat upon Lisbon. But Ferguson was recalled, to his intense disgust, which meant that the impending change of command had been accomplished. Burrard had come up in time to see a part of the action, but had generously left the finishing of the work to Sir Arthur. Now he had taken over the reins, and decided that it would be prudent to remain on the defensive, awaiting Moore with the reinforcements which were known to be off the coast. Then followed the convention, miscalled, of Cintra, which provoked a storm of indignation. The three commanders—for Sir Hew Dalrymple within twenty-four hours had in turn superseded Burrard—were recalled to England to give evidence before the Court of Inquiry.

Moore succeeded to the command of a nominal force of 30,000 foot and 4000 horse. For the calculations were on the imaginary strength of depleted battalions in Portugal, and the contingent of 10,000 under Baird was still at sea. His instructions were to make a diversion in Spain, in favour of the Spanish armies, when the Emperor was in the Peninsula in person, with 180,000 foot and 40,000 horsemen, all disposable, without drawing upon his fortresses or endangering communications. Nevertheless, Moore proceeded to obey orders, and there is no reproaching him with lack of audacity. The rather that he was not of a hopeful spirit, and fully realised the difficulties.

For sound reasons he decided to march towards Madrid by way of Almeida and Ciudad Rodrigo. The direct road from Lisbon lay through mountainous country, and he was informed that it was impracticable for guns. He discovered to his regret that the information was false; meantime he had reluctantly violated a fundamental rule of war, and separated from his field batteries. They were committed to the charge of Sir John Hope, who was to follow the easier and more southerly route to Talavera, and thence crossing the Guadarama Sierra, to rejoin his commander at Salamanca. Hill with the 1st Brigade was a part of Hope's column. They had no fighting, but much hardship and infinite anxiety. From want of supplies and of money to buy them, the small force was broken up in six divisions, each separated by a long day's march.

Hope concentrated at the Escorial beneath the Guadarama, but, having gone to Madrid to interview the Spanish statesmen, he came back with the conviction that nothing was to be hoped from them and that he most look to his own safety. It was high time—he was enveloped by the French, and the 4th Corps in particular seemed to be omnipresent. He dragged his guns and waggons over the mountain, saving them on the northern side by the skin of his teeth. Moore had the guns and ammunition again, of which he had well nigh despaired, and Hope and his generals of brigade had saved the army.

For Hope had reached Salamanca on the eve of the retreat, inevitable after the disaster of Tudela, when Lannes scattered the levies of Castaños and Palafox. We hear little of Hill between Salamanca and Corunna. He played no such sensational part as Paget or Craufurd, who held the pursuers in check and broke down the bridges. But at Corunna he had his share of the glory. Napier, who is not given to exaggeration, describes the situation as dangerous but not desperate. The problem was to win a battle under every disadvantage, and to embark the victors in a crowded harbour, in face of an enemy formidably superior in numbers and covering the heights with heavy artillery. The fighting was very fairly distributed among the 14,000 march-worn soldiers who held the inner amphitheatre of hills.

Hope's division was on the extreme left, resting on the tidal estuary of the Mero, and taking the offensive when Foy's successive attacks had failed, it flung him back in hopeless disorder. The fall of night put an end to the action, but enough had been done for honour and safety. Moore had been laid in a rough coffin, awaiting burial at daybreak: torches were flitting about the field, where ambulance men were seeking to succour the wounded: and a circle of picket fires marked the sweep of the British lines. Soult could believe that he would have another opportunity on the morrow. Then Hope, who had succeeded to the command, set about the embarkation. The great powder magazines had been exploded in the morning: the jaded and foundered cavalry horses had been shot: the heavy guns had been sent on board the transports.

Now shipping the men went swiftly and silently forward, and with the dawn, when the French realised that our pickets had been withdrawn, the only English left on shore were Hill's brigade, who, having covered the embarkation from beneath the ramparts, were in occupation of the citadel. The brigade was quickly embarked in turn, when the bulk of the transports had cleared out of the harbour, though the French had pushed forward a battery which caused considerable confusion in the fleet. Nevertheless Beresford, with the rear-guard, kept possession of the citadel till the last of the wounded were placed in safety.

3

Napoleon's marshals had carried out his orders. They had driven the English into the sea, victorious but discomfited. His admirably devised plan of garrisoning Spain was in full operation; with Madrid for a centre, his disciplined legions in their irresistible superiority were everywhere scientifically disposed so as to crush any serious efforts at resistance. In every engagement the Spaniards had been routed and their levies dispersed. The fall of Saragossa, after a heroic defence, had set Lannes with his 25,000 at liberty. The final subjugation of Portugal seemed assured. Victor in Estremadura was menacing Badajoz; Lapisse in Castile was threatening Ciudad Rodrigo; Soult had peremptory orders to bear down upon the north and seize the great commercial capital of Oporto. The only adverse circumstances were the invincible jealousies of the generals and the condition of Soult's army.

It had been worn out, in strength and spirit, shoes, arms, and clothing, in the hot pursuit of Moore through the highlands of Gallicia. Cradock had been left at Lisbon, in command of the feeble rearguard, and his position was well nigh desperate. He had barely 10,000 British troops, and in the reasonable fear of being abandoned to their fate the violence of Portuguese factions had come to a head. He had so little hope of help from home that there were secret instructions to embark his men in case of necessity, bringing the Portuguese fleet and the contents of the arsenals away with him. Insufficient justice has been done to his constancy, coolness, and military skill. He held tenaciously to his forlorn charge, while taking every precaution against the worst, and his masterly preparations for the defence of Lisbon had anticipated Torres Vedras on a smaller scale. But, at the moment when evacuation seemed imminent, events took a sudden turn.

In the English Cabinet a hot fit had succeeded to the cold, and it was decided that Portugal was not to be abandoned. The immediate despatch of strong reinforcements was commenced: the good news brought a revulsion of feeling with the Portuguese; they volunteered to call out all their levies—ban and *arrière-ban*—and offered the command to an Englishman. Beresford landed at Lisbon, to be gazetted a Portuguese marshal, and proceeded to lick his excellent raw material into shape. But a greater actor was to appear on the scene, for Wellesley superseded Cradock.

Cradock had cause to complain, yet the wisdom of the choice was abundantly justified. Sir Arthur came with the prestige of his former victories, and the patriotism of the desponding Portuguese was warmed to fever heat. They hopefully worshipped the rising star, and prepared themselves for hard times and heavy sacrifices. Moreover, the new general had come with solid pledges of support, for with other troops he brought four regiments of cavalry, and hitherto in cavalry we had been lamentably deficient. Nor did he come a day too soon, for the outlook on all sides had become darker than ever. The Spaniards, thoroughly beaten before, had rashly provoked fresh disasters. Cuesta had been routed at Medellin, and the army of La Mancha had been scattered at Ciudad Beal.

Soult was not only established at Oporto, but by a liberal policy he was said to be conciliating influential *fidalgos* and citizens. Now that Victor had for the time disposed of Cuesta, the road to Lisbon lay comparatively open. But Victor was still obstructed by the frontier fortresses and the barrier of the flooded Tagus. Sir Arthur was in a strait between two decisions, with a confusion of interested counsellors; but he never made more conspicuous display of the daring strategy and imperturbable self-confidence which were invariably tempered by prescience. He came to the conclusion that the more pressing necessity was to rid the northern provinces of the French, which would at the same time liberate Gallicia. There was peril either way, but he decided that there was time to deal with Soult without serious danger from Victor.

Soult, dazzled by visions of a Portuguese crown, had cast longing looks at Lisbon. He commanded all the passages of the Douro; his light cavalry held the fords and bridges of the Vouga; but his further march had been arrested by the prospect of flooded rivers and formidable defiles. Sir Arthur's advance would be so far without military impediment, but when he had negotiated the floods and dragged his guns through the nearer gorges, he would find the enemy on the line of the Vouga, and in occupation of the farther passes. Beyond these was a virtually impregnable position, girdled by the broad and rapid Douro.

Soult might well, to all appearance, have deemed himself secure, and the English general seemed to be courting disaster. But Soult, though fearing nothing from surprise or direct assault, had realised that his position was untenable, and was contemplating retreat on Salamanca. He was being threatened from behind by Spanish and Portuguese partisans; his line of retreat was being menaced by Silviera; and, as Wellesley learned, when concentrating at Coimbra, the marshal was the object of a formidable conspiracy and was being betrayed by the men he most implicitly trusted. Both knew that the evacuation of Oporto was a foregone conclusion; and had Wellesley waited, as the more cautious Cradock would have done, we should never have heard of the "Passage of the Douro."

But time was still of supreme importance. If Wellesley struck fast and hard, Soult's precipitate retreat would result in an immense disaster, and the moral effect would be great. Moreover, if Soult, a master of orderly retiring, took men and guns and military train safe to Salamanca, he would be more formidable than at Oporto: if he were driven over the mountains into Gallicia, he need not be counted with for many weeks to come. And when the plan of operation had once been settled, and when Beresford in relatively slender strength was to be thrown across the Salamanca route, accelerated action became imperative.

The army moved forward from Coimbra in three lines. The main advance took the direct road to Oporto. On the right Beresford's Portuguese, stiffened by two British battalions, marched upon Lamego. The 3rd Division under Hill was to follow the coast road and turn the extreme right of the French, which rested on the Lake of Ovar. Sir Arthur had learned that that long sheet of water—open to the flow and ebb of the tides—had been left unguarded. Accordingly he had arranged an unpleasant surprise for Franceschi, the Craufurd of the French outposts, the dashing leader of light cavalry; and a letter written to Hill on the 8th shows his minute attention to details he might well have confided to subordinates. He tells Hill that he will find a flotilla of boats awaiting him at the foot of the lake, that Colonel Douglas had orders to look up the boatmen, and he recommends the general to cook a day's provisions at Aveiro, and to see that the men had a full meal at Ovar.

As such careful foresight deserved, all went well to Ovar. The Portuguese fishermen toiled at the oars with zealous patriotism, scaring clouds of waterfowl and sea-birds from solitudes within sound of the ocean surf; and the flotilla, timed to reach Ovar at daybreak, had to lie off in the dusk before disembarking. Hill had turned the right of the French, as Beresford by that time had turned the left, and it was only owing to one of the accidents of war that Franceschi with his horse and Mermet with the supporting infantry were not caught in the toils so carefully spread for them. But Franceschi proved himself an apt pupil of Soult in the art of extricating himself from situations threatening destruction.

As it was, he probably owed his safety to Sir Arthur's peremptory orders and Hill's too docile obedience. On the 10th, surrounded as he was by the English forces, he led his horsemen across Hill's front, and led them with impunity. The impetuous Craufurd would certainly have attacked, and if a Nelson had been in command of the division he would assuredly have disobeyed orders. But Hill with sublime self-restraint let the enemy and the opportunity go by. In his implicit loyalty to his chief he refused by a personal success to risk upsetting a complex scheme of operations, and as he knew nothing of the strength of the French supports, even a victorious advance might have sacrificed his division. The decision is characteristic of his temperament: but, when the Duke of Wellington spoke of him afterwards as shirking responsibility, it would be interesting to know whether the inaction at Ovar was in his mind.

That he did not always shrink from responsibility was to be shown at Almarez, and no one ever charged him with lack of spirit. On the 12th, at the memorable passage of the Douro, he was to give his proofs, if fresh proofs were needed. Franceschi and Mermet had crossed the Douro in the night, breaking down the only bridge behind them. Soult believed he had secured every boat on his own side of the river. He had already been sending off his guns and baggage: but, knowing nothing of the rough handling of Loison by Beresford, he decided to delay his march for another day, that that general might draw in his detachments. He might well believe that there was no need to hurry. The broad river was rolling by in angry flood, and his absolute confidence in the impassable barrier was his undoing. His own quarters were in the west end of the city, and all his attention was given to the lower river, for he believed that Hill's division had come by sea and that the ships could be used for crossing at the estuary.

Above the bridge in the centre of the city the Douro makes a sharp bend, and the bend is commanded by the convent-crowned heights of Sarco. Behind those heights Sir Arthur had concentrated his main force, and it was effectually masked. He had detached General Murray to cross at Avintas, three miles higher up, and both Murray and Beresford were in danger if the river were not passed that morning. It is doubtful whether the problem would have been solved had it not been for a happy chance. A barber gave Oporto to Sir Arthur, as a pedlar saved Soult from capitulating. Eluding the vigilance of the sentinels, the barber had brought a skiff across.

Surveying the situation from the convent, Sir Arthur had seen that the sweep of the river was unguarded, though in the distance, through clouds of dust, columns in retreat were to be distinguished. Beneath him, on the opposite bank, was an unfinished building, which seemed designed by Providence for a *tête de pont*. It would offer shelter for a considerable force, and to the west was an open space which could be swept by musketry. If the head of a column were lodged there, the rest would be comparatively simple. There was the little skiff, and Colonel Waters, famed for many daring exploits, volunteered to go with the barber on a quest for boats. The Prior of Amaranta made a third in the party.

The adventurers, successful beyond hope, brought back some barges in tow. "Let the men embark" was the curt order when someone suggested difficulties. Some troops of Paget's and Hill's divisions were cautiously advanced to the bank. One officer and twenty-five men of the Buffs were the first to land. Boat-load after boat-load was ferried over before the garrison took the alarm. Then there was the roll of drums, beating to quarters, and a confused noise of shouting as regiments rushed to arms. A mixed multitude passed out of the city, and throwing out swarms of skirmishers, came surging up to the walls of the seminary. The fire swept the walls and searched the loopholes. Paget, who was among the first to cross, was one of the first to fall.

Hill took his place in directing the defence. By this time the enemy had brought cannon into play, but their fire was kept down by the British batteries on the height, and these swept the exposed *terre pleine* in such deadly fashion that the assault on the seminary was confined to a single side. Still the assault was so sustained, and the situation so critical, that, as Napier says, "Sir Arthur would himself have crossed, but for the earnest representations of those about him and the just confidence he had in General Hill."

Already, as he was hesitating, the crisis had gone by. The citizens were signalling from roofs and windows that the enemy had abandoned the lower town, and already they were bringing over many boats that the evacuation had released from embargo. Sherbrooke, near the broken bridge, was busy embarking his battalions. Murray's division was seen descending the opposite bank: and again, beyond the seminary through the clouds of dust, other columns were seen retreating. They were not suffered to pass unmolested, for Hill, pushing forward to the enclosure walls, kept pouring in a steady fire. He could not venture to quit his cover, for with him were only three regiments, and one of these was Portuguese. But all the time the army was crossing: Sherbrooke, with the guards, as he gathered additional strength, was pressing hard on the rear of the enemy, while shell and shot were being showered on them from the guns on the crest of Sarco. Confusion and panic would have been changed to utter rout had Murray's division been handled by Hill or Craufurd.

Hill kept up regular correspondence with a favourite sister. Nothing can be more modest than the descriptions of his own doings, and we may add that his letters of that period show that even generals of division were little in the confidence of the commander-in-chief. Sir Arthur kept his own counsel, and in the campaigns of the Douro and Talavera, Hill can only hazard surmises as to what may happen next. Modest as he was, he felt he owed it to his family that he should have his fair share of commendation. He resented Lord Castlereagh's public comments on Sir Arthur's hurried despatch on the passage of the Douro, and he wrote:

> No officer is more deserving of praise than General Paget; but he was wounded so very early in the business that he was not present when the serious attacks were made, which indeed did not take place till after the greater part of the 66th and 48th had come up, although Lord Castlereagh would wish it to be understood that General Paget and the Buffs resisted the whole

French army.

Hill, though generous, was only human: it may have been the undue credit attributed by Castlereagh to the Buffs which inspired a rather spiteful remark on the eve of Talavera.

The soldier still interested in his poultry and pheasantries at Hawkstone had not been parted from all his pets. As he asks anxiously after the kennels and the chicken coops, so even in the swing of rapid movements he reports on Dido, his spaniel bitch, which had been confined during the advance to the Douro, and his brother Clement, who was one of his *aides-de-camp*, writes:

> I must tell you how careful Dido is of her family. Two of them have been brought in a basket, and the other morning, when the baggage was going off, she went upstairs by herself, and brought the basket in her mouth for the puppies to be put in.

Marshal Beresford, a *connoisseur* in wines and *cuisine*, was noted for keeping the best table in the Peninsula. He had his French *chef* with a *batterie de cuisine* in his baggage. But if we may take Hill's own word for it, though hospitable to excess, he lived very frugally. He writes in one of his letters:

> Mr. Mackworth[1] is a fine young man: I wish I had it in my power to show him more civility. All I can do for him is occasionally to give him a very bad dinner.

Larpent, Judge-Advocate-General to the armies, once excused himself from dining at headquarters, as he was engaged to Hill. "Very well," said Wellington, "but I advise you to come to me nevertheless, for Hill gives the worst dinners in the army."

Soult had been driven out of Portugal and hunted back into Spain. By something like miracles of skill, coolness, and daring, he had saved the bulk of his army, but they were reduced to worse condition than when he was beaten at Corunna. He had lost his guns, his stores, and his baggage. Sir Arthur's calculations had been justified by events, and now he could turn his attention to Victor. On 17th June Hill was writing from Abrantes, where the victorious army was encamped, short of money, and shoes, and everything else, but full of spirit and eager to advance. He had his quarters in a small house in the town; his men were in temporary huts they had run up for themselves. He thought it probable they would tarry there for some time: but ten days later the camp was broken up.

---
1. Afterwards Sir Digby Mackworth.

In strange ignorance of the strength of the northern French armies, in reliance on the fallacious assurances of the Spaniards, Sir Arthur meant to move on Madrid by the valley of the Tagus. When he met Cuesta, their staffs intermingled to the thunder of the cannon, the beat of the drums, the music of the bands, and the shouts of the Spaniards. It was the meeting of mediaeval and modern war; of age, infirmity, and antiquated methods, with energy, stern simplicity, and prompt decision. Sir Arthur may have rued his advance and foreseen his retreat when he saw the unwieldy figure of the Spanish veteran in slashed doublet and trunk hose, with an *aide-de-camp* in superb accoutrements walking on either side of his saddle in readiness to lend support to the tottering horseman.

The interchange of courtesies did not reassure him, nor was he misled by the magniloquent vaunting of his vain-glorious colleague. Cuesta failed him on every occasion. The sullen old valetudinarian who went to "observe" the enemy in a coach and six had alternate fits of sluggishness and frenzy: one day nothing would induce him to move; on the next he would risk his men with the harebrained valour of a Don Quixote. Though the rich Vera of Placentia was near, the English were starving, and Hill wrote on 25th July:

> Instead of our having supplies to take on, the soldiers have not yet had meat or bread for *yesterday*.

In that letter he ventured on a rash prediction. Victor was in retreat, and he says:

> If we can get the French out of Spain without an action, which I do not think unlikely, I shall be satisfied.

Napoleon showed greater prescience. Dictating minute instructions to Soult from distant Germany, he had said: "Wellington will probably advance by the Tagus against Madrid; in that case, pass the mountains, fall on his flank and rear and crush him."

When Sir Arthur with barely 20,000 men was pressing forward to meet Victor, he little realised the danger impending from the north. Soult had 50,000 bayonets and sabres at Salamanca: the very day the British passed the Tietar he was threatening the defile of Baños in the *sierras*, and Cuesta, who had undertaken to guard it, had only sent a couple of weak battalions. Had Joseph had anything of the genius and energy of his brother, the avalanche must have fallen and the victors of Talavera must have been crushed. But the usurper was distracted by conflicting counsels and disposed to sacrifice everything to the safety of his capital.

Hill had no part in the operations when Victor was retiring and returning. The French marshal had fallen back on the central army led by Joseph and Jourdan, and it had been joined by the fourth corps from La Mancha under Sebastiani. The allies, who had taken positions at Talavera, found themselves confronting 50,000 veterans. In numbers the armies were not unequally matched, but the brunt of the battle impending was to be borne by 19,000 British. Sir Arthur had begun to understand the fighting worth of his allies, and made his dispositions accordingly. The Spaniards were in positions virtually impregnable, their right resting on the town and the Tagus. The field of operations was enclosed in a square, about two miles in diameter either way.

To the north lay the Alberche: to the east the Tagus: to the south the line of defence held by the allies. To the west was the ridge of a lofty *sierra*, which sunk at half distance into the plain. The British aligned to the west of the Spaniards had their left on a detached hill which proved to be the key of the positions and pivot of the fighting. For immediately in front of it was a dominating height, which when it fell into possession of the enemy searched the British lines with an oblique fire, and threatened to make the lower eminence untenable. Sir Arthur made at least one serious mistake. He neglected the deep ravine lying between those confronting heights and the loftier *sierra*, and had hastily to modify his arrangements when his left was menaced by a turning movement. It was broken ground, between the Alberche and the town, thickly covered by olives and oak trees, which masked the evolutions on either side, as it broke the order of the attacking columns. General Campbell's division stood next to the Spaniards; then came Sherbrooke, and Hill was to the extreme left, with the cavalry massed behind him.

At three in the afternoon the enemy crossed the Alberche in two columns, and stealing onward under cover of the trees, surprised our outposts at Casa Salinas. Indeed we narrowly escaped an irretrievable disaster, for Sir Arthur himself was nearly taken prisoner. But his presence restored order; he rallied the old 45th with some companies of the 60th, and brought them to the support of the younger battalions which had been thrown into confusion. Moreover the cavalry came to the rescue, and the British withdrew fighting, having sustained heavy loss. Mackenzie fell into line behind Sherbrooke; Donkin, with his brigade, took post on the lower hill on the left.

It seems to have been assumed by Sir Arthur that the approach of night would suspend the battle. For Hill was not called up to the support of Donkin, and nothing was done to secure possession of the dominating eminence in front of Donkin's position. But the French were blooded and full of fight, and Victor had no mind to restrain them. On our right the mere show of an attack had thrown the strongly entrenched Spaniards into a panic, and the panic would have ended in a rout had not the onset been checked by flanking movements of the English cavalry.

That onset was the mere impulse of a wild rush; scarcely even a feint: Victor never expected to storm those formidable positions. The serious attack was directed to our left, where, seeing the weakness of the force with which it was held, he hoped to seize the key of the positions. He came very near to succeeding. Leading Villatte's division across the plain, hurrying up all his field pieces and light cavalry, he established his guns on the isolated hill and concentrated a tremendous cannonade upon Donkin. Fortunately Donkin's hill was a natural redoubt Steep and rugged where it faced the French, it was skirted at bottom by a deep ravine. On the southern side, towards Hill and his division, the slope was comparatively gentle. Under cover of the vehement cannonade, Ruffin and Villatte rushed to the storm. Donkin forced back the frontal attack, but the assailants had swept round his left and seized the summit above him.

Hill had been dining in Talavera. No one had dreamed of an attack that evening, and he was riding quietly back with Major Fordyce when he heard the firing. He reached the encampment to meet an order to hurry up with supports. It was fast drawing towards dusk, and objects were barely distinguishable. He was hastily giving instructions to the colonel of the 48th, when, as he tells himself in a memorandum drawn up in 1827, for the satisfaction of an officer of high rank, he "observed some men on the hilltop fire a few shots at us. Not having an idea that the enemy were so near, I said at the moment I was sure it was the old Buffs as usual making some blunder."

When he rode up the hill to stop the firing, he discovered his mistake. He was in the midst of the French. "I turned to ride off, when they fired again and killed poor Fordyce and shot my mare through the body. She did not fall, but carried me to the 29th Regiment, which by my orders instantly charged the French and drove them from the hill." It was a narrow escape, for a Frenchman had seized his bridle, and only lost hold when Hill set spurs to his horse. Had he been captured then, it is certain he would never have been commander-in-chief of the British army.

His brief, blunt memorandum gives but a faint idea of what happened in that critical half-hour. The enemy had won the heights, and had no mind to abandon them. The other British divisions, looking anxiously to their left, saw the hill-crest illuminated with incessant flashes, now advancing and again receding. For half-an-hour the combatants had been exchanging volleys point blank, and ever and again came the clash of bayonets. But at length arose the British cheer of victory, when the assailing column, in shattered fragments, was hurled down into the depths below. It was a near thing at the best; the position had been well nigh lost, and it was fortunate that the supporting regiments of Baffin's division had gone far astray in the ravine to the left. But in the fighting of that half-hour nearly 2000 combatants had fallen.

Victor was piqued by a failure, where he had only been baffled by ill-luck. He proposed to renew the attack next morning: Jourdan opposed, but Joseph acceded. His reasoning was sound, but the favourable opportunity had gone by. During the night Sir Arthur had altered his dispositions. Now the flanking ravine was guarded by two regiments of horse, and the mountain beyond was watched by a Spanish brigade. Nevertheless the renewed attack on the key of the line was sufficiently formidable, and for a time the issue was in doubt. Victor had been as active through the night as Wellington. He had massed all the guns of the 1st Corps on the eminence commanding Hill's position. With the dawn they simultaneously opened fire, scattering death broadcast among the defenders of the British hill, and raking our entrenchments to the right, up to the great redoubt in their centre.

Simultaneously, too, the dim plain in front was darkened by Ruffin's division coming on, two regiments abreast, supported by heavy masses behind. The roar of the French guns lulled when their own attacking columns crossed the line of fire. But it was succeeded by sharp exchanges of musketry. Then the ranks were broken on either side, and it became a soldier's battle—a sort of Inkerman. And, as men fell fast, the ranks were replenished by the supports on one side and the reserves on the other. Hill, who was everywhere in the front—it was no time for the coolest general to spare himself—had his horse shot under him and was slightly wounded. But again British obstinacy carried the day, again the French were precipitated down the fatal hillside. Their retirement was covered by the fire of their cannon, to which there was nothing more than a half-dozen of field pieces to reply, but they had left 1500 of their comrades behind.

For a space after that sanguinary prelude, the opposing hosts rested on their arms. In that informal truce, the soldiers of both armies, parched with thirst under the burning sun, amicably intermingled on the banks of the brook which traversed the plain between the outposts. Meantime the French leaders were consulting. Jourdan gave the wise advice to retire on the Alberche and there await the operations of Soult, when Wellesley, unless he fell back from Talavera, must have been caught in a vice between two armies; but his counsels were rejected and the pertinacity of Victor prevailed. Thus the real "Talavera" began at noon. This time the battle raged furiously along the whole line, and there were no feigned attacks. To the right the British everywhere held their ground, till the impetuosity of Sherbrooke's Guards, scattering in hot pursuit, invited disaster, and they were swept back in confusion on the surge of a returning tide. The centre was broken: the onset was not to be stemmed, and for the moment victory inclined to the French. Sir Arthur had taken his station on the height held by Hill, and thence he was surveying the scene.

On that hill the attack had been fierce as before, and it was menaced besides by a formidable flanking movement along the ravine to the left. But it was so firmly held that at that supreme crisis Sir Arthur could spare the 48th to support his centre, and in the centre the 48th restored the battle. To the left, in the great ravine, the brilliant though reckless courage of the cavalry had amazed Villatte's division and checked its advance. To the right ten of the guns of the 4th Corps had been captured, and the fall of Lapisse had disheartened the soldiers he had so gallantly led. The musketry fire slackened, sputtered, and died out.

The Frenchmen limbered up and withdrew their guns. Joseph decided to fall back to make sure of Madrid, and Wellesley was in no condition to pursue him. More than a third of his soldiers were *hors de combat*, and the others, who had fought the battle with empty stomachs, were exhausted by hunger, thirst, and hard fighting. If Talavera was a bloody and barren victory, that was the fault of our allies. It gave Sir Arthur. Wellesley his peerage, and General Hill carried off the second honours. He was rewarded with the colonelcy of the 94th Regiment, and was gratified by the graceful compliments of the Premier, when the army received the thanks of the House of Commons.

Talavera proved a barren victory, yet Joseph and Victor had saved the Peninsula for Spain. Had Joseph listened to the counsels of Jourdan, or had Soult been left untrammelled in the direction of operations, the result would have been different. But Victor was hot-headed, and Ney was jealous, and Joseph was a reed shaken by the winds. Between the perversity of crabbed old Cuesta and his strange misapprehensions as to the strength Soult was bringing to bear upon him, Sir Arthur, with the effectives of his victorious army, was in a situation of the utmost peril.

But his genius was always inspired by emergency, and he was never more admirable than when apparently cornered. With a skill and swiftness which remind one of Montrose's eccentric campaigns in Scotland, he not only carried his own troops across the Tagus between the converging armies of Victor and Soult, but shepherded the recalcitrant Spaniards into strong positions. Of course they rushed on disaster immediately afterwards, but for that he was in no way to blame. When Soult had crossed the Vera of Placentia to the Tagus, he found the allies impregnably posted. He might pass the river with risk and loss; but only to find himself within the sweep of *sierras* whose scarped sides were practically inaccessible. Lord Wellington had proved the faithlessness of his allies.

With rare exceptions they were little to be trusted in battle, and Cuesta seemed to take pleasure in crossing his plans. He had decided to fall back upon Portugal, and was only induced to delay by the representations of his brother, who had replaced Mr. Frere as envoy to the Seville Junta. Meantime he had taken up the line of the Guadiana, and the retrograde movement had been accomplished with no little difficulty. Critics have attributed misfortunes in recent wars to a system which undoubtedly fell far short of perfection. Wellington had no regular transport at all; the Spaniards would neither lend nor sell either mules or horses: he could not carry away the guns captured at Talavera: he abandoned stores and ammunition waggons at Arzobispo. His men were always on short rations, and often starving. Craufurd's experiences, when his ravenous brigade bayoneted the swine in the Estremadura woodlands, were but a sample of what all had to suffer.

Headquarters were established at Merida. The battalions, billeted to right and left, enfeebled by the wear of war with semi-starvation, were exposed to the malarious influences of the Guadiana marshes. The mortality was frightful. Hill wrote that of an army of 23,000 they could not bring 13,000 into the field. The rest were buried or in hospital. He had neither the knowledge nor the foresight of his chief, and he showed himself no prophet. "The cause is *hopeless*"—so he emphatically expressed himself, for the Spaniards had proved worthless on the field, and the numbers of the English were lamentably inadequate.

And he might well have thought so, when the united French might have launched upon Portugal ten times the numbers of the effective English. It is clear that Wellington had only Job's comforters about him when the man whom he trusted the most was *hopelessly* despondent. But we must remark that the chief kept his own counsel so closely that he made no confidants among the generals who stood nearest him. Hill wrote in the same letter—it was dated 10th November—"I do not know whether our future plans are fixed upon." He knew as little as the Madrid Intelligence Department of the lines of Torres Vedras.

The soldiers on the Guadiana were sickening and dying like flies, but Hill had his divisional headquarters on the comparatively salubrious heights of Mondego. There, in his enforced leisure, he was the sporting Shropshire squire. His brother writes:

> We lead quite a country life, going out coursing three days a week, though I should not wonder if Buonaparte gave us a chase of another sort one of these mornings.

They seem to have got together a scratch pack of hounds, for the general wrote that they now and then indulged in a fox-hunt, sometimes attacking a boar or a deer. And he sent home a portrait of his Spanish huntsman, sketched by his brother, remarking that the Spaniard dispensed with the orthodox horn, preferring a sort of pipe-lute which animated both the dogs and the field. Clement Hill with his satirical talent might have caricatured the sheep, for, like Skye-terriers, their beauty seems to have been in their ugliness. Nevertheless, the general bought four of them to lead with the milk goats, with the idea of sending them to England "to improve the Shropshire breed." From which we gather that a taste for acclimation must be hereditary in the family, for the late Lord Hill imported elands from South Africa. While Hill was killing time and foxes at Mondego, he had the satisfaction of being gazetted lieutenant-general.

A more important charge was now to be confided to him. Wellington, after tarrying at Merida against his better judgment, carried out his original resolution of evacuating Spain. The final decision was precipitated by weighing probabilities and by reports of the enemy's menacing movements. There were various lines by which they might attack, and he had to take his precautions against many contingencies. Yet when he went into winter quarters with his main force in the valley of the Mondego, he was compelled to break it up for the sake of the commissariat. Himself took post at a commanding centre, whence concentration could be most easily effected. The rear of that widely scattered army must be guarded against the French, who were in great strength in the south. For the most part he employed secretaries, but with his own hand, and on the eve of the retirement, he wrote to Hill the following flattering letter. For the first time he gave a general of division an independent and most responsible command.

Badajoz, December 18, 1809.

My dear Hill,—In the arrangements for the defence of Portugal, I shall form two principal corps, both consisting of British and Portuguese troops, the largest of which will be to the north-west, and I shall command it myself; and the other will be for the present upon the Tagus, and hereafter it may be moved forward into Alemtego; and I will not make any arrangement as to the troops that are to compose it, or as to the officer who is to command it, without offering the command of it to you.

At the same time, I will not separate you from the army, and from my own immediate command, without consulting your wishes, &c.

Needless to say, Hill accepted joyfully, and a letter to Hawkstone shows how deeply he was touched and gratified by the unexpected proof of confidence. He adds:

I am aware of the importance of the situation I am placed in, and trust I shall be attended with the same good fortune I have hitherto experienced.

It was a post demanding vigilant generalship. Regnier in Estremadura was a dangerous enemy, fertile in expedients, swift in evolution, and of the impetuous temperament that lost him the battle of Maida; and between Regnier and Hill nothing was interposed but the bands of Romana, who dared not face the French in the field, but was waging a partisan war in the sierras. Hill took post at Abrantes, on the southern bank of the Tagus, at its junction with the Zezere, where the broader river was spanned by a bridge of boats. His own division mustered 5000 men, and he had as many of the Portuguese. He set to work to strengthen the fortifications, and his engineers were busied over new works, a part of Wellington's general schemes for the defence of Portugal.

When Mertier from Andalusia, joining his division to that of Regnier, was threatening Badajoz, the appeals of Romana induced Hill to move to his support: but, id strict conformity to Wellington's intentions, he declined to entangle himself in the Spanish operations. With Regnier there was an amicable interchange of courtesies, though the French general in somewhat sarcastic letters taunted the Englishman with keeping his distance. But Hill, like his commander when facing Marmont on the Coa, was not to be provoked into fighting against his judgment

Wellington after long correspondence had obtained the assurances which decided him to maintain the defence of Portugal. Masséna, having superseded Marmont, was at the head of nearly 70,000 men of all arms, and had completed his dilatory preparations for an advance. Wellington had had ample time to think out everything, and had decided on his counter dispositions. When Masséna crossed the frontier, the allied positions extended from Almeida to Castel Branco, on the royal road from Spain to Lisbon, running north of the Tagus and parallel to it. The orders were that, if there was a serious attack on any point, the line was to bend back and not let itself be broken. There was to be a general retirement, converging towards Torres Vedras, though the army generally was contemplating the possibility of an embarkation.

Hill, with his independent command, had to act on his own judgment. It was to be apprehended that the enemy might seek to sever the communications between the two armies of the allies, but his line of retreat was marked out from Sazedas to Abrantes, whence he could cross the mountains and meet Wellington in the Mondego valley. He wrote on the 12th September that as Regnier seemed to have moved to the north, to unite with Masséna, he had prepared to pass the Zezere. Should the news prove false, he would be still in a position as effective. Masséna's whole army was on the Mondego by the 17th. Giving each man fourteen days' rations to carry, he was pressing forward by forced marches. Hill was ordered to Espinhal, there to await further orders. On the 24th Wellington had taken his stand at Busaco, willing on political grounds to blood his Portuguese and confident of victory, if his challenge were accepted. Again was his military sagacity justified, for Napoleon in urging Masséna on had virtually ignored the Portuguese in his calculations.

At the battle which covered some of the lieutenants with laurels, Hill looked on as a spectator, though neither an idle nor a useless one. On the 25th, having been disappointed of an interview with Wellington, for which both generals were equally anxious, he was over the Mondego; and on the following day, he had taken his stand where the sierra sloped to the river. Masséna made a direct frontal attack on the allied right, and Hill's corps never came into action.

When the battle was raging, the corps was shifted to its left, behind the screen of the mountain ridge. At what Masséna believed to be the extreme of the allied right, the 74th had repulsed an attack of the enemy, and were retiring in perfect order to this crest Wellington had galloped up, expecting the attack to be renewed. "Hill," he said, "should attempt this point again. Give them a volley and charge bayonets." But the presence of this fresh reinforcement was enough, and the French had no stomach for further fighting. With such a position against them, held by such men, they had done as much as might be expected of mortal soldiers.

Hill's unbroken division recrossed the Mondego to observe the enemy. Wellington wrote that if Massena also passed that river a special message was to be sent at once, and "you may depend on my being with you in a few hours." But the marshal turned the northern extremity of the *sierra*, to make his flank march between the mountains and the sea.

Ten days afterwards the allied army was behind the lines of Torres Vedras. Hill had his post at Alhandra, on the right front, a formidable position washed by the Tagus and pronounced impregnable by the engineers; yet it is characteristic, that he remarked, with his habitual caution, "It is too extensive for my numbers." At Alhandra he was in clover. His brother wrote in high spirits: "We get all good things from Lisbon, and are living in a palace." He added in another letter:

> The people in Lisbon have quite got rid of their alarm, and the ladies come up by water to look at the French. Rowland is just gone down to do the civil to the admiral's family, who are come up on a party of pleasure.

"Rowland" was once more opposed to his old antagonist Regnier, who, after reconnoitring the position, resigned himself to sullen observation. Supplies were abundant with the British, but the French were in evil case. Sometimes they were indebted to our soldiers for little luxuries. A trace had been virtually proclaimed, and, as on the

Coa and elsewhere, the men met on a friendly footing. Sir Rowland wrote:

> We are perfectly good neighbours and never think of molesting each other. On the contrary, I have been obliged to put a stop to the intimacy that was going on. It was by no means uncommon to see the soldiers of each army getting grapes out of the same vineyard, water from the same well, and asking each other to drink wine. Indeed I know of some instances, though not quite correct, of our officers sending to Lisbon for boots and shirts for some of their friends at outposts.

When Masséna had been starved into a retreat, at Santarem the tables were turned. The allies remained inactive in their encampments before frowning heights bristling with cannon, and an enemy too formidable in numbers to be outflanked. Sickness spread in the encampments skirting the Tagus, and Hill was prostrated by an attack of the country fever. A change to sea air failed to cure him, and the illness was complicated by an attack of jaundice. Letters from Wellington were full of sympathy and regret, but begged him not to return till his health was re-established. And it was only at Wellington's pressing entreaties that he consented to take orders from the doctors and sail for England on furlough.

4

A year was passed at home, and he was welcomed back by Wellington in a letter written ten days after Albuera, the bloodiest and most fruitless battle of the war:

> You will have heard of events here, which I hope will enable us to obtain possession of Badajoz.

The hope was frustrated, and indeed the attempt seemed a desperate one. When Wellington made a snatch at the fortress, with an inadequate battering train, the armies of Soult and Marmont were within easy relieving distance. He was forced to raise the siege, for he was in no condition to risk a battle on the plain with their united forces. Hill had been again placed in command of the covering army, which held the country from Albuera to Merida. Wellington fell back to positions on the Caya River, where he could venture to await a battle, if the enemy chose to challenge it. He had no desire to hazard an engagement where defeat must have had far-reaching consequences and where the odds were terribly against him.

But, as at Busaco, he made the stand from political considerations. Fortunately the French were deceived as to his strength and disheartened by recent reverses Moreover, as they had been concentrating on the frontiers of Portugal, they were uneasy about their communications and their garrisons. The great combination was broken up when it had the fairest opportunity of crushing the allies. Soult was recalled by troubles in Andalusia: Marmont had evil tidings from the north. But Phillipon was given time to revictual his fortress, and Drouet was left with the 5th Division to mount guard in Spanish Estremadura.

The deadly repute of the valley of the Guadiana played no little part in all the operations. Both the combatants avoided it when possible; the ravages of fever and dysentery among British and Portuguese had been frightful, and now Wellington gladly withdrew to healthy stations in the interior. Hill was again charged with the duty of observing Drouet. As the frontier had been cleared of enemies, he could choose his positions, but his strategy was always influenced by regard for the health of his troops. He had 10,000 infantry, a division of cavalry, and four brigades of artillery—a force strong enough, not only for defence, but for demonstrations.

Napier writes that "that bold and vigilant commander, having 10,000 excellent troops, was a dangerous neighbour to Drouet." His information was good, for Morillo and his Spaniards were perpetually harassing the French general, and his movements were marked by extreme elasticity. When Drouet advanced, he withdrew his outposts; when Drouet fell back, he concentrated to follow him. Till the beginning of September his headquarters were at Villa Viciosa, a sylvan hunting palace of the Portuguese Royal Family, surrounded by extensive preserves. There he indulged in his favourite amusement of the chase, and the excellent discipline he enforced was rewarded by the abundant supplies brought in by the peasantry.

Meantime Wellington, who had been menacing Ciudad Rodrigo, had borrowed several of his battalions. They were returned when there were rumours that Napoleon, pending negotiations with Russia which were tending towards peace, intended to torn his whole attention to the Peninsula. Drouet had become more active, General Girard was occupying Zafra with several thousands of horse and foot: Soult had returned from Eastern Andalusia to Seville, and Hill, when he had his soldiers back, was ordered forward to Portalegre. It was in the middle of October that he had the opportunity of showing that, with all his coolness and caution, he had something of the dash of Craufurd and the fighting lust of Picton.

Girard had passed the Guadiana at Merida and was ravaging Northern Estremadura. Hill advanced to repel the invaders in conjunction with the Spaniards under Castaños. He knew that Girard was supported by Drouet, but he resolved nevertheless to endeavour to make him pay for his temerity by the capture of a part or the whole of his forces. He was fettered to a certain extent, for he had been ordered not to pass Caceres, where Girard was now established. But notwithstanding Wellington's *dictum*, then as afterwards at Almarez, he accepted responsibility and used his discretion.

On his approach upon the 26th, Girard abandoned Caceres, but the weather was terrific, and Hill, knowing nothing of the route the enemy had taken, halted his exhausted troops for the night at Malpartida. He knew next morning, and when taking a shorter hill road to cut them off learned that Girard was at Arroyo de Molinos, and in absolute ignorance of his movements. Indeed the French general believed the British were following him on the Caceres road.

Hill pressed onwards through the mountains, and the march was made doubly difficult by the weather, for the rain was still descending in torrents; but when the men bivouacked that night they were within four miles of Arroyo. Every precaution was taken to avoid discovery. Companies of light infantry occupied the adjacent villages, and kept the villagers under surveillance. All fires were forbidden, though the gusts of the storm blew down the tents and the men had to shiver under soaking canvas. There was no sound of bugle when in the darkness and in perfect silence they fell into their ranks.

In silence they marched down the long village street, crossed the valley, scaled another mountain, and at daybreak were looking down on Arroyo, where the French were resting in fancied security. Then the weather, that had tried them sorely, turned in their favour, for a blinding hail-storm coming from behind drove full in the faces of the French pickets. They had formed, under a sheltering eminence, in three columns. The left column plunged down into the steep main street of the village: the right marched eastwards to the spur of the *sierra*, where it was turned by the Truxillo road: the cavalry kept touch between both.

The surprise was complete; yet Girard's veterans, suddenly aroused, though scarcely startled, maintained their high reputation. If the onset was furious, the resistance was stubborn. It was a battle where the game was being driven by the beaters to the guns. But it was no helpless victims that were caught in the toils. With the hailstones driving through the street, with a dense mist rolling down from the crags of the sierra, as two British regiments came charging with fixed bayonets, the French were already standing to their arms. Their cavalry, hastily bridled, were covering the retreat of the foot, who were forming in squares beyond the village.

But the squares, suffering heavily from a galling musketry fire, were broken and forced back when our guns were brought up: the French cannon were captured and their horsemen cut to pieces or ridden down. Girard's nerve had never failed him: he sought valiantly to retrieve the disaster his carelessness had caused, and rallying his broken infantry into column, commenced his retreat on the road to Truxillo. But there the allies were already *a cheval*: the cavalry and artillery were closing up on his left, the captors of the village were coming up behind, and he had to choose between surrender and flight. Promptly he gave the word to disperse, and forthwith his soldiers, casting away weapons and knapsacks, were scrambling up the sides of the Sierra de Montanches—renowned for its swine and its hams.

The pursuit was hot and persevering, and many prisoners were made. But it was no even race between the fugitives and men weighted with arms and heavy packs; man after man succumbed to fatigue and breathlessness, yet the hunt was only ended on the crest of the mountain, where General Howard judiciously called a halt. Fifteen hundred prisoners were taken, in the village or on the hills, and among them sundry officers of rank, including the Prince d'Aremberg and General Brunn. Girard lost guns, small arms, and stores, with the contributions which had been the fruit of the foray, escaping himself by the skin of his teeth, with a handful of his men, by the bridge of Merida. Hill was the more gratified that his losses were of the slightest. Letters of congratulation poured in from brother generals, who appreciated the difficulties of the exploit and the glory it reflected on the British arms. Wellington immediately forwarded a despatch to the Prime Minister.

> It would be particularly agreeable to me if some mark of the favour of the Prince Regent were conferred upon General Hill: his services have always been meritorious and very distinguished in this country, and he is beloved by the whole army. ... In recommending him, as I do most anxiously, I really feel that there is no officer to whom an act of grace and favour would be received by the army with more satisfaction than on General Hill (*sic*).

The answer was the conferring of the Knighthood of the Bath. Hill and his staff were invited to headquarters at Elvas, where he was invested by the commander with the insignia of the order, and the ceremony was celebrated with a grand military banquet.

The dignity had been bestowed with due pomp and ceremony, but Hill is said to have carried his characteristic modesty to excess. For months afterwards, according to a distinguished officer on his staff, the most good-humoured of men was obviously irritated if anyone ventured to address him as Sir Rowland, "and it was only very gradually that he could be driven to bear the honour."

While Wellington was occupied with the siege and storm of Ciudad Rodrigo, Hill had given the French another surprise in Estremadura. General Dombrouski had a narrow escape; he saved his men, but he lost his magazines. Ciudad fell, and Wellington was already meditating a more daring venture. On 28th January he sent Hill a letter, marked "secret and confidential." He said: "I am turning my mind seriously to Badajoz," and suggested that Hill should seize upon Almarez and hold the passage of the Tagus. That was the shortest route by which the army of Portugal could advance to the relief of the Spanish fortress. We say he " suggested," because everything was left to Hill's discretion, and at that time he deemed the attempt impracticable, a decision in which Wellington concurred. Nevertheless, no rescue reached the beleaguered stronghold. Badajoz fell like Ciudad; yet Wellington was compelled by the inaction of his allies to renounce his hopes of invading Andalusia, and move northward to make sure of the northern fortresses.

Badajoz had fallen, partly owing to the hesitations of Marmont, partly to the weakening of Soult by the withdrawal of troops for Russia. Divided counsels still prevailed. Marmont, cowed by his dangerous adversary, was holding back; and the Spaniards, always restless, though never reliable, were again finding Soult occupation. Wellington had dispersed his army into winter quarters on a line extending over four hundred miles. The impossibility of concentrating in a devastated country had compelled him to violate the first principles of war; but, as the enemy was likewise in evil case, he rightly counted on impunity. With the opening of a new campaign in the spring, he decided on the aggressive, for if the French were to be driven out of the Peninsula they must be beaten in pitched battles.

The question was whether his march should be into Castile or Andalusia, and he resolved on the former plan. Hill had been left to superintend the repairs of the Badajoz works, and to guard the place on the sides of Estremadura and Andalusia. But when Wellington marched into Castile the army of the centre would be left free to act and might strike at Hill by the bridge of Almarez. If the covering army met with disaster, Wellington's right flank would be imperilled. Wherefore the capture of Almarez was now of supreme importance, and with the altered circumstances it seemed feasible. On the 24th of April Wellington wrote urging Hill to make immediate and secret preparations, though he was not to march without further orders. The orders came a week later. But there had been an inevitable delay of twenty-four hours, in repairing the bridge over the Guadiana at Merida, and so nicely had the operations been planned that Wellington feared "Hill would be late."

Secrecy was indeed indispensable, for far superior forces were within striking distance. Foy's division was cantoned in the Tagus valley, and D'Armagnac was in Talavera with detachments from the army of the centre. Drouet was supposed to be watching Hill, and in a position to cut his retreat to Merida. It may be said that, notwithstanding the silence observed, the chances were in favour of failure, and failure might have meant annihilation. At that time, with the nervous apprehensions of the Government, a general, meeting a reverse falling far short of a catastrophe, might consider his career as ended. Yet Hill did not hesitate, and, taking all the precautions skill could suggest, he staked his future on the hazard.

On the 12th, passing his troops across the reconstructed bridge, he mustered 6000 men in Merida. By feigned demonstrations and false reports. General Foy had been deluded into the belief that with thrice his real force he was contemplating an invasion of Andalusia. There was no suspicion that his objective was Almarez, and his purpose was to carry it with a rush, before the enemy should be better informed. On the 16th he was at Jaraceigo, six miles from Almarez, where his operations were still effectually masked by the jumble of rough mountains with their intervening valleys. There he formed his troops into three columns, hoping to take the enemy at unawares after a long night march. Simultaneous attacks were to be delivered at daybreak.

The left column, advancing by side paths, was to assail the Castle of Mirabete; the centre was to force the pass, strongly fortified at the narrowest point, through which the royal road led northward; the right column, commanded by the general in person, following tracks only known to the goat-herds, was to assail the forts at the bridge. The difficulties, serious as they were known to be, were greatly underrated; the combinations failed, and surprise became impossible. For two days nothing could be done, and each day of delay increased the danger. Hill was seeking in vain for a passage by which he could move his guns.

On the third he came to a resolution which might have staggered the most daring leader of partisans. He left his cannon with the central column; he ordered Chowne with the left column to make a feigned attack on Mirabete; and for himself he led his right along the ledges of precipices to storm, with only the musket and bayonet, works defended by heavy guns. As Napier remarks: "A military career hitherto so glorious was likely enough to terminate in shame." But General Hill, being totally devoid of interested ambition, was unshaken by selfish considerations.

He led out his little force on the evening of the 18th, hoping to be in front of Fort Napoleon before daybreak. It gives some idea of the tracks along which he scrambled that the scaling ladders were sawn in sunder, to turn the angles of the cliffs. When day broke, the head of the column was near the bank of the river, but the body was still struggling behind in slow procession. Fortunately some low heights concealed the first arrivals, but there was no time to wait for the loiterers to close up. At that moment Chowne was menacing the Castle of Mirabete, and clouds of smoke from its batteries began to roll along the crest of the *sierra*.

The garrison of Fort Napoleon, aware by this time that the British were in their neighbourhood, crowded to the ramparts to gaze at the spectacle. They were startled to immediate attention by a shout beneath their walls. At sight of the smoke on the heights Hill had let his stormers loose; they came bounding over the nearest slopes, and rushed at the ramparts in open order. Before reaching them, they were welcomed with a heavy fire of cannon and small arms, while the guns of Fort Ragusa on the northern bank began to play on their flanks. Nothing stayed the rush. Headed by General Howard, they leaped down into the ditch and planted the sawn ladders, which proved too short. But the broad ledges projecting from the rampart were turned by an acrobatic feat: the ladders were dragged round them: and the parapet reached by a second escalade.

The garrison, overpowered, fled to the *tête de pont*, and there the pursuers entered with them in hand-to-hand fight. The chase was continued over the boat-bridge, but the pontoons on the farther side had been sunk by stray cannon-shot. Those of the fugitives who did not take to the water were slain or surrendered at discretion. The breaking of the bridge had left Fort Ragusa unapproachable, but, strange to say, the panic had gained its garrison. When it poured out upon the road to Naval Moral, the fire from Fort Napoleon hastened the retreat. Some of the soldiers plunged into the Tagus, breasted the current, and brought back some boats.

Hill, standing on the bank, in great jubilation, paid them handsomely with praises and gold. The bridge was restored, the river was passed, and, without losing a moment, the stores were burned and the works blown up. Finally, the bridge itself was destroyed. No more brilliant feat of arms was performed in the war. It raised Hill's reputation to the highest point, and no one could reproach him afterwards with excess of caution. The decision with which it was planned was equal to the daring with which it was carried out. When baffled by unexpected obstacles which would have driven a weaker man to renounce the enterprise in despair, he was only nerved to new exertions, and where one less fearless of responsibility would have lost his head, his brain was never brighter or more active.

Thenceforth, had he cared for disparaging and ignorant censure, he would have a freer hand in sparing his soldiers, for it was his habit to weigh the death losses against the gains. That the work was not completed as he would have desired was no fault of his. The fortifications at Mirabete were now at his mercy; it only needed a brief time to reduce them, and he was bringing his guns into position when a well-authenticated report was forwarded from Erskine, that Soult had broken into Estremadura, and then, in accordance with his instructions, he fell back promptly upon Merida. The surprise had set all the French in motion. Foy, in self-reproach, was stirred into activity. He passed the Tagus at Arzobispo, and, threading the mountain defiles, threw succours into Mirabete.

Soult was moving on Andalusia, and it was from Soult that Wellington apprehended danger. But there, as ever, French combinations were deranged by the inveterate jealousies. Foy, after his advance, had withdrawn, but Drouet, who had conflicting orders from Soult and Marmont, was still in a threatening position which demanded the utmost vigilance. Not that Hill had any fear of Drouet; on the contrary, he would have willingly offered him battle; but he was doubtful as to the intentions of Soult.

On 3rd June he wrote to Wellington:

If Drouet is not supported, it will not be difficult for me to disturb him in his present position.... On the other hand, if Soult keeps within reach of him, it will not probably be advisable for me to adventure farther.

Believing that Soult was contemplating an inbreak in force, Wellington hastened to send reinforcements. But Soult, with distractions on his flanks and rear, was content to send assistance to Drouet, whereupon Hill fell back. He found further supports at Albuera, and on those formidable heights, still strewn with the bones of the brave who had fallen in the battle, he confidently faced with superior numbers the antagonist who had followed him. Wellington had left him full discretion. He had not only permission, but every personal inducement to fight. The glory of a victory gained on that spot and in the circumstances would, as Napier says, when magnified by malevolence, have placed his fame on a level with that of the commander-in-chief. But his patriotism and chivalrous loyalty rose superior to selfish considerations. He believed that even winning a battle would have interfered with his general's plans.

Hill, who had shown himself so daring at Arroyo Molinos and Almarez, now, with an uncommon mastery of ambition, refrained from an action which promised him unbounded fame.

In July the British forces were nominally 60,000. Of these, 35,000 were with Wellington, 13,000 with Hill, and the remainder in garrison or hospital. Hill could not be withdrawn from watching Drouet, till the victory of Salamanca compelled Soult to concentrate and ultimately to withdraw to the east. In July Hill had written:

It is a most glorious event, but appears to have had little effect on my immediate opponents.

All was changed when in mid-August Wellington made his triumphant entry into Madrid. Joseph had fled with a rabble of soldiers and camp-followers into La Mancha: Soult had gone to join him, having sacrificed his better judgment with his daring scheme of abandoning Madrid and making a new base for French operations in Andalusia. Hill could write to Wellington that he was finally relieved from Drouet, and that he had sure intelligence that not only Estremadura, but Andalusia was being evacuated. He added: "The joy of the people is great indeed"

But the joy of Madrid was damped by uncertainty, to be succeeded by tribulation. Wellington's great schemes were baffled for the time, and the expulsion of the enemy from the Peninsula was to be deferred for another year. It was owing partly to the backwardness of the Spaniards, and partly to the false economy of the British Government, which starved him both in money and reinforcements. Reluctantly he resolved on abandoning the capital. He marched back to the north, driving Clausel and the army of Portugal before him, and laying siege to the Castle of Burgos which blocked his way. Arrived at Burgos on the 17th September, he sent orders to Hill to march on Toledo, and Hill established himself in New Castile, with his headquarters at Aranjuez, the favourite rural retreat of the Bourbons, when the heat did not drive them to La Granja in the hill country.

Hill waited anxiously for the news which never came: Burgos still held out, and his letters show how uneasiness passed into despondency. The failure was due to an inadequate siege train and short ammunition; but it is remarkable that Sir Augustus Frazer, who commanded the horse artillery at Salamanca, attributes the miscarriage "to the want of will to employ sufficient artillery, with the amplest power of having done so." Be that as it may, when Dubreton's obstinacy of defence had brought Wellington to a standstill, by the fortunes of war Hill missed another chance of adding to his renown by a glorious victory. And, strange to say, the chance was missed by the fact that Wellington had at last consented to become the *generalissimo* of the Spanish armies that he might the better secure effective co-operation.

The English at Alicante with their allies found Suchet sufficient occupation, and were even strong enough to assume the aggressive. Joseph and Soult were marching westward, for the usurper's dominating idea was to regain his lost capital. Wellington, whose eye ranged over all the battleground, had ordered Ballasteros, commanding in Murcia, to unite himself to Maitland from Alicante and hang upon the flanks of the French advance. Hill was waiting confidently behind the Tagus with a fine fighting force. He had the Light and three other divisions, with several Portuguese regiments and a strong body of English and Spanish horse.

If the French attacked, as they were almost compelled to do, for when they had come so far they could hardly refuse without fatal loss of prestige, Maitland and Ballasteros should have been ready to fall on their rear. But Ballasteros, in jealous discontent, had refused to stir: he bitterly resented Wellington's being put over his head: and it was small satisfaction that he was summarily disgraced, when the Cortes made him prisoner in his own camp. But the upshot was that Joseph and

Soult came on unmolested, threatening Hill with forces nearly double his own. He had been in constant communication with Burgos. Wellington had sent directions providing for every contingency, but added: "I write, as I always do, to provide for every event, not believing those instructions are at all necessary." Both were agreed that no battle was to be risked, unless with the odds in favour of a victory.

On the 21st the siege of Burgos was raised and the retreat begun. The same day a courier was despatched to Hill, with orders to join at Salamanca. The orders were superfluous, for he was already making his preparations, and it was high time. The heads of the French columns had been seen on the opposite bank of the flooded Tagus. The bridge at Aranjuez had been mined, but he was delayed for a day by the failure of the first explosion. There was some sharp skirmishing with the last detachment of his rearguard. Nevertheless on the last day of the month his infantry were well on their way to the Escorial.

It was a picturesque scene when he looked back from the crest of the Guadarama on his regiments winding their upward way along the zigzags in a snake-like train. And there were dropping shots from the rear, showing that the French were close on his heels. Next day, when on the plains of Old Castile, his scouts reported that French battalions were already ascending the pass. What force was behind them he knew not. Wellington's answer to his report, for now they were in close communication, shows the sagacity with which he calculated on the temperaments of his adversaries. He did not believe Soult was following in force: he must be merely keeping cautious touch. Hill crossed the Tormes at Alba, the same day that Wellington was back at his old position on the heights of San Cristoval overlooking Salamanca. The great victory had proved the rebound of a boomerang. It had forced Soult to evacuate Andalusia, but it had compelled the scattered French armies to draw together, in accordance with Napoleon's principle of operating in masses.

The united armies of the south and the centre were too strong, and Souham, who had seized the passages of the Douro, was within some short marches of his rear. Even then he hesitated as to abandoning Salamanca, and leaving the citizens to their fate after their patriotic demonstrations. For he wrote to Hill, who was to descend the Tormes valley, ordering him to leave a garrison in Alba. In answering, Hill asked if he had ever seen the place: a weak garrison in the castle would not suffice to command the bridge. But Wellington had still a lingering hope that the French might assail the heights of San Cristoval.

Joseph was, in fact, disposed to gratify him, but was over-ruled by the more cautious Soult. That marshal had devised one of his ingenious pieces of strategy by which, by a wide cast of the net of the *retarius*, he might entangle the enemy in its meshes. For by sweeping round upon the road to Rodrigo he made retreat inevitable, and Wellington's escape or surrender became but a question of hours.

It was a repetition of Marmont's fatal flank march, but on an infinitely wider circuit: and if Marmont was too reckless, Soult was too wary. Moreover, the elements fought for Wellington. His movements were masked by dense fog, and in drenching rain his enemies were bogged to the knees and saddle-girths in the tenacious mire of the by-road. Soult missed his cast, and Wellington reached Rodrigo after one of the most miserable marches on record. There was little food for the men and less forage for the horses. The famished soldiers scrambled greedily for fallen acorns, and many lives were saved by their breaking the ranks and shooting or bayoneting the swine in the woodlands. There was no shelter from the unrelenting dampness, and no possibility of kindling fires.

So ended, in mortification to the general and misery to the men, a campaign that had opened so brilliantly and been crowned by splendid successes. Yet Wellington had only to possess himself in patience: the strength of the French occupation had been shaken to its foundations, and to his prescience the issue was only deferred.

5

The army had gone into winter quarters. Wellington's first business was to brace up the relaxation of discipline—always engendered in British soldiers by a mortifying retreat—by masterful edicts and salutary reprimands. He had little to fear from attacks on any formidable scale. He had again dispersed his troops in salubrious quarters, and with due regard to considerations of the commissariat in a country which had been so devastated by the war that Sir Augustus Frazer, when riding from Lisbon to Santarem, had not seen a soul at work in the fields. But he had now distributed them with a view to the campaign of the next summer, which was to sweep the Peninsula clear of invaders.

While the Anglo-Portuguese were in repose, affairs were going badly for the usurper. Wellington had so arranged that the allies in the east found active occupation for Suchet. Everywhere the partisans were numerous, and successful rivalry inspired them to the most audacious enterprises. The insurrection in the north was spreading to the Basque Provinces, where the guerrilla chiefs hung emulously upon the communications with France, and Napoleon considered it of such vital importance that he sent Joseph peremptory orders to crush it. That was more easy to order than to execute. The insurrection gained head and engaged the army of the north with good part of the army of Portugal, when Joseph stood in need of every available man to stem the torrent of war that went surging forward upon Vittoria. Above all, it was Hill who had puzzled the enemy, and who finally crippled their combinations at the critical moment in the spring.

Hill was covering the right flank of the scattered forces. He had his headquarters at Coria, whence he commanded the passes over the mountains to the north or could strike at will up the valley of the Tagus. His exploits at Arroyo Molinos and Almarez had made him a terror. Everything in the way of enterprise was to be feared from a leader at once so calculating and so deliberately audacious. He can hardly have been said to have been a thorn in the enemy's side, for he kept quiet in obedience to instructions. But Napier writes that "the slightest change of his quarters or even the appearance of an English uniform beyond the line of cantonments caused a concentration of French troops as expecting one of his sudden blows."

The demoralisation of the retreat had had grave results. The hospitals were overcrowded: in January there were 22,000 men on the sick list: few of the transport animals had struggled through to Rodrigo. But in March, with bracing air and better food, most of the invalids had rejoined the colours. Beresford's severe discipline had drilled the Portuguese into excellent form. Wellington had clothed, fed, and paid many of the Spanish battalions, so that they were in condition to do good service. In March he had 70,000 Anglo-Portuguese veterans under his hand, with 20,000 fairly efficient Spaniards. Joseph had little more than half the force with which to confront him when he began to develop the plans which were still inscrutable to the enemy.

To the last moment his officers in high command were profoundly ignorant of his intentions. Their letters home were full of speculations, often absurdly wide of the mark. Perhaps Graham, Hill, Beresford, and one or two of his staff were alone in his confidence. He had decided to strike at the north, where he could interpose between Joseph and Bayonne, coming into touch with the spreading northern insurrection and the guerrillas who were swarming on the slopes of the Pyrenees. Hill was employed to mislead the enemy, and to persuade them that the tremendous infall, as in the Talavera campaign, would follow the course of the Tagus.

If Wellington struck north, it seemed certain to military students of the topography that he would strive to turn the left of the French. In reality he was to direct his main attack on their right, which nature had made apparently unassailable by flooded torrents and impracticable ravines. According to the received rules of war, in advancing he would keep his columns in touch. He moved forward to his objective in three bodies, separated from co-operation by mountains, morasses, and rivers. Yet these delicate combinations of his were so nicely devised that the slight delay did not sensibly derange them.

In the middle of May, Graham with 40,000 men was over the Douro, threading the gorges to the eastward. No intelligence of that audacious turning movement reached the unsuspecting king, who in blissful ignorance was slowly concentrating, and meditating new measures of government amid conflicting military councils. He had only eyes for Wellington, who was advancing on the Tormes with the centre, and for Hill, who had at last broken up from Coria and was bringing round his right wing by the passes of the mountains.

Hill's officers delighted in sport, like their hard-riding commander. Many a couple of greyhounds accompanied the march, and many a hare started by the advancing columns was run down in crossing the plains between the *sierra* and the Tormes. A long halt at Galisteo, where the corps was concentrated, was enlivened by a romantic *al fresco* banquet. The 28th Regiment, which had distinguished itself at Albuera, entertained the general and his staff on the anniversary of the battle. The arrangements were original. There were neither chairs nor tables; regimental plate and crystal were conspicuous by their absence. Each guest, from Sir Rowland downwards, brought his own knife, fork, and plate. Trenches were cut for the accommodation of their legs, and smooth sods of fresh-cut turf were the covering of the banqueting board. There was such promiscuous foraging for the miscellaneous *menu* as Lever describes in his *Charles O'Malley*, and the cooking over the camp fires was of the roughest, but the dinner was a great success.

Hill and Wellington met at Salamanca, and Hill was left in temporary command, while Wellington hurried off to the Esla to relieve his anxiety as to Graham. On his return the united armies again moved forward, the French abandoning position after position, as they were outflanked on either side. Not even at Burgos did they make a stand.

Joseph had neglected his brother's repeated instructions to repair the works and revictual the fortress. Breaching batteries and scaling ladders were all in readiness this time, but there was no need to employ them. Clouds of smoke, with a report that shook the ground, were the visible and audible signs of evacuation: the castle had been so hurriedly blown up that 300 Frenchmen perished in the explosion. Hill commanded the column that had followed the royal road, and now on the 13th June filed, unobstructed, over the bridge into the town.

The French had seen the British advance, when they hastily fired the mines in the castle. Nor could they understand why the pursuit was not pressed, for it was two days before Wellington and Hill resumed the march, moving on parallel lines. They congratulated themselves on reaching Pancorbo without losing a gun or a waggon. They knew not that the day of reckoning was only delayed, to give Graham time to pass an impossible country before coming down on their communications with France, and making sure that their defeat should be a catastrophe. On the 13th Wellington's army was in motion by the left: two days afterwards the centre and the right had left Burgos: on the 20th the nets had been drawn around the French, and Joseph was at bay in the basin of Vittoria.

The basin is enclosed on two sides by the Zadora, which was spanned by seven bridges. Vittoria was the Cinque Bras of Spain—the meeting place of five highways. It was traversed by the northern road to Bayonne. On the east were the ways leading to Bilboa and Durango. Towards the north-west two others branched off to Pampeluna and Estella. Two of the bridges were on the western roads, where the river flows due south; three were on the southern lip of the basin, where the river bends to the east, almost at a right angle. The sixth was down stream to the east: it led across to the village of Puebla, beyond the pass of the same name. The narrow defile is shut in by parallel ranges of mountain.

Graham, always pushing his advance, was threatening the bridges on the Upper Zadora and Joseph's direct retreat to Bayonne. Wellington was directing the frontal attack by the three southern bridges. Hill's line of operations was on the extreme right: he passed at Puebla, beyond the eastern ridge, and was to wait in the meantime at the mouth of the defile. Morillo's Spaniards were to scale the mountain to the right of the road; it seemed rather like scrambling than walking. They gained the crest, to be fiercely opposed, and though supported by their second brigade. Hill had to succour them with the 71st Regiment and some light infantry under Colonel Cadogan. For a time the struggle raged with varying fortune: supports were harried up on either side, and then there was a relapse into expectant inactivity. In the rough *Journal of a Soldier* in the 71st, (published by Leonaur as *Bayonets, Bugles and Bonnets*), we have a vivid incident of that weary waiting. Beneath the blazing sun the soldiers were parched. There was one little spring on the *plateau* that was swept with shot and shell. A man more desperate than the rest broke from cover to quench his thirst.

A ball pierced his head—he fell in the well, which was discoloured with brains and blood. Thirsty as we were, we could not drink it.

Having won the heights, Hill had passed the rest of his corps over the river and proceeded to force the pass. It was done with no small expenditure of life, and the village which closed the northern outlet was carried by storm. The French troops on the mountain were outflanked, and then the battle, which for hours had been stationary, went ebbing backwards towards Vittoria. The central columns had passed the Zadora, and were driving the enemy before them. Far away to the north-west the smoke of the cannon showed that Graham was developing his attack. The French had made their last stand on a ridge in front of the town, whence eighty guns belched out death on the British advance through enclosed cornfields.

The old soldiers of Napoleon were still full of fight, but Joseph was panic-stricken and Jourdan in despair. They had good reason. The road to the Bidassoa was choked with carriages. Two convoys despatched the day before were heavily dragging through mud and ruts. Vittoria was a scene of mad confusion: in the general *sauve qui peut* the plunder of years was being abandoned, with the stores and equipment of three armies. Graham would already have swooped down on the line of flight had it not been for the stubborn and skilful opposition of Reille. The beaten army broke away to their left, along the narrow road to Pampeluna, skirted by marshes which protected their flight. All their guns, save one, had been left behind.

At Pampeluna Joseph made no long halt. The Governor, preparing for a siege and short of provisions, refused to admit the rabble. Wellington went in search of Clausel, who had been approaching the field of battle. Hill was charged with the blockade of Pampeluna, but when Joseph had sent Gazan with the army of the south to occupy the Spanish valley of Bastan, which abounded in defensible posts. Hill handed over the blockade to the Spaniards, and marched north to clear the Bastan. He never showed as a strategist to more advantage: with insignificant loss, he drove Gazan from position to position till he lined the crests of the Pyrenees with his pickets. His brother wrote:

> We have gone through a very interesting part of the campaign, having completely driven that part of the French army to which we were opposed over the Pyrenees. Great part of Rowland's corps being detached from him, his force has been greatly inferior to the enemy's, and they have always had the advantage of strong positions.

Soult had been hurried from Germany to supersede Joseph: with amazing rapidity he reorganised an army and in a measure restored its *morale*. Thenceforth between San Sebastian and Roncesvalles there was no rest for the allies. Their scattered forces were always exposed to combined attacks. Soult's strategy was directed to relieving Pampeluna, and in the battles of the Pyrenees which baffled it he lost 15,000 men. Hill, as a rule, held his own, gaining praise from his chief for skilful manoeuvring. Only once was he forced back by superior strength, when the French won for a brief space the passes of Maya and Roncesvalles. The difficulties of the defenders were increased by torrents of rain and by fogs which shrouded the enemy's movements. Impromptu earthworks were washed away, and guns could not be moved from point to point.

The nerves of responsible generals, striving vainly to pierce an impenetrable veil, were perpetually on the strain. The *Journal of a Soldier*, from the soldier's point of view, (published by Leonaur as *Bayonets, Bugles and Bonnets*), gives a graphic account of the surprise and the obstinate, stubborn resistance on the retreat from the Maya ridge.

> Our fatigue-parties were out for forage and we were busy cooking when the signal was given on the 20th of June. . . . The French were in great force, moving up in solid columns. We killed great numbers of them, but they still moved on. We killed great numbers of them, but were forced to give way, contesting every foot of ground . . . We had the mortification to see the French making merry in our camp, eating the dinner we had cooked for ourselves. What could we do? They were so superior in numbers.

The key of the pass was regained before nightfall, and Hill reported that his men had done their duty gallantly. Shortly afterwards he was shifted to Roncesvalles, on the extreme right, and as autumn passed into early winter the sufferings of the troops became intense. The *Soldier* says:

> The weather was dreadful. We had always either snow or hail. We were forced to put our knapsacks on our heads to protect us from its violence.

There are significant touches:

> The mules used to run crying, up and down, hurt by the hailstones.

The Highlanders had to betake themselves to breeches.

> They could not live in their kilts; the cold would have killed them. In bright weather they looked longingly down on the plains of France, and they blessed the day that brought orders for the descent, which was to bring their general an addition to his laurels.

On the morning of the 10th November the armies came down on the Nivelle by moonlight. Hill's troops had been moved back from Roncesvalles to the Bastan. His orders were to deliver a frontal attack on D'Erlon, while Beresford assailed his right. The French had busily employed themselves in fortifying positions which nature had already in many cases made almost impregnable. Two parallel ranges, the Great and the Little Rhune, were precipitous scarps with rocky bastions. Hill, after a long night march, came into touch with the enemy at seven in the morning. Fatigue was forgotten. Covering his flank with the Spaniards, he sent the 2nd Division against D'Armagnac and carried D'Erlon's first positions.

The 6th Division, with a Portuguese battalion, had passed the river lower down, and with left shoulders forward were threatening the bridge above them, defended by D'Erlon's second line of redoubts. Fighting their way through broken ground, the 2nd Division was before the bridge at eleven. The bridge was carried, the flanking ravines were turned, the redoubts were either stormed or evacuated: the French fired their entrenched camp, and beat a retreat with the 6th Division in hot pursuit D'Erlon might have made a more determined stand, but the battle elsewhere to the north of the Nivelle had gone sorely against the French.

Alten with the Light Division had literally rushed the Little Rhune. Nevertheless Clausel with two divisions still stood firm; but when Hill effected his junction with Beresford, and their united columns drove a wedge between Clausel and D'Erlon, the hostile line of battle was broken. Assailed fiercely in front, menaced on either flank, Clausel's men were forced back in disorder, after stubbornly disputing each foot of ground. That rout made the strong positions of Soult's right untenable. The whole French army retired on the ridges before Bayonne, and were followed by the allies in order of battle. Four days afterwards. Hill had established his quarters at St. Pé. In a letter he says: "I do not see any prospect of our having another fight. The glorious news from the north, I trust, will settle Napoleon." Again he was no true prophet: within the month he had fought and won the memorable Battle of St. Pierre.

That was the last of Soult's five days' fighting around Bayonne, and when he broke out on Hill on the 13th of December, it was with every reasonable assurance of victory. From his central position in the city and its entrenched camp he could assail with overwhelming superiority any section of the beleaguering forces. He had tried elsewhere and failed, but Hill's position was exceptionally hazardous. On the morning of the 13th he was cut off from the rest of the army, for the Nive had come down in flood and the pontoons had been swept away. With 14,000 men and fourteen guns he had to hold his own against seven divisions, while a cavalry and infantry division were hovering over his rear.

Strong bodies of horse and foot had been passed from the camp through the city in course of the night. In the early morning they passed out through the eastern gates and formed in columns. Their movements were at first shrouded in fog, but it lifted as they were distinguished by Hill's pickets, and the battle was fought in brilliant sunshine. The one advantage of the weaker was the character of the battle-ground The solid roadway was skirted by swamps and thickets, so that the enemy could only avail himself of his superiority by bringing up his inexhaustible reserves. Hill made the most of his advantages, but never was combat more fiercely contested. His dispositions were skilful. For himself he was omnipresent: he headed the most critical counter-attack in person.

But for once the obstinate resistance was compromised by the timidity of two colonels of English regiments. It is true that the indignation of the soldiers lent fuel to their fire when brought back to the battle; and that wavering was more than redeemed by the stubborn courage of the Portuguese, who nobly sustained the reputation they had first won on the *sierra* of Busaco. Almost every officer on the staffs of the generals was either killed or wounded. The gutters in the High Street of St. Pierre are said to have been flooded with blood. Wellington pronounced it the bloodiest engagement of the war—he made that same remark more than once—and declared he had never seen so narrow a space so thickly strewn with slain. For when he heard the firing he had hurried up, sending battalion after battalion over the pontoons, which by this time had been hastily replaced. He arrived at the supreme moment, but would not interfere.

Hill had won the battle, and Hill should have all the glory. Yet when he came up the moment was supreme, for Hill had thrown his last reserves into the action. He was unusually excited, and for the first and last time was heard to mutter an oath. "Damn it, this won't do."

Wellington smiled and turned to his staff: "Hill is beginning to swear; we had better get out of the way."

"Hill," he said afterwards, "this day is yours," and he wrote joyfully to Sir John Hope and Sir J. Kennedy that "Hill had given the enemy a terrible beating."

The battle was a turning-point in the campaign. Wellington had achieved his grand object of drawing Soult away from Bayonne: now he could strike in either direction, and his advance was only delayed by the rains and the flooding of the country. Hill held a firm grip on the Adour, obstructing the French communications by the river.

There, as when Craufurd was guarding the Coa, the hostile pickets, only parted by a narrow stream, came to a very friendly understanding. Not only was there no sharpshooting, but they carried civilities and a system of barter to such length that Wellington issued a general order on the subject. There was one amusing incident in Hill's corps, and a rather delicate case. On a stone in the middle of the stream a canteen was placed with a piece of money: the coin was removed in due course, and the canteen filled with cognac.

One evening Private Patten, who was standing sentry, found to his disgust that the money was gone and the canteen was empty. In righteous wrath he dashed across next morning, seized the French sentry, stripped him of his accoutrements and carried them over. The consequence was the appearance of a French captain with a flag of truce, who urged that if the accoutrements were not returned he would certainly be court-martialled and his sentry shot. Patten protested that he had the clothes in pawn for the brandy, and was not only induced to give them up under pressure, but was sentenced to three hundred lashes, which was more than he had bargained for.

Though the fault was flagrant, it would have been hard measure had he been punished, considering that his superiors had winked at the abuse. The denouement was the same as that in a very similar case under Craufurd, save that Craufurd acted on an impulse and Hill with benevolent deliberation. Patten was paraded to receive his punishment, when Hill addressed the troops and severely improved the occasion. Then he gave his discourse a more agreeable turn, expatiated on Patten's numerous deeds of gallantry, and to the delight of his audience remitted the sentence. After all, Wellington might have court-martialled himself for similar indiscretions.

Larpent tells us that when before Toulon he rode down to the Garonne, concealed his general's hat with an oilskin, got into conversation with the French *videttes*, looked quietly about him, saw all he wished to see, and then mounted and rode away. As he remarks, it was risking rather too much.

In the second week of February the general advance was resumed. The passages of the Gaves—the wild torrents which pour down from the mountains to swell the Adour—were forced in swift succession, Hill's corps always working round to the right, on the upper waters of the tributaries. There was much skirmishing and some sharp fighting; bridges were blown up; fords depending on the rise and fall of the rivers were found and passed under heavy fire, but Soult made his only serious stand at Orthez, on the Gave de Pau. This is not the place to sketch the battle, where Hill played but a subsidiary part; Beresford and Picton bore the brunt. Hill's charge was to menace the massive bridge, which, though its strength had defied the destructive skill of the French engineers, was so commanded and defended as to be pronounced impassable.

But when Wellington changed his plan of operations, and the scales were trembling, Hill had orders to pass the river at any cost. He was either to cover the flank of the assailing forces from Harispe's attack, or in the event of victory to cut Soult's retreat to Pau. He could not force the bridge, but he forded the Gave higher up. When the day was won and the French were retiring, his rapid advance changed orderly retreat into panic-stricken rout. As he saw the confusion spread he pressed the enemy harder, till it became a race between vanquished and victors for the Adour. Cotton coming up with the cavalry took the lead, his troopers taking fences and jumping water in their stride, while the fugitives flung away muskets and accoutrements.

The pursuit was only stopped when the horses gave in from exhaustion. The flight had been fast, the confusion great, and there were many desertions among the unwilling conscripts, yet Soult rallied his forces again with little show of demoralisation. He had charged Clausel with the defence of his magazines at Aire, on the southern bank of the Adour. Hill was detached to seize them on the 5th March, and mastered the place after some sharp fighting. The bloodshed was greater than need have been, had the assault been more deliberately scientific.

But Wellington was acting on Napoleon's maxim of always driving a beaten enemy, and Hill's orders were peremptory. He was to attack at once, though he had neither knowledge of the ground nor time to examine it. Then Soult was withdrawing sullenly on Toulouse, often facing round, and always defending any position of vantage. The strongest stand he made, and the sharpest affair in which Hill was concerned, was at Tarbes, where he led his centre column down the steep main street, forced the bridge, and charged victoriously up the slopes beyond, to be confronted with solid masses on a farther ridge. Dusk closed the combat, and in the night Soult had retired again, to reach Toulouse by forced marches.

In that great southern arsenal of France, with its massive walls, its circle of heavily armed redoubts and girdling rivers, he turned at bay. He would not believe in the collapse of the Empire: he still hoped that Suchet would respond to his reiterated appeals. His veterans were rather irritated than dejected by repeated discomfiture: he was seconded by such fighting generals as Taupin and Harispe. In the days that were left him he laboured indefatigably at strengthening his outworks. The delay on Wellington's part was unavoidable: his corps were divided by the swift Garonne, and he could not control its rise and fall.

Hill, who had passed it once, was constrained to recross: he had turned engineer for the nonce, and was preoccupied with pontoon bridging. It tested even his proverbial coolness, which, in the consciousness of doing its best, calmly resigned itself to the inevitable. Afterwards, when talking over the campaign, he often alluded to the trouble those bridges had caused him.

> For instance, at a point where all seemed most promising, I found we had not enough to cross by exactly *one* boat, and we had all our work to do over again.

Even when all the bridging was at last effected, Soult had the advantage of working upon the inner radius. He had his divisions under his hand, whereas Hill's headquarters were eleven miles from those of the commander-in-chief, and the only way of communication was by the pontoons of the Garonne. The purposeless battle might have been avoided by telegraphs or a good postal service, but every day was strengthening the defences, and Wellington had good reason for haste. It was fought on 10th April, and on an Easter Sunday.

Again Hill's role was a subsidiary one. Opposed to Soult's left, he hung over the suburb of St. Cyprian, "in order to draw a part of the enemy's force and attention to that side." There were desperate fluctuations in the battle elsewhere. At one time it seemed that repulse of the allies was certain: at another, Soult saw the veterans in whom he trusted hurled down in wild confusion from the heights their gallantry had won. But Hill had the quality of selfrestraint. Unlike Picton, who would always turn a feint into a real attack, he held fast to his instructions unless influenced by unforeseen circumstances. He drove the enemy out of the exterior works, forcing them behind the old city walls, but there he halted. He had been ordered not to assail the second line.

Still hot from the fluctuating fortunes of the combat, next morning Soult was ready to renew the battle. Wellington held back for another day; for one thing, he wished to discuss the situation with Hill. And that day brought wise reflection to the French marshal. Suchet had not come to his succour, and he could not afford to be shut up in Toulouse. With his usual decision he arranged one of his masterly retreats. The morning of the 12th saw Toulouse evacuated, and further bloodshed was happily spared on that side of the battle-ground.

6

The Peninsular War came to an end. The Irishman who had triumphantly carried the British colours from Torres Vedras to Toulouse was rewarded with a dukedom, and five of his chief captains were raised to the peerage. Sir Rowland became Lord Hill of Almarez and Hawkstone. Eager to see his family and Shropshire, he was in England before the end of May. The nation was wildly enthusiastic over the return of the Peninsular heroes, and Wellington's "right-hand man" was overwhelmed with honours and congratulations. Swords were presented to him and Beresford at a great gathering in the Guildhall. He was cheered by excited mobs whenever he was recognised in the streets. His journey to Shrewsbury was a triumphal progress, and at Shrewsbury all Shropshire seemed to have mustered. His modesty was sorely tried, for he was the most diffident of men, and he only forgot his shyness in the heat and bustle of battle.

He had a sad experience of hand-shaking at the London Guildhall, but it was nothing to what he went through when presented with the freedom of his county capital. He declared that he ran away for the first time in his life. "I never fled from the fury of my enemies, but now I have been obliged to do so from the kindness of my friends." His young nephew, who had been taken to breakfast with him on his return by his venerable and reverend uncle and namesake, has an interesting recollection of the conversation.

The spoils of Vittoria were mentioned, which, as he says, seemed odd, seeing that the general prided himself on a china drinking-cup being the only article of booty he had carried off. It appeared, however, that that was not quite the case, for after Vittoria his servant, jealously catering for him, had transferred an ample provision of hams and tongues from King Joseph's carriage to Sir Rowland's—a striking contrast between the conduct of the English general and that of Soult, whose acquaintance he made subsequently at the Queen's coronation.

On that occasion the French marshal had showed his ready wit by paying Wellington a graceful compliment. In the hall of Apsley House he was arrested by Canova's statue of Napoleon, and expressed his admiration. The Duke remarked that it always struck him that the globe in the Emperor's hand was too small for the figure. "*C'est voyez vous, Duc que L'Anglèterre n'y est pas comprise*," was the answer, worthy of Talleyrand. Soult was again at Apsley House during the Exhibition of 1851, when his host, who was always outspoken, hit him hard with a stinging and less courtly repartee. The marshal, who was being shown the collection of paintings, remarked on the absence of important Spanish paintings. By the way, the rich loot he had gathered in Spain must have made him fastidious. "*Ah, Monsieur*," said the Duke, "*Je vous ai suivi*"

A model squire and county magistrate was spoiled when Hill took to soldiering. Self-condemned to celibacy, no man was more inclined to domestic life, and except at the calls of duty and glory it was hard to tempt him from his family circle. Few soldiers of his rank and modest means have been so indifferent to lucrative promotion. On five occasions at least he declined high appointments. Once after the battle of Toulouse; now when he was offered the command in Scotland; again when he had the refusal of the command in India; and twice when the

Mastership of the Ordnance was pressed upon him.

Now, like a boy broken loose from school, he was set upon enjoying himself. He took his favourite sister to London in spring, intending to have a good time. *Dis aliter visum.* He had engaged a box for an evening at the opera. In the afternoon he had a summons to Downing Street. News had come that Napoleon was on the march for Brussels. On the frontier the Crown Prince of the Netherlands was on guard with a motley corps of Dutch and Belgians, English and Germans. It was feared that his youth and impetuosity might hurry him into premature action; nor were the apprehensions groundless, as was shown when he sacrificed a regiment at Waterloo. Hill was charged with the delicate mission of moderating his ardour, for the Prince was known to hold him in high regard.

In that mission he succeeded, but in three days he was superseded by Wellington, who had hurried to Brussels from Vienna. Then the Duke made rapid preparations to meet the impending attack. His mixed army was in two corps. The first, under the Prince of Orange, touched the Prussians on its left flank, extending westwards to Enghien. There Hill took up the line of defence, and his troops were stationed from Alt to Audenarde. He had his headquarters at Grammont. By remarkable coincidences he was again opposed to his old antagonist, Girard of Arroyo Molinos, and was within gunshot of the *château* of the Prince D'Aremberg, who had been taken in the action and sent a prisoner to Shrewsbury, to be made welcome by Hill's Shropshire neighbours.

Wellington was persuaded that Napoleon must assail him on the right, and his frequent and curt despatches to Hill indicate his grave preoccupation. Hence to Hill were assigned some of the staunchest battalions in an unreliable army. Consequently it was the other corps which was engaged at Quatre Bras, and bore the long and stubborn brunt at Waterloo, when the French directed the first of their indefatigable onsets on our left and centre. As the battle shifted towards the left, he gradually brought up his eager battalions and struck in at the crisis with crashing effect

The old chief, who had his quarters at Grammont, was not present at the Brussels ball. On the 16th he had orders from the Duke to move up towards the centre and to charge Prince Frederick of the Netherlands with guarding the extreme right. That night he passed in a little house on the road from Brussels to St. Jean. The evening found his corps posted to the right of the Nivelle road. He took his own stand on an eminence, whence he could command the movements on either side. He kept his station there amid showers of shot and shell, merely descending to restore the battle where any part of his line seemed to waver.

The moment came which he had foreseen, when the Emperor was to make his last desperate effort. He looked anxiously on the stately advance of the Old Guard in solid phalanx. As he saw the head of the column shattered by the fire of the allied guns, he galloped down to put himself at the head of his light Brigade, which had been sheltering behind the brow of a lower hill. That charge of his was decisive. It was such a *mêlée* as will seldom be seen again, in these days of smokeless powder and long ranges. "Volleys at half pistol-shot"—as a staff officer describes it—were followed by hand-to-hand fighting and heroic single combats. It was then that Napoleon dropped his glass, with the despairing exclamation, "*Mon Dieu, ils sont mêlés*." Adams, the brigadier, was struck down, and Colonel Seaton, afterwards Lord Colborne, took his place. Hill had his horse shot under him—the charger had five bullets through the body.

It was so much a case of every man for himself that for half-an-hour the general was scarcely missed. He had not actually been ridden over, like Blücher; he escaped with severe bruises, and when he reappeared the survivors of his staff welcomed him with heartfelt joy. When he fell, he was riding alone: for all his staff had been killed, wounded, or scattered. Maitland's Guards and Seaton's Light Brigade bivouacked on the ground, when sheer exhaustion had compelled them to relinquish the pursuit, while the Prussians, swinging round on the enemy's flank and rear, were following up the chase, sabring relentlessly. Hill, kept awake by the pain of his bruises, passed a sleepless night in the cottage he had occupied on the previous evening, listening to the moans of the wounded who had been carried back, and to the shrieks of the sufferers under the knives of the surgeons.

Three of his brothers had been in the field, and two had been taken to Brussels badly hurt. Next day, with Wellington, he visited Blücher. Neither of the veterans seems to have been much shaken by their falls, for, as Hill wrote to his sister, they found "the old marshal amusing himself with Buonaparte's hat, star, and personal baggage, which with his carriage had been taken by the Prussian cavalry."

Waterloo saw the close of Hill's active career. He took over the French posts around Paris when they were surrendered. At the end of the year he shifted his command to Cambray, whence he was summoned to London on disagreeable business. When Wellington heard that his old friend had suffered serious pecuniary losses, he wrote immediately:

> I have a large sum of money entirely at my command, and I assure you that I could not apply it in a manner more satisfactory to me than in accommodating you, my dear Hill, to whom I am under so many obligations.

The generous offer was warmly acknowledged, but gratefully declined. On his return to Cambray he had a severe illness. "Nothing," he wrote, "could be kinder than the behaviour of the Duke," who begged him to come to his house in Paris for change of scene. While at Cambray he again kept hounds for the amusement of his officers, but his own favourite pursuit was boar-hunting, and he had one narrow escape. The boar charged home: the onlookers were in alarm, but the old sportsman's nerve was firm as ever. Armed only with a short spear, he calmly stood the rush. A thrust in the face turned the charge, and a second went home to the heart Wellington sent him another spear when he heard of the exploit.

On the evacuation of France he left the Continent for the last time. There was a remarkable family gathering at Hawkstone, where the patriarchal father of the household saw himself surrounded by six sons and four daughters. Four of the sons, as by miracles, had escaped the perils of the war. Only the eldest of the family was missing. In his quiet Shropshire home the old soldier passed twelve uneventful years, still walking out with his gun or following the hounds, and interesting himself in the farmyard and garden. His kindness to his poor neighbours was unfailing; he was munificent in unobtrnsive charity, and it is said that when he bestowed a kindness he was far more embarrassed than the recipient

Nor was he to be tempted away by the tenders of honourable and lucrative posts. It was then he declined the Indian command and the Master-Generalship of the Ordnance. The latter would have made a sojourn in London compulsory, and he hated city life. But circumstances alter resolutions, and in 1828 he could not resist the offer of the blue ribbon of the army, which Wellington had honoured in the wearing. In that year the Duke consented to charge himself with the destinies of the country, and as Prime Minister he invited Hill to replace him at the Horse Guards. He answered immediately, and with his habitual promptitude of action brought his own letter to London.

All I shall say at present is that I accept the flattering offer with pride and gratitude, and that it shall ever be my anxious study to fulfil your Grace's expectations and wishes, which I trust I shall be enabled to do by unremitting attention to my duties.

He kept his word: he renounced pleasures for duty: he made his home in town, and thenceforth his visits to Shropshire were few and far between, except when health made change of air imperative. The part of his duties he disliked the most was rejecting incessant applications. The widows of officers besieged his door; the ladies were voluble, and it was not in his nature to listen to them with anything but kindly sympathy. When asked how he managed to get rid of these supplicants, he answered with a twinkle in his eye that he received them in a room with a single chair, and insisted on their being seated.

"Then they are sorry to see me standing, so they do not stay very long."

Both George IV. and his brother were exceedingly gracious, but the old soldier had less hesitation in dealing with the monarchs when they hinted at patting pressure on his conscience. Twice with King William, though he had strong personal regard for him, he gave unmistakable proof of his independence and straightforwardness; and it is but fair to say that His Sailor Majesty respected him all the more. The first occasion was when the king said with his seamanlike bluntness that he was "positively decided" that a certain officer should be promoted. Hill, couching his refusal in respectful terms, was as positively decided he should not; and when the king gave way, he sent straight for the officer, to report the interview and explain his reasons.

The second was when he was urged to vote in the Lords for the Reform Bill being remitted to Committee. "I said that, if I were to act contrary to my conscientious feelings and my known declarations, I should so lower myself in the eyes of the world and the army that I should not be able to render service to His Majesty or the country. The king said he could understand my feelings, and that everyone had a right to have his own: he had his." A very amenable man he was, but no one stood more stiffly on his rights or on the dignity of the office he safeguarded for his successors. In his diaries there is one significant note.

Came to town to see the king on the subject of orders issued without my knowledge. The interview was satisfactory, and I am inclined to think nothing of the sort will in future occur.

Firm as he was where a principle was involved, he had the old chivalrous loyalty. After his death a purse was found, with a crown piece enclosed in paper. On the paper was written:

> This crown was won by Lord Hill from His Majesty, King William IV., at Windsor Castle. I will do my best to preserve *it* for him.—H.

He had an anxious time when political ferment ran high and rioters were abroad. He made his old military chief the confidant of his troubles and his counsellor. And Wellington wrote in his off-hand style:

> Never mind, Hill: you have enough to satisfy your conscience. Everybody knows the army under your charge has saved the country.

His old age was green, but strength was failing: Peel's accession to power gave him a fresh lease of encouragement, and perhaps he held to office too long. He kept on at the routine of work in spite of a growing sense of exhaustion, but nature would not be denied, and the end came in the summer of 1842, when he sent in his resignation. It was accepted with flattering expressions of reluctance, and he was touched and gratified by an autograph letter from the young Queen. He was created a viscount when he took leave of the Horse Guards, and compliments, condolences, or congratulations showered in upon him from many old comrades.

He only survived his resignation for a few months, and on the 10th December 1842 passed peacefully away. He had lost the years of quiet rustication he had looked forward to, and worn himself out in the service of his country. We read only half his character in the portrait that has been bequeathed us. The face is that of a benevolent divine, rather than of the general who had led armies in the field and never spared himself in the hottest of the battle. We see nothing of the firmness that never failed in emergency, of the iron determination that held to the hill at Talavera, or of the fiery dash that swept all before it on that wild autumn morning at Arroyo Molinos.

General Craufurd

1

Among Wellington's lieutenants in the Peninsula two figures stand out conspicuously, as striking the popular fancy—the stern Craufurd and the rugged Picton. With no claim to the highest order of military genius, it must be admitted that Craufurd in special embodies the romance of the war. It was emphatically a war of surprises, of manoeuvring in a mountainous country of almost unexampled difficulties. Rugged *sierras* with few practicable passes, traversed elsewhere by paths only known to the *contrabistas* and goat-herds— rivers running in their deep and rocky beds, rising and sinking with the rainfall and the melting of the snows—opposed themselves to swift and sudden combinations and effectually screened the hostile operations.

Sure intelligence was of supreme importance, but intelligence was seldom trustworthy and often altogether lacking. The master mind might be there to direct from headquarters, but the person of the commander-in-chief could not divide itself. He could hazard little, nor could he afford to throw away a chance, when, with an undecided Cabinet at home, a serious reverse might lead to his recall and even to the withdrawal of the British from the Peninsula. His reputation and the fortunes of the war were staked on the guard maintained by his outposts. The dashing leader of the Light Division was the man on whom that responsibility chiefly devolved.

In the most critical emergencies, in advance or retreat, in directing the scouting and mounting the guards, in protracting the audacious games of bluff before the overwhelming forces of a vigilant enemy, Craufurd was the soul of the Field Intelligence Department, wielding a sword that was ever ready to feint, to strike, or to parry. The surest proof of his rare genius for outpost duty is that Wellington was content to overlook his indiscretions and on one memorable occasion to condone disobedience which gravely endangered far-reaching plans, when temper and patience had been strained to the uttermost. With the soldier-like faults which were the causes of continual anxiety, the commander-in-chief knew what he must lose by superseding him, but it would have been well for the fame of the leader of the Light Division had he had more of his chief's self-control and imperturbable coolness of judgment

When at the age of fifteen he was gazetted an ensign in 1779, favouritism went far at the Horse Guards. For the most part the men who distinguished themselves in the Peninsula, who held important commands or prominent staff appointments, were of high birth and breeding, or backed by the influence of relatives conspicuous in fashionable society. Young Craufurd was fortunate. He was descended from an old family in Ayrshire, and his father, who had sold his estates and become a man about town, was an intimate of a Scottish neighbour, the notorious "Old Q." That was enough to mark his position. His sons inherited hereditary qualities, and Robert had a double portion of his father's impetuous temper, but all had the energy and gifts to avail themselves of the paternal influence. They were pushed by their friends, and they deserved pushing. Robert's elder brother, Sir Charles, was the favourite equerry of the Duke of York, so was able to give the young cadet a powerful helping hand. But Robert, though hot-tempered to a vice, grappled friends to himself with hooks of steel, and owed much to the admiring partiality of Wyndham—"the most accomplished gentleman of his time."

In those days boys were gazetted to the army as children were sent to sea. Craufurd was barely fifteen when he got his commission, and in four years he had his company, though, indeed, promotion was almost as rapid in the Crimean campaign. Naturally most of those youngsters were absolutely untaught. British pluck and common sense were their simple stock-in-trade, but Craufurd had gone through a course of training more practical than any that can be taught in staff colleges. like others of the future heroes of the Peninsula, he had wide experience of foreign service.

As captain of the 75th he was with Lord Cornwallis through the first war with Tippoo Saib, and in a warfare where ambushes and surprises were frequent, and when the columns advancing through jungle and *nullahs* were often enveloped in clouds of irregular horse, he mastered the duties of a regimental officer, and graduated in the science of scouting. Returning to England in 1794, he was saved by his brother

General Crauford

from rusting in barracks. Charles, though a favoured boon companion of the commander-in-chief, was a scientific soldier, profoundly interested in his profession, and had been sent as military *attaché* to the Austrian headquarters. He was present in the first memorable and fatal campaign, when the fortunes of the Hapsburgs waned before the rising star of Buonaparte. Perhaps there can be no better schooling for an intelligent student than looking on as an interested but dispassionate spectator at a succession of mistakes, reverses, and disasters.

The venerable methods and sluggish movements of the Austrian *martinets* were utterly upset by the startling innovations of the terrible incarnation of war who set precedents at defiance. Playing a game that was contrary to all the received rules, he scored nevertheless at every point as if he were indeed the omniscient man of Destiny. When the Austrians were being out-generalled, out-manoeuvred, and out-flanked, Craufurd was learning the invaluable lessons he practised when holding the line of the Agueda. And all the time he was acquiring the knowledge of German which stood him in good stead at more than one critical moment, when the German Hussars formed a part of his Light Division. When Charles Craufurd was severely wounded, his brother replaced him as *attaché*, and gained no little credit by his reports of the operations.

A zealous soldier, if ever there was one, he spared no trouble to perfect himself in his profession. Recalled in 1797, he was promoted lieutenant-colonel, and next we see him playing an important part in an ignoble but anxious warfare. In the rebellion of 1798 he was Deputy Quartermaster-General in Ireland under his old friend and commander, Lord Cornwallis. Colonel Craufurd was in no way responsible for the "Race of Castlebar" and the other untoward incidents before Humbert and his handful of French surrendered to irresistible force.

On the contrary, he had high commendation from his superiors. Another swift shifting of the scenes, and next year he was again on the Continent as military *attaché*. It was his good fortune to be present at the most romantic of campaigns, when Suwarrow, leading his ragged legions from the plains of Italy, made his startling descent from the Alpine glaciers on the valleys at the head waters of the Rhine and Rhone. Thanks to the habitual tardiness of the Austrian advance, he missed the satisfaction of seeing the Russian veteran at close grips with the spoiled child of Fortune.

But he saw Suwarrow extricate himself from the Shackenthal

when apparently entangled hopelessly in the toils—perhaps the most brilliant retreat that was ever executed. He may have remembered that lesson of the rough old master when snatching the Light Division from the consequences of his rashness on the Coa. Again he was on the staff of the Duke of York in the expedition to Holland, when the Duke, like the Austrian field-marshals, showed how things ought not to be done, though, unlike His Royal Highness, he came home with enhanced reputation.

By a strange coincidence, both the brothers, though far apart, were married on the same day of the same year, the 7th February 1800. The marriages had no little influence on Craufurd's career. For himself, thenceforth he was torn by two conflicting passions—devotion to his wife, and ambition of glory. There never was a more loving, a more uxorious husband. Yet his whole soul was in the service, and when the Continent was on fire, it would have broken his heart to miss any opportunity of distinction. Had he accepted the lucrative appointments within his reach at home, the laurels of his comrades would have left him no peace. Yet once indeed, and sorely against the will of Wellington, he asked and obtained furlough from the Peninsula, when his division was sure to be in the front of any fighting. But the home sickness had become unendurable: at any cost he must hurry back to embrace his wife. She mingled with the disturbed dreams of the bivouac, and the soldiers who feared and the officers who shrunk from the lowering brow of their stern commander little suspected that the gloom had been deepened by the tender emotions he severely repressed.

Anything in reason he asked at home might have been easily obtained, for his brother's marriage with the Dowager-Duchess of Newcastle had greatly increased the family influence. In those days, there was nothing to refuse to the man with nominations to many pocket boroughs, and when it was a case of a soldier with the record of Robert Craufurd, the most inveterate malignity of party could not have taxed the Government with favouritism. Craufurd asked for nothing, nor is it easy to conceive why he should have consented to be returned for East Retford, though he only followed the fashion of others of the lieutenants. He was no politician and no orator: his fiery appeals to the men of the Light Division were always brief, though much to the point.

He sat for a few years, a silent member, and gave up the seat in 1806, in the assurance of being sent on active service. For he had been fortunate, as we said, in winning the friendship and confidence of the all-powerful Secretary at War. Wyndham, as a politician, was the most brilliant of failures, the victim of his versatility of talent. He was lacking in concentration of mind and decision of character: he had a fatally inveterate habit of hesitation. But he was a strong War Minister, who had the good of the country at heart, and when he made choice of a man for a definite piece of work, he was not to be turned from his purpose. Craufurd had been promoted in 1805, and in the following year he stood at the bottom of the roll of colonels. Nevertheless Wyndham selected him for the command of a force intended to carry out critical operations, to the intense disgust of the seniors who were passed over.

Both Wyndham and Craufurd had to take their chance of the responsibilities of failure, at a time when the levees at the Horse Guards were overcrowded with clamorous applicants, strong in parliamentary influence and confident in the strength of their claims. Craufurd was made a brigadier and confirmed in a command which should have ordinarily fallen to a lieutenant-general. The force with which he embarked at Falmouth in November 1807 consisted of four regiments of Foot, five companies of the 95th Rifles, now the Rifle Corps, and two squadrons of Dragoons, in all over 4000 men. There is still a mystery as to the original object of the expedition. It is said it was intended for a descent on Chili. Nor is the matter of any consequence, as it was diverted elsewhere, but considering our relations at the time with Spanish America, whether it was ever intended for Chili seems more than doubtful.

In the beginning of the century, when there were neither telegraphs, steam posts, nor war correspondents, admirals on foreign stations and generals in distant commands had necessarily wide discretionary powers. If they chose to play for fame at the risk of courts-martial, they were free to do it. As it chanced, in the year when Craufurd sailed, three of the most daring spirits in the service had come together at the Cape. Admiral Sir Home Popham proposed to General Sir David Baird a scheme as daring as any which had ever suggested itself to Drake or Raleigh. It was nothing less than to drain the slender garrison at the Cape for the storm of the great and wealthy city of Buenos Ayres, and the occupation of the vast territory thereto appertaining. Baird was enchanted by the very audacity of the idea, and Brigadier-General Beresford, who was called into their councils, eagerly volunteered for the command of the troops.

All the ships of the fleet were taken up for the expedition, though the admiral had strict orders to confine himself to the protection of the Cape. The expedition succeeded beyond expectation: the Spaniards were surprised and their city was captured. When news reached London of the departure of the adventurers, orders had been immediately despatched for their recall. Of course the orders arrived too late, and the answer from Popham was a glowing report of the value of our latest annexation and of the friendly feelings of our new subjects. The flood of national jubilation swept the ministers along with it, and the gross violation of imperative instructions was not only condoned but commended.

Unfortunately our grand acquisition had scarcely been won when it was lost. The Spaniards, rallying from their panic, realised the weakness of the occupying force. They were happy in having a Frenchman in their service, a man of spirit and capacity. Liniers reinforced his few regulars from other garrisons, mustered levies from the country, and fomented an insurrection within the city walls. The English after a gallant resistance were compelled to capitulate, and Beresford and 1300 men became prisoners of war, after putting more than half that number of their assailants *hors de combat*.

Craufurd had landed at the Cape and was awaiting instructions. Apparently even he had been kept in the dark as to the intentions of the Government. Then came a letter from the friendly Wyndham, beginning with a characteristic apology for procrastination. The same procrastination had nearly driven Sir Gilbert Elliot to despair, when, as Commissioner in Corsica, he was impatiently expecting directions as to accepting the cession of the island. Wyndham began:

> Though I have often reproached myself for not having written to you, I am very sorry for having occasion for retrieving my fault, such as is now presented to me.

Vague rumours of the disaster in Buenos Ayres had reached London, and Craufurd was directed to act as if they were true. He was immediately to embark his troops for the La Plata, having previously effected a junction with Sir Samuel Auchmuty, who had sailed from England in October. Craufurd was to hunt up Auchmuty, who was missing, and he succeeded in the search. Their forces were united at Monte Video, and had the expedition been left to those capable officers, unquestionably the upshot would have been very different. But, at the critical moment, there was a shifting of generals, as after Sir Arthur

Wellesley's victory of Vimiero.

In May the *Thisbe* dropped her anchors off Monte Video, being freighted with two of the most incompetent seniors that favouritism and parliamentary influence could possibly have selected. General Whitelocke was not only incapable but a coward—as was proved to demonstration when he was subsequently brought to a court-martial, and Leveson-Gower, though not lacking in courage, was in all other respects a worthy second.

The little army moved forward on Buenos Ayres. Craufurd, in place of commanding as he had hoped—he had left Falmouth with the complete staff of a general officer—was leading the light Brigade, which formed the advance. In the brigade, by the way, were eight companies of the 95th—a regiment which fought under him in all his Peninsular engagements. Gower was in command of the division, and directed the operations. The Spaniards began the fighting when the British approached the city. Craufurd countered them with an impetuous charge, drove them from all their positions, captured their guns and entered the gates, sweeping the fugitives before him in wild confusion.

Had he pressed home the charge, as he said deliberately afterwards at Whitelocke's court-martial, the panic-stricken city was at his mercy. But Gower, in an excess of caution, gave orders to sound the recall. It might have been better had Craufurd been deaf, as Nelson was blind to the signals at Copenhagen. But Gower's action was not unjustifiable, for he had been left unsupported, and Whitelocke with the main body was lagging far behind.

When he did come up, he still hesitated and delayed, giving Liniers the breathing time he wanted. Liniers rallied his soldiers and reassured the citizens, who had everything in their favour when standing on their defence. Though there were few of the massive convents which could resist the fire of siege batteries, to all intents Buenos Ayres was another Saragossa. The broad, straight thoroughfares could be raked by cannon, and each of the flat-roofed houses was a fortress, with parapets offering effectual protection from musketry. When Whitelocke at last decided to attack, he made masterly arrangements for failure.

As if to make his dispositions the more inexplicable, he was fully alive to the dangers he had to face. Craufurd said, in evidence, that when accompanying him round the works at Monte Video, the commander-in-chief called his attention to the construction of the houses. He added that he never would risk his troops in the more populous city of Buenos Ayres, where the streets would be swarming with armed defenders. Nevertheless that was exactly what was done. The plan of attack had at least the merit of simplicity. The force was broken up into weak detachments; no arrangements were made for mutual support; each separate regiment was divided into wings; each section was to follow the street in front of it, till it reached one of the many open *plazas*; there it was to form up, and wait for orders.

There was to be no firing till the columns reached their destinations, and none of the muskets were loaded. The troops, if resisted, were to rely on the bayonet against bolted doors and shuttered windows. At the head of each column were a couple of corporals, provided with tools for breaking in the doors; but had all the soldiers turned pincers for the nonce, they would have been barely equal to the occasion. The Light Brigade advanced along parallel streets, each section followed by a three-pounder.

The attack commenced soon after daybreak in the summer morning. It encountered neither pickets nor sentries; not a soul was to be seen in the silent streets; the columns might have been moving through a city of the dead. Yet there were signs that they were treading towards the verge of a volcano, for the vistas in front of them were cut by trenches and blocked by barricades. Suddenly a shot broke the stillness. At the signal, the city burst out into explosion. The barricades belched fire from cannon behind them. There was a rush in the houses to the parapets and upper windows; converging showers of ball rained down on men with uncharged muskets, who were powerless to force the solid doors.

Without pausing to load, they pressed on to the storm of the barricades, only to be riddled by a flanking fire tram musketry in the side streets. Liniers had made his dispositions with consummate skill, and the Spaniards shot steadily from under cover. Officers and men were falling fast: still the street-fighting went on with varying fortunes. There was no room for generalship; the word of order was " Onward." Each section of combatants was acting for itself, knowing nothing of what was befalling its comrades. Auchmuty had made his way to the great *plaza*, taking prisoners and many cannon, though his columns were fearfully cut up. The 88th—the Connaught Rangers—was nearly annihilated, and the few survivors were forced to surrender.

The same fate befell a part of the left of the Light Brigade; the rest, led by the gallant Pack—afterwards Sir Dennis—fought their way to their comrades of the right, commanded by Craufurd in person. His position seemed desperate, but he had been brought to bay near a convent, and he threw himself into the building, on the chance that the reserves might come to his rescue. Bat the roof was swept with grape and ball; guns were brought up to breach the gates; there was neither food nor water, and the ammunition was running short. Elsewhere the sound of firing had ceased, and the choice was between massacre and surrender. After hasty consultation with his officers he chose the latter alternative, for, stern disciplinarian as he was, he was always regardful of the lives of his men, and never wasted them wantonly save when his fighting instincts got beyond control.

The humiliation to his proud spirit must have been almost intolerable, and we may learn something of his mood in that bitter moment from the report of one of his rank and file, who published interesting *Recollections,* (also published by Leonaur as *The Compleat Rifleman Harris*), which have all the stamp of veracity. Rifleman Harris says that when the confusion of the fighting was at its height he and others of the Rifles had orders from their "fine and chivalrous officer" to shoot the general if they saw him.

For Craufurd in vindictive indignation had persuaded himself that Whitelocke was a traitor as well as a coward. Craufurd's captivity did not last long. Within twenty-four hours Whitelocke had assented to all the humiliating conditions of Liniers. The prisoners of the previous day, with those who had been taken under Beresford, were handed over, on the understanding that the British troops were to be withdrawn from the La Plata.

The whole business had been one of unmixed mortification for Craufurd. He had been reduced from the chief command to the leading of a brigade, and that magnificent brigade had been lamentably mishandled: in the outbreak of indignant disappointment in England which welcomed the return of the force, he smarted from the sense that his courage was impeached, and that he was sharing the infamy of the generals who had victimised him. The impression was absolutely erroneous, and at Whitelocke's trial Colonel Pack bore testimony to Craufurd's eagerness in courting death when he consented to save the lives of his men. But his grandson shrewdly surmised that the misfortune had an evil influence both on his character and career.

The cloud that settled on him then never altogether lifted, and it deepened the constitutional gloom of a naturally saturnine temperament Moreover, the lesson on the deplorable consequences of timid vacillation was the last he needed to learn. His spirit wanted the curb rather than the spur, and the memories of Buenos Ayres may have hurried him into the audacities which compromised his reputation as a lieutenant of Wellington. If he had not passed under the Caudine Forks in South America, he might never have risked his rash engagement on the Coa.

2

The Argentine adventure had been discreditable to the English arms, but Craufurd had rather gained than lost reputation. His conduct, like that of Auchmuty and Pack, contrasted with the misconduct of their commander, and feeling in England ran all the higher that the failure was rightly attributed to his unseasonable supersession. The unlucky expedition had been an improvised interlude in the troubles that were then convulsing Europe and imperilling the very existence of the British Empire. Wide opportunities for distinction were opening, when the battle of continental markets and maritime supremacy was to be fought out in the Peninsula.

Moore had been recalled from the mad expedition to Sweden to take command of the army in Portugal. He was to be reinforced by 10,000 troops from England, and they had sailed from Falmouth in October 1807 under Sir David Baird. Baird and Craufurd were congenial spirits. Both were men of iron resolution; both carried courage in action almost to excess; both were stern to a fault in enforcing discipline, and yet had a kindly regard for the welfare of the soldiers they never spared in battle. Baird was delighted to have a man after his own heart, and on whom he could rely in all emergencies, in command of the Light Brigade.

But the fates were against them throughout that unfortunate campaign. They reached Corunna, to be forbidden to land by the allies they had come to succour. When permitted to disembark after a fortnight's delay, the military chest was empty. The Home Government, which had just shipped millions of dollars to be squandered by the Spaniards, had neglected to supply their own general with the sinews of war. Had not Moore managed to spare him £8000, he would have started penniless. While he and Craufurd were chafing on the transports, their involuntary inaction delayed the operations of Moore. Nor were Spanish petulance and financial embarrassments the most serious obstacles to be surmounted.

In that wet and stormy climate, the march had been undertaken far too late. The streams were rushing down in flood, and the roads were well nigh impracticable for wheels. While Baird was pushing forward with dogged determination, he had repeatedly to act on contradictory orders. Now he was advancing, now he was retiring, and again he was concentrating in expectation of battle. It was no fault of Moore's, who was modifying his plans on the receipt of conflicting information, and who had reason to believe that Baird was being threatened by Soult. But at last, on the 20th December, his division was united to the main army at Mayorga.

Up to the 23rd, Sir John Moore's mind was still set on an advance. Deluded by false assurances, he had believed in the effective support of the Spaniards: and, deceived as to the Emperor's intentions, he had hoped to strike at Madrid and menace the enemy's communications. Of a sudden he awakened to the fact that the whole strength of the French was to be concentrated on crushing the English invasion. Napoleon was swooping down with his accustomed swiftness, and his divisions, set in motion from all quarters, were being directed towards their objective by the genius of that master of combinations. Nevertheless, he had partially achieved his purpose. He had proved his allies and found them wanting, but he had given them breathing time: the pressure on Saragossa was relieved, and Andalusia was saved in the meanwhile. If he were to save himself not a moment was to be lost, for already his army was grievously imperilled. He had been lost had he hesitated.

Napoleon had already sent his orders to Soult: "If the British retreat, pursue them closely." For himself, he hurried forward from Tordesillas, barely taking time to eat or sleep. Yet he arrived too late on the scene of action, for he learned at Valderas that Moore was already beyond the Esla.

The disappointment nerved him to redoubled efforts, and the chase to Corunna might have ended differently had not more urgent affairs recalled him to Germany. His presence animated the ambitious rivalry of his generals: in his absence their jealousies revived. Yet, with Soult in supreme command, he had left an efficient substitute, and Soult, though specially excelling in retreats, was nevertheless a terrible pursuer.

Indeed he was already in pursuit before the Emperor's prescience sent him orders. His advance was pressing hard upon Moore at the difficult passage of the Esla. Baird's division formed the British rear, and Craufurd with the light Brigade was covering the rearguard. There could hardly have been worse weather for marching. The Gallician-winter had set in with premature severity: already the country was being covered with snow, and the Esla, a capricious mountain torrent, was rising fast, so that the doubtful fords were almost impassable.

On the 26th, the troops and the baggage train were being slowly passed across the single bridge of Castro Gonzalo. Everything was enveloped in. drizzling mist, but already dropping shots could be heard, where the enemy's cavalry patrols were in touch with our pickets, and threatening the lagging baggage guards. The main army was passed over in safety, but the cavalry watching the enemy was still on the farther bank. On the next day the cavalry followed, and when the last of the stragglers had crossed the bridge, Craufurd had orders to destroy it.

It was his first experience of those grave responsibilities in the Peninsula which it became his habitual business to face. He was left isolated with his brigade and a couple of guns, with a raging torrent before him, in front of an enemy of whose movements he was ignorant, but who were gathering, as he knew, in overwhelming strength. He set himself at once to the work of destruction, in such a scene and such circumstances as Salvator Rosa would have delighted to depict. Rain mingled with sleet was descending in torrents: the troops were drenched to the skin and chilled to the marrow. In the darkness of the night he heard the wheels of French waggons: their escort detached itself, and broke down upon his pickets in a desperate attempt to seize the bridge.

The charge was repulsed and the firing slackened, though skirmishers were still shooting out of the blackness. Meantime his pioneers were hard at work, but the Spanish bridges were built of massive masonry. The tools made slight impression, and each moment was precious. He decided to concentrate his efforts on two of the arches, blowing up the buttress, yet it was not till midnight that the mine was fired. Then planks were thrown across the yawning chasm, and the troops were ordered to steal down from the heights in silence. Facing the gusts of wind and rain tearing down the river channel, they trod the trembling and slippery planks in single file, and, strange to say, passed over without a casualty. Craufurd rejoined the cavalry and reserves at Benevente, and it was a marvellous example of the chances of war. Had the enemy taken the alarm from the explosion and attacked, few could have escaped either death or capture.

At Benevente there was another wonderful escape from disaster, due to the presence of mind of one of Moore's most gallant officers.

The brigade was quartered in one of the great convents, built round a vast quadrangle, with a single entrance. The horses of the cavalry were stabled in the apartments on the ground floor, and crowded so closely together as effectually to block egress. When all the wearied men were in profound slumber, two officers chanced to return from patrol. They saw that one of the large shutters had caught fire, and if the flames had spread to the horse litter on the floors, nothing could have averted an appalling catastrophe.

Happily Captain Lloyd was not only a man of nerve, but a famous athlete. He vaulted on the nearest horse, ran along the backs of the others, tore the blazing shutter from its hinges and tossed it out; then, quietly awakening a few of the men, he quenched the smouldering embers without exciting alarm. Not till the reveille was sounded did any of the others know that they had been sleeping quietly in what had been the deadliest of death-traps.

Moore, falling back through the Gallician defiles, had hoped to embark without being forced to a general action. On the 31st December, partly to relieve the strain on the commissariat, partly to secure his left flank with an alternative line of retreat, the Light Brigade under Craufurd, with the German Brigade, were ordered to march on Vigo. Thus Craufurd was left in independent command of battalions of three of the regiments which gained him his distinction in the Peninsula—the 43rd, the 52nd, and the 95th, afterwards the Rifle Brigade. The names that they bear on their colours are so many tributes to their fighting general.

Craufurd had parted from the main body before the wine caverns of Benbibre had for a time turned disciplined soldiers into a horde of mutinous ruffians. But his own men, the very pick of the army, though they had escaped that carnival of mad debauchery, were irritated and demoralised by being driven to retreat. They had scarcely left Bonillas, where they diverged into the road to Orense, when they heard heavy firing behind. Soult's advance was again assailing the British rearguard. They looked wistfully back, and murmurs were heard in the ranks that they would rather have it out with the foe than face the troubles before them. Their fiery general shared their feelings, but showed no signs of it in his impassive features.

From that day till the other when he led them into Vigo, he was stern, unfaltering and self-contained. He had few friends and no confidants among his officers, and to the soldiers he would only unbend in rare moments of sympathetic expansion. Like Napoleon, he remembered many of his best men by name—though Napoleon is said to have been prompted by Berthier—and he would cheer them and hand them his canteen when spirits were hard to come by. The difficulties to be surmounted were appalling, and the little column was in poor condition to face them.

Already the mountains were covered with snow, and the valleys were being blocked by drift The men were in rags; the most of them were going barefoot, and their tattered uniforms were always soaking. The country had been laid under heavy contribution, and the peasants had driven their cattle into the hills. All were on short rations, not a few went without, and they were pressing forward by forced marches to Orense to secure the passage of the Minho, where they feared the French might have anticipated them. There they fortunately found some supplies, for they were on the verge of starvation. When the march was resumed, the extreme of severity failed to keep order. Some would struggle to search the farms and hovels for food: others dropped from sheer fatigue and had to be brought along by the rear-guard.

Under a weaker leader there must have been a catastrophe, but Craufurd's apparent cruelty was real kindness. He was learning the lessons he put in practice on his memorable march to Talavera, and rankers who were thoroughbred soldiers like himself admired his spirit as they feared his frown. Rifleman Harris gives a graphic account of the proceedings, and says that no man not formed of stuff like Craufurd could have saved the brigade from perishing. Yet Harris had made his chiefs acquaintance under unpleasant circumstances. He was told he was to sew up some barrels in hides, with the warning that if the job was not done in half-an-hour the general had sworn to hang him. "Knowing the stuff that Craufurd was made of," Harris thought that the threat was serious, and the job was duly finished in the time.

Harris says that the commander's fiery spirit was by no means uncongenial to his fierce followers, who would have cared nothing for a meek and mild general, and adds that his solicitude for their comfort, with his keen sense of the humorous, secured him their affection as well as admiration. When demoralisation had made inevitable progress, under circumstances scarcely less trying than those of the retreat from Moscow, he had formed a bodyguard of some veterans of the Rifles, whom he seemed to regard as his familiars. There is a striking passage.

If he halted his horse to deliver one of his stern reprimands, you would see half-a-dozen lean, unshaven, shoeless, and savage riflemen standing leaning upon their rifles, and scowling up in his face as he scolded, and when he dashed the spurs into his reeking horse, they would throw up their rifles upon their shoulders and follow him again.

Still we held on resolutely—and Craufurd was not to be daunted by long miles, fatigue, or foul weather. Many a man in that retreat caught courage from his stern eye and gallant bearing. Indeed I do not think the world ever saw a more perfect soldier.

The severity, almost approaching brutality, reminds us of the dealings of some notorious private captain with a crew that could only be controlled by sheer terror. Here is a specimen of his summary "justice," when one unlucky individual was singled out for an example. Two men had been seized in the act of straying. Craufurd halted the brigade in a voice of thunder and ordered a drumhead court-martial, when they were sentenced to 100 lashes apiece. The misconduct was flagrant and the punishment fair. But, disgusted at the offence and the halt, Craufurd dismounted and stood a spectator of the trial, "looking angry as a worried bull-dog."

The whole brigade was as much out of temper as himself, and he chanced to overhear a good soldier grumble: " D—n his eyes: he had much better try to get us something to eat than harass us in this way." A more equably tempered man would have heard nothing. Craufurd snatched the rifle from the nearest soldier and knocked him down with the butt. The man picked himself up and denied having spoken.

"I heard you, sir," said Craufurd.

"I am the man who spoke," said a comrade.

"Very well," returned Craufurd, "then I'll try you."

Tried he was and summarily sentenced to 300 lashes, which were duly inflicted in cold blood next day, with his wife in the front rank of the spectators. The story is little to Craufurd's credit, for though it is notorious that he never could curb his temper, the night should have brought reflection, and his behaviour had been as undignified as ungenerous. But there was the dark side of his character—he was not only passionate, but he nursed his wrath; he was an ill man to have for enemy, either by equal or inferior.

And his moody spirit had been chafed into sullen moroseness long before he set eyes upon Vigo Bay. His was a race against time, with famine urging him forward. In alternate frosts and thaws the precipitous hills had been coated with ice: the men, staggering under their heavy knapsacks, lost their footing and rolled down, to gather themselves up painfully, all bruised and bleeding. Dysentery was busy with them, and when the sufferers dropped they gave themselves up to despair and refused to be assisted. Moreover the march was encumbered with many women and children, whom the follies of the war administration had permitted to accompany the advance. Yet Craufurd on his horse seemed omnipresent—now in the front ranks and now in the rear. He set the example of endurance and unflagging energy; personally he was always whipping in the stragglers, and was as peremptory with his officers as with the rank and file.

At the crossing of a river he saw one of them being carried on the back of one of his men. Characteristically, he did not shout his orders from the bank: he spurred in himself, and went splashing after the pair through the floating ice. "Put him down, sir, put him down; I desire you to put that officer down instantly!" And the soldier, gladly dropping his burden in mid-stream, scrambled out on the other side. Craufurd was unharassed by the enemy, and he fought no Corunna, but his conduct of that retreat was a masterly piece of service, and it was duly set down to his credit at the Horse Guards.

3

When the wrecks of the Light Brigade landed in England, they showed their countrymen the seamy side of war. A rough voyage had prolonged mitigated sufferings: they still wore the rags of the march, and these were burned immediately to disinfect the tormented wearers, who were literally swarming with vermin. Squalid, ghastly, and spectre-like, the men had thrown away their kits in Gallicia, and many had even parted with their rifles. Bat their martial spirit was unquenched, and they were still the strong skeletons of wasted battalions. Recruiting went briskly forward, and in March 1809 the battalions were again up to their normal strength, when they re-embarked full of enthusiasm at Dover to join the army under Sir Arthur Wellesley. Craufurd was again in command, and under him were many non-commissioned officers who had not only gone through the horrors of the retreat to Vigo, but shared the humiliation of the surrender in the Argentine. The men knew their leader, and the leader trusted his men.

They landed at Lisbon and were towed in boats op the Tagus to

Santarem, and there in three days Craufurd had his orders to join immediately. He knew that a decisive battle was impending. Victor was confronting Wellesley; Joseph was coming up behind; and Soult, having mustered his forces at Salamanca, was threatening a descent on the Vera of Placentia. Craufurd left Santarem, to advance by forced marches. The heat was intense: the longest marches were made at night, and in the prolonged noon-day bivouac the soldiers sought shade and sleep. The lessons practised in the Gallician retreat were enforced more severely than ever. No man was permitted to quit the column, on any pretext, without special permission. Petitioners and stragglers were passed under review by the surgeons. Men parched and perishing with thirst were tantalised by the sight of gushing fountains, and looked up longingly at the signs of wine-shops.

Sometimes the seductions would prevail and the men break away. Then the shirkers went before a drumhead court-martial, were triced up to the halberds, and flogged to their hearts' content. These punishments were so common that Costello says, in his *Life of a Rifleman*, (also published by Leonaur as *Rifleman Costello*), it was not unusual at the halt to see many victims with their knapsacks on their heads and their bodies enveloped in loose great-coats—"to ease the wounds inflicted by the lash." Through it all, nevertheless, the men, like a savage but devoted bulldog, fawned at the feet of the master, and were ready to lick the hand that beat them.

The pace had been severe enough up to Malpartida. There rumours of a battle reached the bivouac, and then Craufurd, as his countrymen would say, was neither to hold nor to bind. On the moment the bivouac was broken up. The sick were left behind, and the rest set forward on one of the most memorable marches on record. In twenty-six hours, sixty-two miles were covered. As Napier observes: "Had the historian Gibbon known of such a march, he would have spared his sneer about the delicacy of modern soldiers." Wonderful as it was, however, it was far surpassed by one of Colonel Wellesley's in India, when he did seventy-two miles in seventeen hours. We should have classed that with the fables of a Baron Munchausen, but the Duke has told the story himself.

As Craufurd hurried on, his impatience became intense. The rumours that fly fast told him that Sir Arthur had been crushed. The news, such as they were, were confirmed by flying Spaniards. They were the fugitives from a part of Cuesta's army, which had really been defeated on the previous day. Nor did the fugitives come empty-handed; they were laden with the produce of pillaged farms, and many of the foot soldiers were mounted on stolen horses. Soon they were mixed with camp followers and deserters from the English host, and all had the same tale to tell. But the ebb tide slackened; more trust-worthy information was obtained; it was known that the British were holding their positions, and that the French had been beaten in a stricken field. Then ringing cheers resounded from the ranks; the hunger and thirst and fatigue were forgotten.

Craufurd led his column on to the battle-ground where the hill on the British left had been so fiercely contested. He came up soon after daybreak, but there was no rest after the night march. The men who had won Talavera were dead beat, and the new arrivals were told off for the outpost duty. The enemy were numerous; some of their regiments were unbroken, and yet it was hard to keep up the vigilance of the pickets or to prevent the sentries sleeping on their posts. But there was more active and repulsive work for them next morning. Seldom has there been a more horrible aftermath on a battlefield.

The plain stretching between the town and the heights held by the French was covered with grass as dry as tinder. It was strewn besides with the dead and wounded of both armies, with crippled gun carriages and shattered ammunition waggons. The grass had caught fire the evening before, and the burning wood lent fuel to the flames. There was a holocaust of the dying who could not help themselves, and the stronger of the wounded were shrieking pitifully, as they strove to drag themselves beyond reach of the fires. It was in such a scene that Craufurd's brigade was stimulated to fresh efforts, when transporting the victims to the town, in the absence of stretchers or ambulances.

It is known how Sir Arthur was compelled to retire, with little but the prestige of a barren victory, when he came to learn the actual strength of the forces enveloping him. Cuesta, as always, proved a broken reed, and there was nothing for it but to retire beyond the Tagus. Sir Arthur shifted headquarters from Talavera to Deleytosa, but Soult was interposing between him and Portugal from Placentia, and would have cut the British line of retreat could he have passed the river at Almarez. Craufurd was ordered to seize the boat-bridge there and to defend the defile through the Puerto de Mirabete, through which Hope afterwards delivered his brilliantly successful attack.

It was a rugged road to traverse, but Craufurd moved over it with his accustomed celerity, to occupy Almarez barely in time. His men were almost unprovided with rations, but fortunately they came upon herds of swine in the oak glades; for once discipline was set at defiance, and the pigs were bayoneted right and left. For three weeks he was encamped on a romantic knoll, embosomed in woods and overhanging the Tagus. The swine were still the staple of subsistence; for bread the men gathered the ripening corn from the fields, rubbing the grain in their hands and pounding it between stones. But when they marched on to Campo Mayor, the tough soldiers of the memorable Talavera march were so lowered in condition that it was with difficulty they could drag themselves to the summit of the Mirabete, though only four miles from the camp.

Epidemics followed in the train of exposure and famine. At Campo Mayor, where they were encamped for three months, dysentery and brain fever were raging, and the hospitals filled to overflowing. Such was the enfeebled condition of the brigade when it was ordered north to cantonments before Almeida to play the leading part in the campaign on the Coa. In February it was reinforced by 300 convalescents.

For many months in 1810 Craufurd maintained himself on shifting lines between the Agueda and the enemy. His forces, always slender, though subsequently increased, were doing outpost duty beneath an impending avalanche. Masséna, "the spoiled child of Fortune," had been appointed to supreme command with a view to the invasion of Portugal. He disposed of some 85,000 veterans, to say nothing of his strong reserves between Salamanca and the French frontiers. Ney, who like Blücher might have been called Marshal *en Avant*, was to the front with 30,000 horse and foot and thirty cannon. The Light Brigade by a general order had become the light Division; it had been strengthened by the German Hussars—the crack cavalry corps of the army—and by some squadrons of British Light Dragoons, and two Portuguese battalions were attached.

As has been remarked, nothing shows more forcibly Wellington's appreciation of Craufurd than his anxiety to keep him in command. In private letters he repeatedly expresses a fear that the claims of meritorious seniority may compel recognition, with assurances that he will do his best to avert such a contingency. As a matter of fact, Craufurd was retained in command, though at the cost of provoking the jealousy of other generals, as he found in the crisis of his action on the Coa. It must be remembered that for the most part, throughout his operations, there were no available supports within his reach.

Wellington had advanced to the relief of Ciudad Rodrigo, gallantly defended by the veteran Harrasti, who sent urgent messages for help. Craufurd's instructions were to give moral support to the garrison, to keep open the communications with Almeida, and to command the resources of the country. He could never have accomplished what he did, had it not been for the accurate information he received as to each movement of the enemy. In the middle of March he picketed his cavalry along twenty-five miles of the convex reaches of the Agueda. Behind the cavalry the infantry were distributed in the villages. There were but four bridges in these twenty-five miles: those bridges were carefully guarded, and at first the defence was comparatively easy, for the river was in flood and unfordable. When it began to shrink in the heat of early summer, his anxieties were infinitely increased.

Already the enemy had attempted one surprise at the bridge of Barba del Puerco, and it had well nigh proved successful. It was the first and only time when the Rifles were nearly outwitted. But, with the dwindling of the water, surprises might be expected at any point, and then the whole force seemed to be working on a masterly arrangement of springs which the slightest touch from the centre could set in motion. Still the river swelled in freshets or fell alternately. When there was a fall, the outposts were withdrawn and the scattered parties concentrated.

The standing orders were working automatically—in seven minutes the whole division was standing under arms: in a quarter of an hour it had mustered at the alarm posts with the baggage ready packed for retreat. The general alertness and the abiding sense of insecurity are illustrated by a dialogue between Beckwith, the fighting colonel of the 95th, and the chief of the German Hussars. "Well, colonel," said the German, "how do you do?"

"Tolerably well, thank you, considering that I sleep with one eye open."

"By *Gott!*" was the retort, "I never sleeps at all."

So Craufurd might have said, for he was always in the saddle, riding from one end of the line to the other, and invariably turning up at any threatened point. Nothing short of his iron frame could have stood the strain on brain and body. And the warfare of 1810 was very different from that of these days of smokeless powder and rifled guns. The bivouac fires blazed on either bank of the Agueda, and the sentries could exchange greetings across the stream. Sir George Napier, who with his brothers was serving in the Light Brigade, tells good stories of amusing personal experiences—of exchanges of courtesies and luxuries—though the old soldier shakes his head over the escapades, and relates them for warning rather than example.

That amicable intercourse was abruptly broken off when in the second week of June the French cavalry passed the Agueda in force. The enemy was already opening trenches against the fortress, but Craufurd still held doggedly to his positions, till their batteries opened fire on the 25th, when he sullenly withdrew to the left of the Azava River. He was the more reluctant to retire that Wellington had advanced his headquarters. At that time the commander-in-chief still hoped to save the place, and every personal and political consideration urged him to a strenuous effort It is clear from his private letters that he gave more encouragement to his venturesome lieutenant than has been generally believed. Even so late as the 10th June he wrote:

> I don't give over all hopes of attempting relief, at least by throwing in supplies, which might possibly be done without a general action.

The fortress still held out; Ney pushed his infantry after his cavalry to the Azava, but Craufurd only yielded foot by foot In the end of June, Charles Napier, who was not a timid man, pronounced the positions eminently perilous, predicting that the allies would be attacked and lose many men. Yet Wellington wrote so late as the middle of July that he was desirous of holding the other side of the Coa a little longer. On the 10th July there was an unfortunate affair, making great noise at the time and provoking no little censure, when Craufurd failed in an attempt to cut off a French foraging party. After all, the attempt should have proved successful had it not been for the extraordinary gallantry and skill of the French captain. But as the courage bordering on rashness was notorious, Craufurd was sure to be severely blamed for any mishap. In this case he was consoled by the approval of Wellington, who remarked in a long letter:

> As soon as an accident happens, every man who can write sits down to write his account of what he does not know, and his comments on what he does not understand; and these are diligently circulated and exaggerated by the idle and malicious, of whom there are plenty in all armies. The consequence is that officers and whole regiments lose their reputation.

At that moment Wellington, smarting from stinging reproaches himself, could specially sympathise with the victims of undesired obloquy.

Ciudad Rodrigo fell on the day that letter was written, and the Spanish auxiliaries, in not unnatural irritation, separated from the Light Division. On hearing the news, Wellington wrote that nothing was now to be risked beyond the Coa. These were the instructions that Craufurd was bound to obey, though again on that very day, when his temper had betrayed him into fighting, the commander-in-chief had written another letter and in a less decided tone; but, as that letter reached him too late, his instructions had never been modified.

On the 24th of July 1810 he fought the combat of the Coa. Napier admirably sums up what he had hitherto accomplished.

> He had kept a weak division for three months, within two hours' march of 60,000 men, appropriating the resources of the plains entirely to himself.

He adds, however:

> But this exploit, only to be appreciated by military men, did not satisfy his feverish thirst for distinction. Forgetting that his stay beyond the Coa was a matter of sufferance and not of real strength, he with headstrong ambition resolved, in defiance of reason and the reiterated orders of his general, to fight on the right bank.

It would seem that the judgment is over severe, for, though Napier admired Craufurd, he never liked him, and was inclined to judge with something of professional pedantry a man whose deliberate tenacity had achieved marvels, setting strict rules of strategy at defiance. His brother, Sir George, takes a juster view of the business, when he says that "Craufurd let his vanity get the better of his judgment, and delayed so long that at last the enemy made a sudden attack." And Lord Wellington wrote to Lord Liverpool: "Unfortunately General Craufurd did not begin to retire till the last moment:" from which it is clear that the commander-in-chief did not believe that there was deliberate purpose of provoking a battle. Craufurd was there in accordance with Lord Wellington's great plan, and the repeated expression of his wishes to prevent or delay the investment of Almeida. If it were impossible to relieve the fortress, it was desirable to prolong the defence. Doubtless his natural audacity was stimulated by the successful impunity with which he had hitherto acted in front of an enemy who had made hesitating use of infinitely superior forces.

He had played the perilous game too long; his imprudence might have resulted in a great disaster, and he escaped with a comparatively light penalty. On the night of the 23rd, the Light Division was in observation, with its left within cannon range of Almeida. By a remarkable coincidence, many of the great Peninsular engagements were preceded by violent storms, but the weather was never wilder than on that night of the 23rd. The rain came down in torrents, the roar of the thunder was deafening, and the blackness was fitfully illuminated by vivid flashes of lightning. It was not only the unfortunate soldiers who could not sleep: by the lurid flashlights they could see snakes and lizards running about in all directions, for the creatures had been flooded out of their holes in the tree-roots.

It was but the customary reveille—though now they needed no rousing—when at daybreak they heard the rifle-fire at the pickets. But this time, when the pickets fell back on the supports, it was soon known that it was the prelude to a regular engagement. Ney was advancing with the full strength of his division, 20,000 infantry and 5000 horse, to complete the investment and annihilate Craufurd ere he could cross the Coa. In both objects he seemed certain to succeed, for nothing could be apparently more desperate than the British position. Victory in fair fight being out of the question, retreat was inevitable, and retreat was barred by the river, swollen by the recent rains and running deep between its rocky banks. The fords were impassable, and the chasm was spanned by a single narrow bridge. Sir Augustus Frazer has sketched the scenery in his *Peninsular Campaigns.*

> The bridge is curved and is in the most romantic glen: the green water, the purple rocks, the din of dashing waves, the wildness of the scene, and the abruptness of the craggy cliffs give a character of terrific grandeur which is indescribable.

The bridge was only accessible by a narrow defile over a mile in length, and if the heights were turned by Ney's clouds of sharpshooters, they could rain down rocks as well as bullets.

Craufurd, though surprised at the last, was by no means taken unawares. He had made the best dispositions possible in the circumstances, and with his feeble means. His left, as has been said, was resting on Almeida, and his line inclined backwards and convexly towards the river. His cavalry posts on the plain in front of him were soon driven back, and then with his six guns he began to answer the French field batteries. The infantry were aligned on rocky ground and among stone enclosures—a strong position for defence, but embarrassing when it came to extricating themselves.

Meantime the belated preparations for retreat were in full progress. The baggage, the two Portuguese battalions, the cavalry, and finally the guns were sent back towards the bridge, with orders to gain the other bank without delay. It was easier to order than to do, for the narrow pass was encumbered, and confusion threatened to turn to panic. Ney had no mind that his enemy should escape him; he began by fiercely pressing the attack on our left, and soon afterwards the swarms of sharpshooters who assailed the centre and right gave way to more serious attacks in column. It became a rearguard action, causing the confused retirement which threatened to degenerate into a *débâcle*.

Still stubbornly contesting the ground, the rear-guard fell back, though the impetuosity of the French rushes threatened to overwhelm them. The horse were actually charging them among the ditches and walls; the batteries galloping forward were pouring down shot from the heights. When they emerged on a little space of more open plain, they could see that the bridge was choked, while many of the infantry and cavalry, with the artillery, were still on the farther bank. The left of the retreating line had joined the surging crowd; the right, broken up in sections and hard pressed, was in imminent danger of being cut off. Ney had been sending impatient messages to Montbrun, urging him to bring down the whole body of French cavalry, and had Montbrun acceded the effect might have been decisive. Happily, then as often, jealousies proved our salvation: the attack had been made without Masséna's orders, and Montbrun refused to take orders from any but the marshal in command.

On the other hand, we are driven to conclude that Craufurd's generalship never showed to less advantage. We hear little of him as a directing force, when a Wellington could have calmed the turmoil and restored the battle. That he was somewhere in the front of the combat we may well believe, but his battalions were broken up and intermixed. Like Inkerman, the Coa was a soldiers' battle, saved by the sheer gallantry of the rank and file and the coolness and ready inspiration of certain regimental officers. It was the prompt initiative of Major Macleod of the 43rd that seized a golden opportunity and held on to a small eminence commanding the passage of the bridge, and consequently the key of the situation. Colonel Leach, who led the 95th, bore generous tribute to Macleod's heroism:

> How either he or his horse escaped being blown to atoms when in the most daring manner he charged on horseback, at the head of a hundred or two skirmishers of the 43rd and of our

regiment mixed together, and headed them in making a dash at a wall lined with French infantry, which we soon dislodged, I am at a loss to imagine. It was one of those extraordinary escapes tending strongly to implant in the mind some faith in the doctrine of fatality.

If the soundest military critics may be trusted, Craufurd's detailed dispositions were faulty. The unnecessary extension of his slight line of defence encouraged Ney to drive home the attack, though indeed it would appear that in any case the opportunity was too tempting to be ignored. But in nothing, according to Napier and other writers, was his conduct more blameworthy than in his disposal of the 43rd, when he withdrew it before the French advance. He is said to have ordered the regiment into an enclosure of masonry, more than ten feet in height, with a single narrow entrance. There it remained "imprisoned," seeing nothing, but guessing by the firing that friends and enemies were sweeping past. It was only saved and brought into action again at the eleventh hour, by some of the officers directing the breaching of the enclosure, when the companies were broken up into a confusion of skirmishers.

Napier's circumstantial story is confirmed from other quarters, but it is startling to note the very different colour given to the incident by Craufurd himself, when contradicting Masséna's official report, in a lengthy letter addressed to the *Times*.

> Some companies, which formed the left of our line, were in a vineyard so completely enclosed by a high stone wall that it was quite impossible for cavalry to get into it: but the preceding night had been excessively severe, and some of the troops stationed in the vineyard had unfortunately pulled down the wall in many places, to make use of the stones to form a shelter against the violent rain. This wall, which Brigadier-General Craufurd had considered a complete defence, was accordingly no longer so, and after our artillery and cavalry had moved off, the enemy's horse broke into the enclosure and took several prisoners.

So difficult is it to get at the truth of history. We have never heard Craufurd's veracity impeached, and he should be trustworthy as to the leading incidents of the engagement; yet he not only assumes the wisdom of his order, and blames the men or the storm for interfering with his plans, but asserts that the regiment had taken post in the vineyard during the night preceding the battle.

Major Macleod gallantly held his own against attacks repeatedly renewed: when the bridge was clear he crossed in turn, still showing so determined a front to the enemy that for a time there was a pause. If they had a chance of forcing the passage, they missed it. Craufurd immediately aligned his regiments along the almost precipitous face of the mountain: his guns were on the summit, converging on the bridge, and elsewhere on his front the flooded river was impassable. But as it had been fordable higher up on the previous day, and as there was another bridge at Castello Bom, in the apprehension that his retreat to Celorico might be endangered, he threw out his cavalry pickets in that direction.

Had Montbrun responded to Ney's appeals, Craufurd's communications must have been seriously imperilled: as it was, the French marshal confined himself to desperate efforts to storm the passage. They were foredoomed to failure, and the carnage was frightful. A converging fire of musketry was directed on the bridge: the cannon had got the exact range, and in the second and third attempts the gallant French grenadiers were arrested by a moaning barrier of their own dead and wounded. It was an anticipation of the scenes to be enacted in the great breach at Badajoz. Nevertheless the combat did not end, as it might have done, with the last repulse. Some of the stormers had struggled through the belt of fire, and found shelter among the rocks beneath the British positions. Napier says the French continued fighting, from a point of honour, to cover their comrades' escape, and as the bottom of the ravine was enveloped in smoke the British appear to have been ignorant that any of the stormers had passed the river.

The firing was continued through the afternoon, with no little loss on both sides, when another downfall of torrential rain quenched the ardour of the combatants. Then the Frenchmen, emerging from among the rocks, were permitted to escape unmolested, and the fighting ceased. The needless and worse than fruitless engagement cost Craufurd over 300 in killed and wounded, of whom twenty-eight were officers: it was small consolation that the French loss was more than twice as heavy, owing chiefly to the wanton butchery on the bridge. Under cover of the night Craufurd withdrew behind the Pinhel, and Ney made no attempt to follow him.

Pinhel was the headquarters of Picton's division. That general rode up in the hottest of the battle, and in the circumstances it would have been more to his credit had he refrained. Craufurd, who was hard pressed, asked for effective assistance, or at least that some demonstration might be made in his support. Hard pressed he must have been to beg Picton for aid, for no love was lost between them, and Picton had never concealed his jealousy of his junior. The answer is said to have been emphatic and blunt to brutality: "I'll be d——d if I do." Campbell, Craufurd's brigade-major, and one of the most chivalrous and popular officers in the service, who described the interview to Napier, merely avers that Craufurd's rejoinder was hot, and that we may well believe.

Undoubtedly Picton's conduct was wrong as it was ungenerous. Even had his orders been more peremptory, he should have used his discretion in an emergency when the peril of the Light Division was extreme. It was a standing complaint of Wellington against his lieutenants that they shrank from responsibility. But as matter of fact, in a letter to Craufurd written on 4th July, Picton had owned to having been permitted a certain freedom of action:—

> Sir,—It being important that I should communicate to you with as much expedition as possible the events that may take place on these parts of the Coa which I am instructed to observe . . . I have to request as early information as possible of your movements, that I may be enabled to co-operate with them, in obedience to his Excellency the commander of the forces' instructions.

Had Craufurd's temerity sacrificed his division, the loss might have been fatal to Wellington's scheme. That the general was seriously irritated is very visible in a note in the despatches. It was addressed to the Right Hon. W. Pole.

> Although I shall be hanged for them, you may be very certain that not only I had nothing to do with, but had positively forbidden the foolish affair in which Craufurd involved his outposts. . . . You will say, If this be the case, why not accuse Craufurd? I answer, Because, if I am to be hanged for it, I cannot accuse a man whom I believe has meant well, and whose error is one of judgment and not of intention.

But Wellington remembered the good service that had been done on the Agueda in forming the regiments of the light Brigade, trained under Moore, into a division perfect in all its details, and invaluable as the outworks of the army in action. He addressed to Craufurd no word of reproof: he only indicated displeasure by omitting to thank him in the general orders that commended the division—and indeed it was the officers and privates who had saved their general's reputation. It has been said that Craufurd was serenely indifferent to the praise or blame of the commander-in-chief.

On the contrary, we can see from his private letters that he was almost morbidly sensitive to the censures of the leader he admired. Till he had nobly redeemed any loss of fame on the ridge of Busaco the correspondence with Wellington—formal and constrained, whereas formerly it had been frankly confidential—had been generously reticent, but Craufurd knew himself in fault, and perhaps he was not thoroughly re-established in his own good opinion till his chief had made earnest protest against his going on furlough.

The fall of Almeida followed that of Ciudad. It was precipitated, to Wellington's disappointment, by the explosion of a magazine which left the place indefensible. Masséna delayed to follow up his successes for some weeks: but the old smuggler had abandoned himself to luxury in his age: he brought a mistress along with him to do the honours of his table, to the scandal of Ney and Regnier, who were not over particular, and he is said to have regulated his operations according to the lady's caprices. When he began his advance on the 16th September he moved forward in three columns. Regnier's corps marched by Guarda and Celorico; and on that line Craufurd, who had been in occupation of the latter place, was protecting the retreat. There was little or no skirmishing, for Masséna, deeming the evacuation of Portugal a foregone conclusion, did not care to press the retreating allies.

No one except the confidential engineers who fortified the lines of Torres Vedras was in the secret of Lord Wellington's plans. The shrewdest of his staff seem never to have penetrated them, and considering that Lisbon swarmed with spies, it is a mystery how the secret was kept from the enemy. Wellington's scheme, like other conceptions of genius, was simple in the extreme. He was to place his own army in safety and plenty behind works which could neither be stormed nor tamed, and where it could not be starved as long as England kept command of the sea: and he was to lure Masséna into a desolated country where famine and sickness would be the allies of the British. It was neither his game nor his wish to fight, and Busaco was really a political battle.

Various circumstances conspired to induce him to make a stand there. Constrained by iron necessity, nothing could have been more mercilessly severe than his orders for laying the country waste. Mills were to be burned, cattle were to be driven away, the peasants and the townsfolk were to abandon their homes, and the grain that could not be carried off was to be destroyed. But a hostile faction at Lisbon crossed his plans: the orders were very imperfectly carried out, and the French need never have been reduced to extremities had they economised the supplies left within their reach. Moreover, he desired to conciliate popular feeling in Portugal, disgusted by the fall of the fortresses, and to silence the croakers in his own army, many of whom had influential friends in the Cabinet. Had he hesitated, he might have been confirmed in his resolution to fight by coming upon a position so exceptionally advantageous as Busaco.

We need not retell the story of the battle, except in so far as it concerns Craufurd. With the affair of the Coa still fresh in his mind, again his impetuosity had nearly compromised the situation. General Pack had destroyed the bridges on the Criz, a tributary of the Mondego, and fallen back on the Light Division. The enemy, restoring the communications on the following day, debouched on the plain, and had driven in Craufurd's pickets, when he took up a strong position on the hills behind Mortagon. He was well in advance of the general line, and again he had orders to retire without risking an engagement On the morning of the 25th he saw the enemy's cavalry massing before him, and behind them were the heads of three infantry columns, emerging from heavy clouds of dust, which showed that the whole French army was in motion.

Even had he had no orders to retire, that should have been warning sufficient. It only excited him to accept a challenge, and his conduct was indefensible. He had a few squadrons of Light Horse and a regiment of Heavies: he sent them down into the plain, and already they were exchanging shots with the enemy's skirmishers. The whole of the Light Division would have been drawn on to engage the united corps of Ney and Regnier, when by a fortunate chance Wellington rode up. He ordered immediate retreat, taking personal charge of the covering forces. As Napier writes in one of his most brilliant passages:

> Nor was there a moment to lose: the enemy, with incredible rapidity, brought up both infantry and guns, and fell on so briskly that all the skill of the general and the readiness of the excellent troops composing the rearguard could scarcely prevent the division from being dangerously engaged. Howbeit a series of rapid and beautiful movements, a sharp cannonade, and an hour's march brought everything back in good order to the great position.

Busaco might well have tempted Wellington to a stand, even had he not decided to hearten his troops and to silence the grumblers. With the right of the ridge rising abruptly from the Mondego, with the left merely divided by some impracticable ground from a loftier *sierra*, ragged in itself, it effectually barred the march of Masséna. Yet had the French pressed home the impetuous attack which drove in the Light Division, they might have rushed it on the spur of the moment, for then, the corps of Hill and Leith not having joined the main body, the ridge was only partially occupied. But Masséna, loitering ten miles in the rear, would not listen to the solicitations of Ney and Regnier.

The day of the 26th was passed in inaction, and when the marshal tardily gave his assent to the attack, the favourable moment had gone by. Then even the fiery Ney preached prudence, but Masséna was obstinate: probably in self-reproach he had lost his temper, and with good reason, as their fighting was to prove he had implicit faith in the prowess of his soldiers.

The task then assigned them was well nigh impossible; but as it was they came so near succeeding as to justify Ney's advice. With his soldier's eye he had seen on the previous day that the formidable position could not be adequately defended with the forces at Wellington's disposal. Now the whole army of the allies was being ranged in line of battle along ramparts that seemed engineered by nature for defence. A road running along the rugged crest maintained communications in the rear of the divisions. On the eastern face the descent to the ravine at the bottom was by a succession of gigantic steps: in many places the precipices rose almost sheer: here and there the rocks were scarped, and where the ascent was practicable it was raked by the fire of guns that had been planted on rocky salients. The intervening chasm was so narrow that our artillery could play on the enemy when they emerged from the broken ground beyond it, and then they were entangled in the copse-wood that clothed the bottom, before forming up again for the concerted assault.

Crowning the summit of the ridge in the centre was a convent. The gardens are described by Sir Augustus Frazer in his *Peninsular Campaigns* as a very Paradise. The oak and the cedar, the cypress and the pine flourished in profuse luxuriance. From the heights, on a clear day, the Rock of Lisbon could be seen in the distance. Within the garden walls which shut out the world, "little chapels at every turn invited meditation, and all was peace and silence." On the 27th of September the silence was rudely broken. There Spencer was posted with the 1st Division; to his left was the 4th Division; to his right, Picton with the 3rd. Pack's brigade was in advance of Spencer, and Craufurd was on a jutting promontory beneath the convent, sheltered in the interior of an obtuse angle, where the ridge begins to trend to the north-west.

If his temperament sometimes betrayed him into acts of folly, his faults were more than redeemed by his cool judgment in situations like the present He could seize at a glance the advantage of his ground, forecasting the course of the battle and taking his precautions against all contingencies. At Busaco his dispositions were admitted to be masterly, and his genius had prepared a dramatic surprise which snatched victory from the enemy in the moment of apparent triumph. His British riflemen with the Portuguese *caçadores* were scattered along the face of the mountain: his guns were in battery behind a convex sweep of rocks, breached, as Napier says, with natural embrasures; and the only solid force visible to the assailants was the brigade of Germans, assigned him in support.

But between him and the convent the ground sank away into a rugged basin, and there, and a quarter of a mile before the Germans, the 43rd and 52nd Regiments were effectually concealed. All the dispositions for next day were made before sundown, and soon the darkness was illuminated by the blaze of innumerable bivouac fires. But the soldiers of the Light Division had little sleep, for they were disturbed by alarms which seemed to portend a night attack, when their pickets were incessantly exchanging shots with the French sharpshooters.

All were on the alert long before dawn, and before daybreak the attack had begun. The French had advanced in five columns—three of them under Ney, two under Regnier. Regnier's impetuous attack had well nigh carried all before it. He had actually gained the heights, forced back the 3rd Division, broken a Portuguese regiment, and threatened to sweep the crest, taking the line of defenders in rear, when Wellington came up to restore the battle. The heights were recovered and the French hurled down them.

Ney had a more difficult task than Regnier, for beneath Craufurd's position the ascent was even more precipitous. Marchand's column inclined to the left, as if to turn the right of the Light Division: Loison's Bet their faces straight to the mountain before them. It would have been a stiff and breathless climb had there been no defence. Like Regnier's column, they had to face a rain of musket balls: the showers of grape tore through them from front and flank; but they only closed up their broken ranks and nothing arrested the steady scramble.

The allied skirmishers driven in before them were tumbling over the lip of the basin behind the guns; the guns were rapidly limbered up; and the French, with such breath as they had left, were already shouting victory beneath the edge of the crest. Of course they could see nothing, but they believed there were only the scattered sharpshooters between them and the solid German brigade.

Craufurd had waited calmly to explode his mine. Standing alone on a rock to the side, the French in their last fiery rush had taken no note of the solitary figure. Of a sudden, above the din of the fight, and when, it is said, they were within a dozen yards of him, his voice rang out sharp and clear, giving his regiments the word of command.

Sir George Napier, who was there, tells the story with the dramatic details.

> When all our skirmishers had passed by and joined their respective corps, and the head of the enemy's column was within *a very few yards of him*, he turned round, came up to the 52nd, and called out, 'Now, 52nd, revenge the death of Sir John Moore! Charge! charge! Huzza!' and waving his hat in the air, he was answered by a shout that appalled the enemy.

Next moment "eighteen hundred British bayonets went sparkling over the brow of the hill." Napoleon's veterans stood up to them undauntedly, but the shock was irresistible. The head of their column was crumpled up and borne back; the wings of the concave British line were overlapping them on either flank; volley after volley was poured into them point-blank; the bayonet, with advantage of the ground, did the rest, and pursuers and pursued went headlong down the hill, till Craufurd halted his main body in mid-descent. Some of the light companies still followed up the chase till entangled in the woods at the bottom, when Ney brought his guns into play and set his reserves in motion. Then the division returned to its former position over rocks slippery with blood and strewed with the dead and wounded. They had covered themselves with glory: their losses had been slight, and, emerging from partial and temporary eclipse, never had the star of their chief shone out with more brilliant lustre.

Loison showed no inclination to renew the attack, although the day was yet young: but Marchand, who had suffered less severely, again pushed forward through the copses in the ravine to a pinewood on the right flank of the Light Division, whence he sent up a swarm of skirmishers. It was a wild attempt, and the wood proved untenable. Pack's brigade sufficed to check the advance, and Craufurd, turning his guns on the pines, speedily cleared them of the enemy. Soon afterwards his righteous wrath was characteristically excited by an insulting incident. Loison had shown no signs of activity till towards dusk a company of his *voltigeurs* had the audacity to seek to make themselves comfortable for the night in a hamlet on the British side of the chasm.

They had counted without Craufurd. There was no serious menace in the act, but he resented it as a piece of impertinence. He concentrated all his guns on the hamlet, expending a vast deal of shot and powder; for the Frenchmen, from a point of *punctilio*, held doggedly on. Then he sent down a company, which would have been the advance-guard of the division had not the French promptly evacuated their perilous billets.

A more cold-blooded man would have spared his shot when ammunition was precious. But, in the words of the Chief Justice to Falstaff, the day's service at Busaco had gilded over all previous indiscretions. If there had been coolness between Craufurd and his chief since the affair of the Coa, thenceforth all traces of it disappeared. Their correspondence became as cordial as it had ever been, and, *à propos* of Busaco, Wellington wrote in the following month:

> If you would come over here someday I would show you Masséna's despatch (on Busaco), which I have got, from which it appears that you attacked Loison *en deux columnes serrées en masse*.

For the marshal's despatches were as mendacious as the Emperor's *bulletins*, though on this occasion Craufurd, not being the party principally concerned, did not care to contradict them. But that friendly note had been long anticipated by Lord Wellington's warm commendation of the Light Division and its leader, published in general orders.

Busaco was evacuated immediately after the battle, while Massena, turning the ridge, as he had been urged to do originally, made his hazardous flank march between the mountains and the sea.

After the sanguinary interlude, Wellington returned to his plan and was rapidly withdrawing to his stronghold. But the inevitable horrors and terrors of his stern orders had been aggravated, if possible, by their imperfect execution. The news that the French had been beaten in a pitched battle had reassured the peasants and townsfolk, who had neither destroyed their property nor abandoned their homes. When they realised that the retreat had only been delayed, panic and confusion were universal.

The streets and solitary bridge of Coimbra were encumbered by mobs of fugitives and trains of ox-waggons and mule-carts. The defile of Condeixa, eight miles beyond, was choked, and the road between was a scene of confusion, through which the troops were unable to force a passage. The Light Division, as usual in the post of danger and honour, was the last to cross Coimbra bridge. A detachment was halted on the farther side of the river, on an open space overlooked by the prison. The jailers had fled, leaving the doors locked. The prisoners were in despair, clinging in agony to the bars of the windows, or striding to wrench them away.

They had good reason for their fears, for at that time the ferocious enmity between French and Portuguese was at its height, and the brutality of the invaders had provoked barbarous retaliation. The captives were saved by the humanity of one of Craufurd's most distinguished staff officers. In that moment of storm and stress Captain William Campbell—he has left interesting personal reminiscences of his chief—found time and means to burst the doors of the prison and release the inmates.

Extricated from the defile and the confusion, the army retired in fair order, the Light Division still as the rear-guard. Masséna, who had wasted time and squandered great stores of provisions at Coimbra to his subsequent embarrassment, had nevertheless caught up the allies by more excellent marching, and was pressing Wellington hard when close to the first of the lines. To Craufurd had been assigned the guard of Aruda, a townlet in the mouth of a pass traversed by a road practicable for artillery and only defended by feeble redoubts. He was in charge of six miles of front: it was considered the weakest part of the line, and especially likely to tempt an enemy who found himself brought up by a barrier whose existence he had never suspected.

Craufurd ought to have entered by Aruda on the 10th, but on the 10th he was still at Alemquer, a long march to the north, for the weather had been vile and the roads were horrible. Impunity in the retreat seems to have made him careless, for though the darkness, the storm, and the situation of the town were all favourable to a surprise, he appears to have neglected even ordinary precautions. No pickets were placed; there was no patrolling; and indeed he had sent his cavalry before him to Aruda.

Nor can one help surmising that the narrow escape from disaster was due in some measure to the strained relations between him and his subordinates. For his officers are said to have been apprehensively on the watch, when late in the afternoon, on the heights in front of them, they observed a handful of the French cavalry. The alarm was given; the men sprang to arms, but the only egress from the town was through an ancient archway. The troops were ordered to break and re-form beyond it, and for the moment the confusion was extreme. The baggage animals were still being laden; the enemy was massing on the hill, and the infantry, coming down in force, threatened to strike at the flank of the retreat. They were already pouring into the streets, while their guns from above were playing on the gateway.

But the admirable training of the division served it well. The old soldiers fell in without orders and faced round; and, with his front ranks in disorder and his rear hard pressed, Craufurd resumed his retreat. He escaped lightly, thanks to the weather, for as the wind became more boisterous and the rain fell in torrents, the pursuit slackened and gradually ceased.

Again he had imperilled his division, and his unnecessary delay had come near to compromising the lines at another point. Yet Wellington, making no allusion to the incident, wrote him a friendly letter a day or two afterwards from an adjacent village near Sobral.

> I hope your men are well put up in Aruda in this terrible weather. I don't think the enemy's plan is quite decided yet. . . .
> I mean, however, to hold the town of Sobral as long as I can.
> The peasants say they are marching this morning upon Villa Franca, which is to attack our right, where Hill is. They can make no impression upon the right by the high-road, positively: and they must therefore endeavour to turn Hill's position upon the *sierra* of Alhandra by its left This is a tough job also, defended as the entrances of the valleys are by redoubts and the villages by abbatis, &c. However, that is what they must try. From this statement you will see how important the situation of Aruda and the possession of the Pass of Matos (which, by-the-bye, itself turns Hill's position) are to our operations.
> Aruda itself I don't think could be held for any length of time against a superior force; but the Pass of Matos can, defended as it is by the two redoubts. . . . I need say nothing to yon about the defence of the Pass of Matos.

Both Sobral and Aruda were slightly to the front of the foremost line, and indeed Craufurd had only occupied Aruda as an advanced post. To the eastward was Hill, his right on the sea at Alhandra, and holding five miles of almost unassailable front to the head of the Calandrix Valley and the Pass of Matos, where they came into touch. Craufurd realised the defects of a breach in the lines, which apparently had been unaccountably overlooked by Fletcher, who had superintended the fortifications, and which had already attracted the attention of Masséna. He set himself to strengthen his defences with the skill of a trained engineer, and his men were immediately at work. The forests which clothed the heights were echoing to the axes of his riflemen, while other fatigue parties were engaged in rolling down boulders from the slopes. In vain did Masséna seek to reconnoitre and feel the approaches. Craufurd, still holding the indefensible Aruda, refused to show his force, unless Masséna risked a regular engagement. Meantime, as Napier says:

> In an incredibly short space of time he had secured his position in a manner worthy of admiration. Across the ravine on the left a loose stone wall, 16 feet thick and 40 feet high, was raised: across the great valley of Aruda a double line of abattis was drawn—not as usual of the limbs of trees, but of full-grown oaks and chestnuts, digged up with all their roots and branches, dragged by main force for several hundred yards, and then reset and crossed, so that no human strength could break through. Breastworks at convenient distances to defend this line of trees were now cast up; and along the summits of the mountain, for a space of nearly three miles, including the salient points, other stone walls, 6 feet high by 4 in thickness, with banquettes, were piled up.

At Aruda, as at Busaco, Masséna missed his chance—if chance there was—by delay, but at Aruda he never attempted an attack. The longer he sat and looked at the lines, the more formidable they appeared. The Portuguese irregulars were pressing upon him from all sides; the country behind him was a scene of desolation, and as the area of devastation expanded the more precarious his foraging became. Sickness was enfeebling his army and starvation staring it in the face. In the middle of November he recognised his failure, and at last relaxed his tenacious grip. Then he made one of those masterly retreats in which Napoleon's marshals excelled, and adroitly stealing a march and a half on his adversary, fell back upon Santarem. Then their respective positions were reversed, and Santarem for a time was Masséna's Torres Vedras.

When Wellington started in pursuit, the Light Division followed the French on the road through Alemquer. When the French passed through Sobral, Craufurd was close upon their heels, and his horse made several hundred prisoners. Wellington at first had moved cautiously, fearing that Masséna was luring him away from his lines, in the hope of forcing him to fight at disadvantage. He had changed his mind and decided that the enemy was in full retreat for the frontiers, when Masséna was fortifying the position where he meant to make a stand. This time the astute marshal had doubly overreached him. He had stolen away from before the lines, and he had been long looking back over his shoulder to Santarem, where he had already established hospitals and magazines. It was a position that could be defended indefinitely, so long as his troops could be fed and the communications with Spain kept open; and it commanded many diverging roads by which he could strike out in all directions. Sir Augustus Frazer is enthusiastic over the scenery:

> A finer prospect or a stronger position can hardly be imagined. Abrupt rocks, rugged mountains, and hills clothed with olives, with orange groves and vineyards in the valleys, and the majestic Tagus rolling at one's feet.

However, Wellington, believing he had only to deal with a rearguard, made his dispositions on the 19th November for a general onset. The French, with their headquarters on a mountain and their wings on its spurs, were covered by the Tagus on one flank and the Bio Mayor on the other. These rivers embraced a marshy plain, and over that the Light Division was ordered to advance, while the 1st Division followed the Lisbon high-road, which crossed the swamps on a raised causeway. The attack was carried out in tentative fashion, and it failed; but from all the signs Wellington was well nigh persuaded that he had the whole French army in front of him. He was entirely satisfied when he renewed his demonstrations next day, but Craufurd still doubted. He obeyed the orders to halt, but with the fall of night he went scouting on his own account. Attended by a single sergeant, the general of the Light Division crept in the darkness across the causeway till, challenged by the French pickets, he exchanged shots with them. It was by a miracle that he escaped death or capture, but he had got the information of which he went in search.

For a time there was stalemate between the combatants. Craufurd's spirit chafed in enforced inaction, and the abiding home-sickness got the upper hand. A letter from Wellington, written on the 9th December, gives some notion of the struggles through which he must have passed before he came to a final decision. Wellington, who was very loath to spare him, knew how to touch him on the most sensitive point. He reminds him that, owing to the number of senior general officers, it had been no easy matter to keep him in command of a division—as, indeed, their previous correspondence shows; and adds that, if he were resolved to go, it might be impossible to replace him on his return.

However, Craufurd was obdurate, and sailed in the beginning of February. Had he foreseen the honours his division was to win, though under the far less competent leading of Erskine, he would certainly have seen reason to decide differently. When Masséna was being driven back upon the frontier fortresses, the news from the front must have been bitter reading to him. Never did his division distinguish itself more than at the combat of Sabugal, when it faced the full strength of Regnier's corps, and won the warm praise of Wellington, who with unwonted enthusiasm pronounced it "one of the most glorious actions in which British troops were ever engaged."

4

Masséna had fallen back upon Salamanca to reorganise his shattered strength and recruit his depleted legions. Wellington had closely invested Almeida, and had disposed his army so as to cut off all the communications of the garrison. Towards the end of April, the French marshal returned, determined to relieve the beleaguered fortress. On the 25th he reached Ciudad Rodrigo. On the news of the advance, the Light Division had resumed its former positions, behind the Agueda—the left established at Gallegos, the right at Espeja. Wellington had hastened from the Guadiana to meet the impending attack and confront his old antagonist. Craufurd was already hurrying back to resume the command of his division. Wellington welcomed him heartily. He wrote on the 14th April, from Villa Formosa:

> My dear general, I received this morning your letter of the 9th. You will find your division in your old quarters at Gallegos, and the sooner you can come up to them the better.

He came up with all speed, and fortunately rejoined immediately before Fuentes d'Onore. It is safe to assume that Fuentes could not have been even a drawn battle had the Light Division been mishandled as at Sabugal, where, nevertheless, it had covered itself with glory. Craufurd made his dramatic appearance on the scene on the very morning of the battle. He rode on to the ground on his famous bay cob, where the 95th was posted to the left of the blackened ruins of Fort Conception. When the men recognised him, he was greeted with ringing cheers, and his reception recalls that of Marmion when welcomed by Lord Surrey to the field of Flodden. Costello, the non-commissioned officer of the regiment, tells us that the Portuguese *caçadores* cheered even more lustily than the English, shouting: "Long live General Craufurd, who takes care of our bellies."

Indeed, Craufurd, who dealt so sternly with defaulting commissariat officers, always saw that the rations were regularly served out, often achieving the apparently impossible. And in that respect his absence had been sorely felt, for on one occasion, on the march from Santarem, for four days the division had been literally starving. He was genuinely touched by the warmth of the welcome. As he rode along the ranks, his features were wreathed in smiles, and he bowed repeatedly, raising his hat.

He was rejoicing besides in the prospect of immediate action, after a winter of restful but irritating inactivity. On the moment he gathered up the reins he had dropped six months before, grasping the whole situation intuitively, and before that eventful day was over he had need of all his promptitude and knowledge of war. Wellington had accepted battle under unfavourable conditions. His dispositions were faulty, as he admitted afterwards in conversation; and his line, covering a distance of seven miles, was dangerously extended to his right. The French infantry, as compared to his own, was as four to three, and Masséna was infinitely superior in cavalry.

Yet it was an action in which cavalry was of supreme importance, for on Wellington's right flank was a broad plain or plateau commanding the roads leading to two of the three bridges over the Coa. Masséna saw the blots and made his arrangements to take advantage of them. Had it not been for the insubordination of the generals acting under him, there can be small doubt that he would have succeeded. As it was, it was chiefly the coolness of Craufurd, the discipline he had established in his division, and the confidence of his soldiers in their chief which averted a fatal disaster.

Masséna meant to hold the British left in check with one corps, while he turned their ill-covered right with the rest of his army, utilising his 5000 horse, which were opposed by but a fifth of their number. Thanks to the nature of the ground, there was no concealing the operations on either side. The French were seen moving off in masses to their left, supported by Montbrun with all his cavalry. The British divisions opposite made a corresponding movement, but Houston with the 7th was already hard pressed when the Light Division and the cavalry were sent forward to his support.

The 7th, driven from the shelter of a village, was being forced back into a wood, when Craufurd's riflemen, skirmishing forward among the trees, restored the fight. Galloping in loose order through the village and the wood, the French cavalry had formed up upon the plain beyond, where Julian Sanchez, the guerrilla chief, had been holding an eminence on the extreme right. Sanchez retired fighting across the Tarones, and then Montbrun, who had wasted time in trifling with the *partida*, turned the right of the 7th Division and threw his whole strength on our cavalry. Overwhelmed by weight and numbers, it yielded to the shock, withdrawing behind the Light Division. Then Montbrun turned to charge the infantry. The division had time to throw itself into squares, and escaped almost scathless. The 7th faced the attack in line, supported by some stone enclosures, and though it suffered severely, the horsemen were repulsed.

But the battle was going against his centre, and Wellington, in order to save the day, decided to concentrate on his original positions round Fuentes. The 7th Division was ordered to cross the Tarones, and retrace its march to Fresnada on the left bank. Craufurd was to cover the passage, and then withdraw over the plain, having the cavalry flanking his right. On that open ground Montbrun, with his 5000 horse and fifteen field pieces, might well have made sure of his prey. The plain was covered with a mixed multitude of fugitives—camp followers, servants, peasants, broken pickets, and soldiers who had lost touch with their colours—all taken by surprise and in mortal panic. Through them all, or rather behind them, in martial procession moved Craufurd's squares—so many shifting and impregnable fortresses.

Time after time Montbrun's horsemen swooped down, yet, though they lacked neither courage nor incentives to action, never venturing an actual attack. They lacked neither incentives nor support, and had these squares once been broken, the right wing of the British would have been rolled up on the centre in hopeless disorder. For the wood which had been the scene of the earlier struggle was now full of

French skirmishers, and behind it were two entire corps in solid formation, abstaining mysteriously from joining in the *mêlée*. The plain was cleared: Craufurd's covering squares, retiring still in their perfect order, closed in upon the right of the 1st Division, and throwing forward riflemen among the rocks, connected the 1st with the 7th, which was already safe in Fresnada.

Wellington was once more concentrated, showing the enemy a formidable front. There was a furious cannonade; the battle raged in and around Fuentes till nightfall; but the French had waited too long, and could never force the passage. The unflinching firmness of the Light Division had retrieved the day and won a doubtful victory. After the battle the Light Division resumed its former positions. On the 10th of May, the French commandant of Almeida succeeded in escaping with the bulk of the garrison, after spiking his guns and blowing up the bastions. The generals responsible for the blockade were severely blamed, and various historians have implicated Craufurd in their censures, but he is clearly exculpated by Napier's narrative. His division was only covering the blockading troops. Believed from anxiety as to the fate of Almeida by its evacuation, the French had again retired on Salamanca, when Masséna was superseded by Marmont.

Wellington had hurried south to confront Soult's menacing operations in Estremadura, but arrived too late to avert the bloody and useless battle of Albuera. The Light Division had been left with others to observe the northern French army; towards the end of May it was ordered south to the support of Hill, who was facing superior forces of the enemy. They had passed Sabugal, crossed the Coa, and were bivouacking in a chestnut wood hard by the scene of their fighting in 1810, when one of those extraordinary panics occurred which were not infrequent in the war. There seems to have been no sort of occasion for it, and it was the more surprising that the veterans of the division were the watch-dogs of the army, who prided themselves on being always on the alert, yet never giving false alarms.

At midnight the cry was raised, "The French are upon us." It might have come from an uneasy sleeper, awaking from a nightmare. But in a moment all the regiments were afoot, falling into their ranks and standing to their arms. One of the riflemen says that the general shouts of alarm caused a terror that was never felt in battle. Nor did Craufurd escape the contagion; or rather he may have taken it for granted that his veterans would not have been scared without reasonable cause. Springing to his horse, he hurried from place to place, ordering all the soldiers he met to fall in and load. They spoiled their night for nothing, and very foolish they felt when, after passing an hour or so in serried battalions, the order was given to dismiss. Among many similar alarms was that on the wild night before Salamanca, when the breaking loose of some horses of the Dragoon Guards from their picket ropes was construed into an onset of the whole French cavalry.

The division marched towards the Guadiana, only to be marched back again, having gone through a sadly distressing experience. For six weeks they were bivouacked, in the height of summer, on what is said to have been "the hottest and most parched piece of ground in the Peninsula." The malarious low grounds were fruitful of the "Guadiana fever," and there were sown the seeds of a virulent epidemic which sent many of them from the camps on the Agueda into the hospitals.

For in the second week of August they were again on outpost service on the north-eastern frontier. Wellington had come back to find Ciudad Rodrigo revictualled, and consequently too late to blockade the fortress, as he had intended. However, in September he had drawn his forces closer round the place, establishing his own headquarters at Guinaldo. As in the Talavera campaign, from imperfect information he had once more underrated the strength of the enemy. Marmont outnumbered him by nearly two to one; for, being joined by Dorsenne, he had assembled 60,000 infantry and 6000 horse. But Wellington misdoubted his intelligence and was troubled in mind, and in August he had written to Craufurd, who was keeping watch on the northern plain, and on whose sleepless vigilance so much depended:—

> I heard last night (but not from good authority) of a party being collected at Granadilla, probably for another reconnaissance. I am going over to Cesmiro this morning, in order to look at the country on the other side of Ciudad Rodrigo, and I shall not be back till to-morrow: but if anything comes near enough to you to enable you to strike a blow without incurring much risk, I wish you would do it. . . .
>
> It is not impossible that they might wish to establish a communication with Ciudad Rodrigo, in which case I mean to assemble the army about Pedro de Toro; and you might collect your division at once in Zanorra and be in readiness to fall upon anything not too large for you which should attempt to cross the plain. I consider Monsaggo to be a point at which you ought to have an intelligent officer, who could be able to give you information of all that passes in the *sierra* on that side.

Marmont, in fact, was then determined on raising the blockade, and was concentrating with the intention of throwing convoys into the fortress. Wellington's line was of necessity unduly prolonged, and his right wing, composed of the Light Division and some squadrons of cavalry, was dangerously posted, beyond the Agueda and behind the Vandillo, a rugged watercourse debouching into the river, three miles above Ciudad.

When Marmont advanced, Wellington disputed the ground in three successive positions. El Bodon was fought on the 24th: Craufurd, still on the Vandillo, only heard the distant cannonade, and was naturally in extreme anxiety as to his communications. In the afternoon he received a message, saying that the army was falling back on Guinaldo, with orders to join it there. He had every reason to hasten, and can have had no inducement to loiter. Napier says that, had he marched at once and marched straight forward, he might have reached Guinaldo by midnight. Colonel Leach, who was serving with him, mentions incidentally that the division set out "the same night," and the delay seems inexplicable.

At whatever hour he started, it is clear that Craufurd only moved forward a league, for he halted at *Cespédosa*, and when called on afterwards for an explanation he said that he feared a night attack, which directly conflicts with Leach's statement. Be that as it may, the missing division threw Wellington into great embarrassment. His situation at Guinaldo was ill assured: he was audaciously disguising its weakness, and on the 25th he would have quietly withdrawn to the strongly defensible position of Aldea de Ponte. But Craufurd had not yet turned up, and he would not sacrifice the division. While he held on to Guinaldo, the French marshal hesitated, and, as Napier expresses it epigrammatically, "Marmont's fortune was fixed in that hour."

It was the delay of Craufurd that gave the opportunity he missed. When Craufurd did arrive, late in the afternoon, he met the commander-in-chief with his habitual imperturbability. Impatient expectation, when the fate of the war was trembling in the balance, must have taxed Wellington's self-control to the uttermost; and we are persuaded that Craufurd was keenly sensitive to the censure of his superior. Yet, according to unimpeachable authorities who were present, what passed between them was this.

Wellington: "I am glad to see you safe, Craufurd."
Craufurd: "Oh, I was in no danger, I assure you."
Wellington: "But I was in great danger from your conduct."

Craufurd (aside): "He is d—d crusty today."

By saying so little and taking no action at all, Wellington gave another unmistakable proof of the value he set on his headstrong lieutenant. Whatever the failings of the leader of the Light Division, it would have been difficult or impossible to replace him, though the day was close at hand when Fate was to take the matter out of the hands of the long-suffering commander-in-chief.

Nevertheless a time of intense anxiety is not lightly forgotten, and the grievance may have rankled in Wellington's mind. Sent back to perfunctory blockade duties, Craufurd was in low spirits and homesick, and a letter to his wife, written on New Year's Day, gives evidence of extreme depression:

> I cannot say that Lord Wellington and I are quite so cordial as we used to be. He was nettled at a report which I made of the wants of the division.

He appears to have contemplated applying for furlough again, but events were to be otherwise ordered. After El Bodon, Ciudad Rodrigo had been loosely observed by the British. Had Marmont struck home after that engagement, the fortress need never have fallen. At one time Wellington had serious apprehensions that he might have to retire again to his refuge in the lines. But the winter brought unlooked-for changes. Napoleon, in a moment of insanity, decided on the invasion of Russia, and 50,000 of his choicest soldiers in Spain were withdrawn for the march to the Vistula The Spanish partisans were incited to fresh activity, and the French communications were in greater danger than before. With the Emperor absent from Paris and preoccupied elsewhere, the incapable Joseph was replaced in supreme command; the jealousies of the marshals broke out afresh; Marmont actually seized by force at Toledo the contents of the magazines which the king had sold when reduced to desperate straits for money.

Wellington welcomed the unexpected opportunity, and resolved by a series of audacious combinations to recover the frontier fortresses. In his silent preparations for the siege of Ciudad, the unsuspecting enemy was as completely deceived as when Masséna had been astounded by the works of Torres Vedras. The regiments he had been forced to scatter widely, for the sake of sustenance, were unobtrusively drawn in: a heavy siege train was brought up from the coast, ostensibly for re-arming the repaired works of Almeida, and he succeeded in keeping the secret of the pontoon bridge to be thrown across the Agueda.

The eccentricities of that river embarrassed him sorely; one day it might be in flood, and the next nearly dry; and he was so short of ammunition that he served his guns with shot that were gathered from the ruins of Almeida. Moreover, time was precious, for the news of the siege would assuredly set Marmont and Dorsenne in motion. On the other hand, and it was the sole point in his favour, whereas the *enceinte* of the fortress was great—two outlying convents with redoubts had been armed—the garrison had but 1700 available men. It was only the weakness of the garrison which encouraged him afterwards to change his plans and to carry it by storm with immediate sacrifice of life, instead of proceeding according to rule by sap and parallel.

The enterprise was hazardous at the best, and the secrecy which enveloped his plans had its disadvantages. His engineers were as much in the dark as to his intentions as the French. Larpent tells us that at the last moment the indispensable scaling ladders were not forthcoming. Wellington was equal to the occasion. "Well," he said, "you have brought up your stores, so never mind the waggons. Cut them up directly: they will make excellent ladders."

By the 1st of January he had under his hand 35,000 available troops. On the 6th the pontoons were thrown over the Agueda; on the 8th, after unavoidable delays, the fortress was invested. That day the Light Division with Pack's Portuguese had forded the river above the town, holding hands in the icy water which came nearly to their waists and well nigh swept them off their legs. Circling to the north of the fortress, they took up their positions behind the outlying ridge of the great Teson to the north-west The ridge was confronted by a fortified convent faced by an armed redoubt.

That same evening at nightfall the troops stood to their arms: Colonel Colborne[1] called out two companies from each of the three regiments of the division, and forming them in column, led them at once to the assault. The redoubt was rushed, and the defenders either slain or made prisoners. Not a moment was lost in breaking ground, and ere daybreak a parallel communicating with the Teson had been dug, of depth sufficient to give partial shelter.

Napier says that dashing attack shortened operations by several days. The enemy, realising the advantage we had gained, and amply supplied with ammunition, poured a tempest of shot and shell on the shallow trenches. The arrangement was that the Light Division was to be relieved by the 1st on alternate days, and the relief was always the

---
1. Afterwards Sir John Colborne.

signal for redoubled cannonading. Craufurd had one narrow escape when his horse was killed under him. And each morning the relieved division, wading the river again, and under fire, was marched back to its quarters in a distant village.

But that strain on strength and constitution was not prolonged, for Wellington had sure intelligence that Marmont was coming to the rescue. It was then he decided to cut the business short: to breach the curtain of the works with his batteries and to storm without blowing up the counterscarp. On the 19th the two breaches—the longer and the lesser—were both pronounced practicable, and from that point we may refer to the soldier-like story of Sir George Napier, no man being a better authority, for he had the honour of leading the stormers.

When he heard from the engineers that the breaches were practicable, he hurried off to Craufurd, to beg as a personal favour the command of the storming party, and the general willingly acceded to the request. On the eventful morning of the 19th Wellington issued his orders, and to the Light Division was assigned the left attack on the smaller breach. The orders closed with the memorable sentence: "Ciudad Rodrigo must be stormed this evening."

The orders to the Light Division were to move out of cantonments and march down to the trenches. They were halted a mile short of the town, when Craufurd ordered Major Napier to get one hundred volunteers from each of the three British regiments. His appeal was responded to by half the division volunteering. He picked the men at random, nor could he go far wrong: then he formed them in three companies of one hundred each. The forlorn hope of twenty-five, which took precedence in the assault, was led by Lieutenant Gurwood of the despatches.

> As soon as all was formed, we marched at the head of the division in high spirits, and determined that nothing should stop us from carrying the breach.

When dusk was turning to dark, the division formed up behind the convent of Francisco. The Commander-in-chief was there in person, and calling up Colonel Colborne and Major Napier, pointing in the fading light to the foot of the breach, he said to Napier: "Now, do you understand the way you are to lead, so as to arrive at the breach without noise or confusion?"

As Napier was moving off, one of the officers on the commander-in-chief's staff exclaimed: "Why, your men are not loaded!" Napier answered that if they could not do the business with the bayonet they could not do it at all, and Wellington, who was listening, simply said: "Let him alone; let him go his own way."

It is strange that at this dramatic moment Napier ignores the presence of Craufurd, for he does his gallantry full justice when deploring his death. Costello of the Rifles, a trustworthy authority, not only comments on his presence, but gives fragments of his spirited address.

Soldiers, the eyes of your country are upon you. Be steady, be cool, be firm in the assault. The town must be yours this night Once masters of the wall, let your first duty be to clear the ramparts, and in doing this, keep well together.

He adds: "Craufurd, calling out, 'Now, lads, for the breach!' led the way."

Had we heard nothing of it, we might be very sure that Craufurd was not hanging back at that critical moment; though it may be doubted whether the fiery general, in his chivalrous dash and greed for glory, was in the right place when in front of the stormers. Craufurd made his appeal when the signal rocket shot up, and from four points the storming columns simultaneously rushed forward, for there was a feigned attack on the other side of the town. The enemy had likewise been waiting in expectancy, and, like the British, they answered to the signal. The men of the Light Division had a space of 600 yards to cross, and it was swept by a hail of fire. They crossed it in a marvellously short time, when, on the brink of the counterscarp, they found that the Portuguese, who carried the grain-bags, had been left behind.

It was a drop of 14 feet, and the bottom was paved with spikes and live shells. No matter: they dropped into the ditch, Gurwood and his party leading, and then rushed forward in the darkness, fitfully illuminated by cannon fire and musketry, to the *fausse braie*. The forlorn hope, thrown out for a moment, had taken to the left: the body of the stormers, scrambling straight onwards, found the bottom of the breach. Narrow as it was steep, a single gun laid crosswise almost blocked it: and had it been retrenched and bristling with *chevaux-de-frise* like Phillipon's breaches at Badajoz, no human courage could have carried it.

But Barrié, though a skilful and experienced veteran, was no engineer and no Phillipon. He failed even to make use of a flanking bastion, which enfiladed the ascent. The very steepness saved the stormers. They pressed forward in face of a plunging fire, the men from sheer force of habit snapping the locks of their unloaded muskets. Napier dropped half-way up, his elbow shattered by a grape-shot, shouting as he fell: "Recollect you are not loaded! push on with the bayonet."

He was answered with a cheer; the breach was carried; and then Craufurd's order was obeyed, which bid his men see to the clearing of the ramparts. Dropping into the space between the ramparts and the town, they opened a flanking fire on the defenders of the great breach, clearing the way into the place for the 3rd Division. Simultaneously the explosion of some magazine on the wall swept away the retrenchments which obstructed the division.

Ciudad Rodrigo was won, and the gain was inestimable to the plan of campaign, but the army had a heavy loss in Generals Craufurd and Mackinnon. Craufurd, having headed the rush of the columns to the glacis, took his stand on the brink a little to the left of the spot where they descended. Of course he was fully exposed to the enemy's fire. There he stood, as at Busaco, shouting instructions and incitements to the stormers. His figure seems to have been seen and his shouts to have been heard from the opposite parapets, and they drew an intense double fire from the ramparts and the *fausse braie*. Before the bottom of the breach was well won, a ball passed through his arm, traversed the body, and lodged in the spine. He fell at once, "and the shock was so great," says Sir James Shaw Kennedy, "that in falling he rolled over the glacis." (*Notes on the Battle of Waterloo* by James Shaw Kennedy also published by Leonaur).

Kennedy, one of his *aides-de-camp*, alone was with him, and there was no other help near.

> I half dragged and half carried him to where there was an inequality of ground, in which he was out of the direct fire from the place.

He thought he was dying, and begged Kennedy to tell his wife that he was sure they would meet in heaven.

Napier, suffering agonies, had been supported into the town. He had previously asked the good offices of a surgeon friend to perform the operation he had fully anticipated, if by any chance he should escape with life. His friend was there and willing, but red tape interposed. A staff-surgeon was present, of higher rank, and on him devolved the duty of the amputation. The arm was duly hacked off with a blunted knife: the mutilated patient, as he tells us, at last succeeded in a search for a bed, and after twenty-four hours of delirium calmed down into peaceful sleep. When he woke, he heard moans from the room above him: there Craufurd was lying, in terrible pain.

Yet in that extremity the iron soldier was still himself, and showed the innate kindness of heart which was too often suppressed in his furious outbursts of passion. He learned that the brave leader of the stormers was lying in the room below: he sent down to tell him how highly he appreciated his gallantry: and, regretting that he could never see him again, through the hours of agony in which he lingered on, he kept sending anxious messages of inquiry. "I shall never forget this: I should be, what I am not, an unfeeling brute if I did. Indeed General Craufurd was always kind to me, and ready to do me a service when in his power."

No one lamented the grievous loss more than Wellington. With the captured city in wild turmoil, and the soldiers broken loose from all control, he was almost as unremitting in his inquiries as Craufurd after Napier. And yet it could be only a question of hours, and the best wish of the man who could spare him the least was for a speedy release. In such circumstances the funeral follows fast upon the death, and while the veteran was dying the coffin was being knocked together. like Moore, he was laid to rest in the dusk of the evening, and on the spot which would ever be associated with his memory. The men of the division—those at least who were sober and under control—stood to arms.

The coffin was borne out and carried forward, between a double line of soldiers of the division, standing with muskets reversed. Immediately behind came General Stewart and Shaw Kennedy as chief mourners: they were followed by Lord Wellington, Marshal Beresford, General Castaños, and a long train of staff and general officers. The men of the Light Division brought up the procession, and seldom has there been a more impressive ceremony. For as the bandsmen played dirges and funeral marches, and the chaplain with faltering accents read the solemn service for the dead, the fires in the town were still smouldering, the shouts of the drunken rioters had not been silenced, and the Provost Marshal was busy in the public squares.

According to the evidence of Mr. Gleig, chaplain-general of the forces, then a very young man, who was an eye-witness, the spectators were so absorbed in the dramatic scene that they were indifferent to these reminders of the horrors around them. (*The Subaltern* and *Waterloo and the Campaign of 1815* both by George Robert Gleig also published by Leonaur). "Six rugged veterans" carried the coffin, and all the six were in tears. If we remember what those veterans had gone through, and how hardened they had become to death and suffering, no soldier ever received a more impressive tribute. The emotion was contagions among the privates in the close columns of battalions who were fortunate in getting a glimpse of what was passing. For the grave had been dug at the bottom of the narrow breach, and few could find points of view so commanding as the crest of the glacis whence Craufurd had cheered his stormers to the attack, and where the grass was still red with his life-blood.

Enough has been said to indicate his character. Sir George Napier, who regarded him both with respect and admiration, sums it up truthfully enough. He says that, though Craufurd was a most unpopular man, every officer in the Light Division must acknowledge that he had brought it to a state of discipline and knowledge of the duties of light troops never equalled by any division in the army. In a long course of perilous experiences, he perfected the training Moore had bestowed on them. The severest of taskmasters, he was merciless to faulty subordinates, but they knew that he never spared himself. The most stern of disciplinarians, his soldiers loved him nevertheless, for they had absolute confidence in his watchfulness and prescience, and knew that he looked carefully after their comforts.

If they suffered privations, the privations were inevitable; they might curse their hard fortune, but not their chief. And the faults which might have provoked reprimands from his superiors were such as soldiers are most ready to forgive. Over fond of fighting, he believed in them so entirely that he would pit them against any odds, and they seldom failed to vindicate his audacity.

Like many hot-tempered and passionate men, he was really warm-hearted and good-natured. Cross his temper and you roused the devil; but there were long interludes between the storms, though the face was habitually sullen and inauspicious. He never stood foolishly on his dignity with his inferiors. Costello tells a good story of his unintentionally interviewing the general at Gallegos. Costello and the chief's valet were sworn friends; when either came upon a bottle of wine, they shared it. Once Costello got a bottle from the *patron* on whom he was billeted, and hurried off to the brigadier's quarters. He saw the valet, as he thought, leaning out of the window, and slapped him cordially on the shoulder. The figure turned sharply, with a "Who the devil is that?" and the intruder found himself face to face with the brigadier. He stammered out some sort of explanation.

"And where did you get the wine?" asked the general, with a good-humoured smile at the other's abject plight. He was told.

"Well, well," said Craufurd, "you may go, but don't take me for my servant another time." He had a sense of humour too, and the soldiers knew it: and the foraging and pillaging Irishmen of the division always declared that the grim chief had a laugh in him. One of them was trudging contentedly campwards, towing a captured pig by a string behind him, when by bad luck Craufurd rode up. "Where did you steal that pig, you plundering villain?"

"Whaat pig, gineral?" exclaimed the culprit, turning round with an air of injured innocence.

"Why, that pig you have got behind you, you villain."

"Well, then, I vow and protest, gineral," looking back at the pig as if he had never seen him before, "it is scandalous to think what a wicked world we live in, and how ready folks are to take away an honest boy's character. Some blackguard, wanting to get me into trouble, has tied that baste to my *cartouch* box."

Craufurd burst out laughing, and set spurs to his horse. The humour of the thing on that occasion was too much for him, yet he was the last man to tolerate pilfering or pillaging. One day when Costello was on guard Craufurd came riding up with his orderly, when two men burst out of a house with some bread they had stolen. At that time the division was on very short commons. The men were hotly chased by a Spanish woman, shouting, "*Ladrone! Ladrone!*" The general and his orderly cut into the pursuit; the loaves were given back to the woman, and the thieves sent to the guard-house.

But there was a strange sequel to that incident. Next day the men were tried by brigade court-martial, and sentenced to punishment. The brigade was formed up: the proceedings of the court-martial were read, and the general proceeded to improve the occasion by lecturing officers and men on cruelty to "the harmless inhabitants." "Besides, you think, because you are riflemen and more exposed to the enemy's fire than other regiments, you are to rob the inhabitants with impunity; but while I command you, you shall not."

"Strip, sir," he said, addressing himself, by way of peroration, to a corporal who was one of the offenders. The man submitted to be tied up in silence; then turning to the general, who was pacing up and down the square, he said: "General Craufurd, I hope you will forgive me."

"No, sir; your crime is too great."

If the crime was great, the penalty was severe; he was to be reduced to the ranks and receive 150 lashes.

Then he made another appeal. "Do you recollect, sir, when under command of General Whitelocke, in Buenos Ayres, we were marched prisoners with a number of others to a pound surrounded by a wall? There was a well in the centre, out of which I drew water with my mess-tin, by means of canteen straps I collected from the men who were prisoners like myself. You sat on my knapsack: I parted my last biscuit with you. You then told me you would never forget my kindness. It is now in your power, sir; you know how short we have been of rations for some time."

The whole square were touched, and waited. The bugler told off to inflict the punishment, after an interval, received the usual signal from the bugle-major. The first lash was laid on. Then the general started from a reverie, and turning hurriedly, said: "Who taught that bugler to flog? Send him to drill! send him to drill! He cannot flog! he cannot flog! Stop! stop! Take him down! I remember it well, I remember it well," while he strode up and down the square, muttering inarticulately, blowing his nose and wiping his face with his handkerchief, busily striving to conceal the emotion which was evident to all.

A dead silence prevailed for some time, until our gallant general recovered a little his noble feeling, when he uttered with a broken accent: "Why does a brave soldier like you commit these crimes?" Then beckoning to his orderly to bring his horse, he mounted and rode off.

It was incidents like these that redeemed him in the affections of his soldiers, for he always had their admiration. Other veterans could remember how he had offered them his wine-bottle or lent them a lift by his stirrup-leather, when they were struggling to Vigo through the rocks and snowdrifts of Gallicia. And he was free and generous even to needy stragglers from other corps. On the frontiers of Estremadura he came across one of his pickets, bringing in a cavalryman who had escaped from the French and had been wandering for days in the *sierra*. The man was half-starved and almost naked. Craufurd ordered him to be supplied with clothes from his own scanty baggage.

Wellington and his lieutenants seemed to have charmed lives, yet in those days of point-blank volleys from the musket, with the clashing of sabres and the crossing of bayonets, these were continually in the thickest of the *mêlée*. The Duke was only once hit—by a spent ball at Orthez. Hope, who was the most conspicuous of marks, had seven bullets through his clothes before Bayonne and escaped with a scratch. Not one of them spared himself. Picton lived to fall in the closing battle of the long war, and the others retired on their laurels, to die peaceably in their beds. Craufurd was the solitary exception, and, if his career was prematurely cut short, he died as he had often desired to die.

Had his life been prolonged, it is doubtful whether he would have increased his reputation, for the headstrong and somewhat unmanageable subordinate was unfitted for supreme command. With all his grand soldier-like qualities, he was lacking in coolness, judgment, and temper. But, when his fighting division lost its head, his severity and the strictness of his discipline were not only forgiven but admired. At one time his chief officers had actually consulted as to which of them should be commissioned to call him out. Now they never spoke of him without regret, and were generous in their letters of their tributes to his memory. But by no one was he more missed than by Wellington, whose plans he had sometimes perversely crossed, and whose positive orders he had once at least disregarded. The staunch and tireless watch-dog of the camps could not be easily replaced.

Sir Thomas Picton

1

Picton stands out in military history as the type of the rugged warrior—a figure who deserved a monument that should endure, hewn out of the granite that refuses itself to delicate chiselling. His look was saturnine and sometimes almost sinister, yet it could be irradiated with gleams of the genial smile that indicated a warm heart. The staunchest of friends, he could be a bitter enemy; but no man was more freehanded, and his unknown charities were bountiful. He stood over six feet, and the commanding form in its massive strength was ever a rallying point in the front of the battle. His voice was harsh and his speech abrupt, nor did he measure his language in the savage reprimands he addressed to soldiers who had broken loose from discipline. His rarer outbursts of eulogy were the more appreciated.

"Are we the greatest blackguards in the army now?" shouted the Connaught Rangers, when carrying all before them in a headlong charge at Fuentes d'Onoro. And the general, who had been revelling in the joy of battle, smilingly retracted, with a handsome apology. No wonder he was dear to the fighting soldier, for, like Blücher, he might have been styled General Forward, and, like the true-bred British mastiff, he never lost grip when he laid hold. His weakness was that, when entrusted with a feint, he always pushed it to a very real attack, and it was a fortunate foible at the storm of Badajoz.

His was a strange as well as a stormy career. Near the outset, by an unlucky chance, his zeal lost him a grand opportunity. Afterwards for twelve weary years he was cursing inaction on half-pay, and then promotion came with a steady rush, each step being gained by acknowledged merit. When he had retired, full of honours, to repose on his laurels, he was summoned on brief notice to Belgium, to die the soldier's death he would have desired. But the best of his life was clouded by legal persecution, which impeached his character, his honour, and his humanity, adding the gall of resentment to an irritable temperament, and deepening the shadows on a gloomy brow.

The younger son of an affluent Welsh squire, he inherited money from his mother which made him comparatively independent He was born, as Nelson was, in 1758. He was entered young to soldiering, for he was gazetted when thirteen, though he did not join till two years later. We hear many complaints now of the miserable pay of our officers, but, owing to the eccentric arrangements then existing, Picton for six years drew nothing at all. Yet he was never one of His Majesty's "hard bargains." As a boy he entered with heart and soul into his profession. He had studied at a military school kept by a Frenchman, for when our officers did not go abroad to learn war in France, they were schooled by Frenchmen at home.

When he joined at Gibraltar, as a youth of fifteen, his time was never wasted. Not content with constant examination of the fortifications, he was continually imagining schemes of attack, and devising plans for defeating them: he devoured the books in the garrison library, and is said to have bored the officers of the scientific corps by persistent questioning. Moreover, on frequent excursions into Spain, he acquired the knowledge of Spanish which proved invaluable, and recommended him to high commands in the Peninsula. But the monotonous garrison routine soon palled, and he sought active occupation elsewhere.

He congratulated himself when, in January 1778, he was gazetted captain in the 75th, which was supposed to be on the roster for active service. It was a sad mistake, which he soon had reason to regret, for by a hair's-breadth he missed the memorable siege, when he might have seen his theories tested in practice. On duty at home in dull provincial towns, again and again he cursed his luck, when all the country was throbbing to the bulletins from the heroic defenders of the Rock.

His patience was to be more severely tried. In 1783 there came a sudden reduction of the forces, and the 75th with other regiments was to be disbanded. His first and last military exploit, for the time, was quelling a riot in Bristol at serious personal risk, when the soldiers resented summary dismissal. His great personal strength served him well, when rushing into the throng he seized the ringleader, and when his firmness had covered the retreat to the guard-house, his brief soldierly appeal hushed the murmurs of the mutineers. Picton himself had most reason to complain. Praised for his promptitude and gallantry, he was

Sir Thomas Picton

put upon half-pay, and on half-pay for twelve years he remained.

He found vent for his superabundant energy in field sports, but not for a single moment did he lose sight of the purpose of his life. His leisure within doors was devoted to study of the classics and of books on war. His incessant applications for employment were courteously answered, though never successful. The invariable reply was that he would be remembered for the earliest vacancy. He bore these repeated disappointments the more complacently that for eleven years the world was tolerably tranquil. But when France broke the peace in the revolutionary wars, his fiery spirit boiled over. The first year of the fighting fretted him beyond endurance, and towards the end of 1794 he took the rash resolution of sailing to the West Indies as a soldier of fortune. His sole encouragement was a slight acquaintance with Sir John Vaughan, the commander-in-chief.

The best answer to the malicious disparagement and malignant calumnies of which he became the object is to be found in the friends he made. He may have made mistakes, but Vaughan, Abercromby, Sir Samuel Hood, and General Grinfield stand sponsors for his honour and sterling qualities. For their own sakes they picked out the best men, and Picton was always placed in the most responsible positions. At first sight Vaughan made him his *aide-de-camp*, appointing him to a company in the 15th Regiment. With his foot once on the ladder, he climbed quickly: he was captain, major, colonel, brigadier-general, all in the course of a few years. Within the first year Vaughan was superseded by Sir Ralph Abercromby, and Picton, in the idea that his chances of employment were gone, had thoughts of returning to Europe.

The meeting with Abercromby changed his views: Vaughan must have spoken warmly in his favour, for the new general grasped his hand, begged him to remain for the impending campaign, and promised "to give him an opportunity of returning in more agreeable circumstances." We need not dwell on the ensuing operations, important as they were. At first he had no recognised position; he acted as volunteer *aide-de-camp*, and though repeatedly distinguishing himself for judgment and courage, could not be mentioned in public despatches. But he could have asked for no more gratifying tribute than the sentence in general orders, "that all orders coming through lieutenant-Colonel Picton should be considered as the orders of the commander-in-chief"—the more flattering when it is remembered that Abercromby's brigadiers were Hope and Moore.

At the close of the campaign Picton sailed with Abercromby for Europe, and the tedious voyage changed friendship into intimacy. The favourite subjects of conversation were strategy and tactics, and Picton owned himself deeply indebted for the lessons he received. After a brief furlough they returned together to Martinique—the return was followed by the seizure of Trinidad, and Picton was nominated by his friend to be governor and commandant. The appointment was destined to exercise a chequered influence on his fortunes; but it pleased him none the less that it was one of great responsibility and difficulty.

"Colonel Picton," said Sir Ralph, when Picton officially expressed his acknowledgments, "if I knew any officer who, in my opinion, could discharge the duties better than you, to him I would have given it: there are no thanks due to me."

He showed his absolute confidence by giving the new governor autocratic power, subject to the administration of the existing law. It was a difficult charge, for the island had been notorious as the resort of pirates and the refuge of *desperadoes* from the Spanish main. The mixed population was ready to spring to arms, and on the appearance of the British fleet the French Consul had offered 3000 volunteers to the Spanish governor. Crime was rampant, and there were flagrant outrages. To check them Picton had but 500 men; of these only 300 Englishmen were reliable, and the sinister warning that they would soon be in the cemetery or hospitals was speedily realised. He was threatened besides by descents from the mainland. Nor were any reinforcements available.

Suffice it to say that he not only maintained order, but was devising ambitious schemes of conquest. He urged on his Government the annexation of the fertile territories of Guiana and Caraccas. His proposals seem to have come to the ears of the Spanish governors. At any rate they simultaneously issued proclamations offering rewards of 20,000 dollars for his head. Nor was the offer by any means an idle menace, for Trinidad swarmed with ruffians to whom the reward would have been a fortune. But, though he rode unaccompanied about the island, his intrepidity and prowess were so notorious that no attempt was made on his life. His letters in a variety of styles might furnish models for a complete letter-writer. He answered the Spanish *hidalgos* mockingly, acknowledging the handsome compliment they paid him and challenging them to come over and take his head.

While the meaner whites and half-castes were disaffected to a man, it is significant that he found staunch supporters among Spaniards of the higher classes. They welcomed the change to honest rule from the venal administration under which they had smarted, and it is in great measure to Picton's earnest representations that we owe the retention of Trinidad as a British colony.

Abercromby, with knowledge acquired on the spot, had heartily approved his proceedings, and Abercromby's approval had been endorsed by official despatches from London. Therefore it was a shock and surprise when he received a letter from Lord Hobart, intimating that the government of Trinidad was to be placed in commission, and among the three commissioners Picton ranked third. It was insult as well as degradation, and he was moved the more that the gall was mingled with honey. There was no charge against his administration: on the contrary, the language of the letter was complimentary. A far calmer temper might have been roused to indignation, and he only awaited the arrival of his colleagues to resign. The first was Colonel Fullarton of the East India Company's service; the second, fortunately for Picton, was Sir Samuel Hood.

It is difficult now to decide how far Fullarton was actuated by pure and patriotic motives; certain it is that he began by duplicity, and prosecuted his attacks with rancorous malignity. Aggrieved as he felt, Picton received him with respect and hospitality, as Fullarton acknowledged in letters to Lord Hobart. For a time they seemed excellent friends, but friction succeeded when Fullarton sought to elbow aside the masterful governor. A surprise was sprung on Picton at a meeting of the council. Fullarton moved for the production of statements of all recent criminal proceedings, "specifying every individual . . . who has been imprisoned, banished, fettered, flogged, horned, &c."

It was obviously a declaration of war, and when Hood arrived later, Picton was ready to hand in his deferred resignation and go home to vindicate his character. It is needless to go into tedious details. It is enough now to advert to Hood's view of Fullarton and his proceedings. He said in a fiery speech in open council:

> I am ashamed of you: ashamed to be seen in the same company. Not with you. General Picton. I shall be proud to act with you on all occasions . . . but as for you, sir (turning to Colonel Fullarton), your behaviour has been such that nothing but the paramount obligation of his Majesty's Commission could seat us at the same Board.

Fullarton sat silent. Picton's supersession by the commission can only be explained by a change of ministers and measures on Pitt's resignation; but it may be noted that while Abercromby and General Grinfield— the men best acquainted with Trinidad and the circumstances—never flinched in their friendship, Lord Hobart wrote that "the first official notification of any dissatisfaction with your government has been *from, yourself.*" And General Maitland, who replaced Picton in military command, in a public address paid him the emphatic tribute that he had saved the colony when it was beset by traitors.

He left Trinidad and landed in Barbadoes just in time to offer his services to General Grinfield for the expedition against St. Lucia and Tobago. The islands were captured: Picton was commended in orders as the cause of the prompt surrender of Tobago, and Grinfield showed his belief in the ex-Governor of Trinidad by appointing him Tobago's commandant. But by every post came letters from home, urging him to return to defend himself against infamous charges. He landed in England to find himself under a cloud, which he must have felt could never be entirely dissipated.

There is seldom so much smoke without fire, and he must have recognised that he had made mistakes and laid himself open to misconstruction. But all the good work had gone for nothing, and the public was in one of its spasms of passionate indignation. As in the cases of Warren Hastings and Governor Eyre, for the moment the spring-tide of feeling was rising strong against him. Endless charges had been put forward or trumped up; no allowance was made for a critical emergency; and the witnesses he might have called were in the distant tropics. "The blood-stained governor" had become a by-word; he was to be summoned to answer for his crimes at "the bar of outraged justice"; he was the object of coarse lampoons and the subject for scurrilous caricatures.

He was brought as a criminal to the bar of offended justice; he was not only persecuted but prosecuted, on no fewer than six-and-thirty charges. To sum up, he stood two trials before juries of his countrymen. On the first, he was technically convicted on what was proved on appeal to have been a misrepresentation of the law. The rule for a new trial was made absolute. But the real acquittal came from the slow proceedings of the Privy Council. Through three weary years the Council carefully investigated all the evidence; as with Warren Hastings, those most nearly concerned sent home the strongest affidavits in favour of the inculpated governor. The Council pronounced that "there was no foundation whatever for further proceedings on any of the numerous charges."

That he was blameless we do not say. In his own manly defence, he rather pleaded extenuation. It was incontestable that he had signed an order for putting a Spanish woman of infamous character to the question—or torture. He urged that he had taken the oath of office to administer island law as he found it, and that in that matter he was in the hands of the island judges. Further, that the woman, who was notoriously guilty, was more mercifully dealt with in Trinidad than in England, where she would have been hanged for a theft of more than forty shillings. We take it that he was a man administering rough justice who did not stand upon trifles. Assured of the guilt of the parties implicated, he thought an essential witness might well be brought to give evidence by the summary methods which chanced to be legal.

Be that as it may, if he sinned he suffered. To say nothing of the wear of mind, of the anguish of being received with obloquy when conscious of having done splendid work, the law expenses would have sent a poor man through the insolvent courts to the Fleet or the Marshalsea. They amounted to no less than £7000. Fortunately Picton had a wealthy uncle who stood by his nephew. He bailed him out on his first committal for £40,000, and settled all expenses on his honourable acquittal. Very naturally the envenomed animosity of the crowd excited the indignation of cooler heads.

It is much to the credit of the disreputable "Old Q" that he came generously to the assistance of the persecuted, and in ignorance of the pecuniary circumstances, he placed; £10,000 at Picton's disposal. The munificent offer was gratefully declined, but it was the foundation of a friendship. Though his Grace only once met the general, Picton gladly consented to write regularly on Peninsular affairs, and on the Duke's death he found himself remembered by a handsome legacy.

He had passed twelve of his best years in unwelcome retirement. Now another six years had gone by in continual turmoil and worry. While his comrades were winning distinction in the wars, he was kept in London dancing attendance at the law courts, and a promising professional career threatened to end in disgrace and dishonour. Repeatedly he would have applied to be sent on service; but he was under a cloud at the War Office, and he was dissuaded by the urgency of his friends. They told him that he must look personally to his defence, for the struggle was sure to go against him in his absence. He reluctantly consented, though it is characteristic of the man that he could divert his thoughts from harassing cares to devise great schemes of national defence; but, his record being rather that of a civil administrator than a soldier, these schemes were officially acknowledged and pigeon-holed.

At last the tardy decision of the Privy Council set him free. Forthwith he presented himself as a solicitor at the Horse Guards, where the warm appreciation of Abercromby had commended him to the favour of the Duke of York. The application was so far timely that the unlucky Walcheren expedition was being fitted out under the most incompetent chief who could well have been selected. General Picton was appointed to Lord Chatham's Staff, and he gained as much credit as was to be got in the circumstances with a Walcheren fever besides. From the first he had never augured well of the adventure; he was too shrewd not to form a just estimate of the commander. The delays of "the late Lord Chatham" gave the enemy ample time to make preparation for the defence of Antwerp.

Flushing fell into our hands, after a siege conducted on the most haphazard principles and a bombardment which reduced the town to ruin. Picton, who was appointed commandant, wrote to a friend, five days after the surrender, that the best thing to be done was to destroy the fortifications with the basin and withdraw at once. In fact, he saw that the expedition had failed; but we held on to the malarious swamps with stupid tenacity till half the army had succumbed to the fever and most of the survivors were in hospital. As we said, the general suffered with the rest, and though saved by his sound constitution, he was never again the man he had been. He was lifted from his sick-bed to be carried on board ship, and the doctors sent him at once to Cheltenham.

2

He could hardly have expected to be soon recalled to action. He had been unpleasantly before the public for several years, and the Walcheren expedition had brought him no distinction. In the West Indies he had made his mark as administrator rather than soldier. But the summons came, and it was a very flattering one, for Wellington had made personal application for his services. The manner of the summons was in this wise, as the Duke explained it to Lord Stanhope. Picton:

. . . . was first mentioned to me by General Miranda, who had come over to this country to propose to us to revolutionise the South American colonies. . . Miranda said that he knew an extremely clever man called Picton, a man to be much employed—but don't trust him, for he has so much vanity that, if you sent him out to the Caraccas or the West India Islands, he would attempt to become the prince of them. . . . When we were afterwards in Spain, we wanted major-generals: I remembered what Miranda had said to me, and I wrote to the Government to send me Picton. Well, he came. I found him a rough, foul-mouthed devil as ever lived, but he always behaved extremely well.

No doubt the Duke had remembered also that Picton had been the friend of Moore and the favoured *protégé* of Abercromby. The Duke's reminiscence was by no means an unmixed compliment, yet it gave a rough though rather unfair idea of the man. And Sir Herbert Maxwell has undeniably brought out in his biography that gratitude to those who had served him was not the Duke's strong point. He declared that the Spaniards had never manfully stood up to the enemy, forgetting their fighting at the storm of the Great Rhone and elsewhere, and he abused the rank and file to whom he was indebted for his laurels. Doubtless our army swore terribly in the Peninsula as in Flanders, and the eloquence of most general officers was objurgatory.

A score of years afterwards, it is said that an Archbishop could remark to a Prime Minister that before discussing serious business they might assume everything and everybody to be damned. But Picton, like Pennefather of Crimean fame, was more fierce-mouthed than foul-mouthed. It was notorious that he swore savagely as matter of habit, when milder men would have grumbled. Kincaid, in his *Adventures of the Rifle Brigade*, (also published by Leonaur in *The Complete Kincaid of the Rifles* by John Kincaid), relates the scene in the great square at Ciudad Rodrigo, where drunken soldiers were firing promiscuously and shooting their comrades in sheer pleasantry.

Some heads began to be blown from their shoulders in the hurricane, when the voice of Sir Thomas Picton with the power of twenty trumpets began to proclaim damnation to everybody.

There were various ways of managing soldiers in war time in those days, and Picton's seems to have answered fairly well. Picton's language must have been strong if it shocked the Duke, but he paid him the highest possible compliment when the general was temporarily invalided during the fighting in the Pyrenees. Larpent tells the story. Talking of some blunder that had been made and excusing it, he said: "Why, even General Picton did so-and-so the other day," as if surprised that he should not have acted quite right

He went to the front early in 1810, when Wellington was making his stand against overwhelming forces and a weak-kneed Cabinet. His hands had been strengthened by his brother's acceptance of the Foreign Office, and he hoped for a modest reinforcement of 5000 men to supplement the 25,000 sickly veterans with whom he was facing the 370,000 French whom their Emperor had poured into the Peninsula. He sorely needed fighting generals who had head as well as heart. When Picton arrived, headquarters were at Viseu; he was at once placed in command of the 3rd Division, and his own headquarters were at Colerico. Wellington's immediate object was to retard Masséna's advance: he had put Ciudad Rodrigo and Almeida in a state of defence, but he had no intention of risking a battle to save them.

The lines at Torres Vedras were being strengthened day by day, and he hoped to draw Masséna on to a disaster. It was then that Craufurd, with the Light Division, was audaciously defying whole *corps d'armée*. When the combat on the Coa was at its height, he had the memorable meeting with Picton which Napier relates dramatically and circumstantially. But did that meeting ever come off? We are inclined to trust Napier absolutely as to facts, and he sought access to all reliable sources of information; but, on the other hand, he is distinctly contradicted by an officer on Picton's staff, who declares that, although they heard the firing, they regarded it as an ordinary affair of posts; that the general never went out alone; and that on that eventful day he did not ride more than half a mile from Pinhel.

Nevertheless, assuming that there was a meeting, as we are inclined to do, we can understand the position, and there can be no question that Picton was blameworthy. Two hot-tempered men, with no love for each other, met suddenly face to face, in highly exciting circumstances. Angry words, swiftly interchanged, brought the colloquy to a conclusion, which Picton may have subsequently regretted. We have already alluded to the reported interview. He had reason on his side and might plead orders. He had been ordered to avoid a battle; he understood and sympathised with Wellington's plans. But it was also in his instructions to support the Light Division if necessary, and when Craufurd made the appeal he was in imminent peril.

Masséna, after marches and counter-marches, at last decided to advance. The allies, concentrating, fell back before him, retiring along the southern bank of the Mondego. The French marshal, though choosing the more difficult route on the northern bank, was making a rush to anticipate Hill's joining at Coimbra. In that he failed, and his rapid movements were brought up before the ridge of Busaco. Wellington would not be tempted to fight at a disadvantage, but here he had made deliberate choice of a position. Deeming that Masséna would seek to turn his flank, he had posted the 1st Division on the sea road. When he found he had only to face a frontal attack, he drew in that division, and Hill had come up and was in touch with his right.

It has been told how Masséna missed his chance by delay. At best it must have been a bloody business—the storming of those precipitous heights—but Wellington had been given time nearly to arrange his battle. His weakness was that with but 60,000 men it was barely possible to guard the extended range. Picton held the crest, with Leith and Spencer to his left, and in a letter to his friend Colonel Pleydell he describes his part in the action. He had detached one of his brigades to reinforce Spencer, and:

> ..... there remained with me only three British and two Portuguese regiments to defend the ridge from Saint Antonio de Cantara to the hill of Busaco, a space of above a mile and a half. The enemy were so concentrated as equally to threaten the right, left, and centre of our position.

There was a wide gap between his posts and those of Spencer, and he sent his strongest regiment to occupy it. To the right of that regiment was the yawning chasm of Saint Antonio, the steep corridor by which the enemy were likely to ascend, and he guarded it with the 74th and two Portuguese battalions, backed up by twelve field pieces. The fighting 45th he kept in reserve. Ere daybreak a sputtering of musketry on his left gave him warning: it was followed by discharges from batteries on the opposite heights. The rush in massive column to force the pass was repelled by the deadly musketry of the defenders in front and heavy enfilading fire on the left. It was repelled and never renewed.

But meantime another column assailing the left of his position had swept aside the resistance and established themselves on the summit of the *sierra*. They might have held the position they had gallantly won had supports been forthcoming.

> I galloped towards the left, and to my great surprise found the enemy in possession of a strong rocky point in the centre of my line, and the light infantry companies of the 74th and 88th

Regiments driven in and retreating before them in disorder. With some difficulty I rallied them, drove the enemy from the rocky point with the bayonet, and with the assistance of a Portuguese battalion I succeeded in forcing them to abandon the hill and cross the ravine in great confusion.

That virtually ended the battle so far as Picton was engaged, though there was another half-hearted attack. He had had his first opportunity of showing his mettle under the eye of his commander, and the satisfaction of knowing that he had done his work well.

It is to be remarked that his account differs materially from Napier's narrative, but his letter is confirmed by his report to Lord Wellington. Napier says that the leading French battalions, having established themselves on the rocks, were preparing to sweep the ridge to our right, when Wellington brought up two guns, and the 45th and 88th Regiments hurled the enemy down the hill. According to Picton, those regiments were then hotly engaged half a mile to the left of his division: it was not his right but his left which was in danger: and the enemy were repulsed, not by aid from General Leith, but by regiments of his own division. Picton reports:

> The assistant quartermaster-general having at this time brought up a battalion of the 8th Portuguese Regiment at this critical period, I personally led and directed their attack on the flank of the enemy's columns, and completely succeeded in driving them in great confusion and disorder down the hill and across the ravine.

It is impossible to reconcile the conflicting stories, and we must conclude that Napier for once was misinformed. Nor does it appear that Picton communicated with Leith till he rode back after saving the situation on his left.

There was not much matter for laughter at Busaco, but Picton was for once a cause of mirth to his men, and that when the battle was at the hottest. After visiting his posts through a sleepless night, he had thrown himself down in his cloak to snatch some rest, and had drawn on a coloured nightcap as usual. Like Wellington, he could sleep on the shortest notice. He gave unnecessary orders to be called if there were any alarm, for he was roused by the roll of cannon and musketry. In a moment he was in the saddle, and after riding to the pass of Saint Antonio, where all was going well, he galloped to a slope of the hill where his troops were giving ground. He placed himself at the head of a Portuguese battalion, led them forward, and when within a few yards of the foe gave the word to charge, waving his hat over his head with a loud "hurrah." He had forgotten the red cotton nightcap, and the sight of it so tickled the Portuguese that they charged with shouts of laughter.

On the foremost line of Torres Vedras the 3rd Division was posted round a mountain commanding the village of that name. General Campbell holding the extreme left. Notwithstanding the strength, natural and artificial, of the position, Picton seems to have doubted whether the numbers of the allies sufficed to protect so great an extent of front. The Portuguese were fast being brought into fighting trim, though he pronounces the Spanish auxiliaries "a miserable mob." But after the engagements with the Light Division Masséna was content to watch and wait, and Picton's duties were confined to mounting guard. "Nothing," he writes, "could exceed the misery of this part of Portugal. Every article of human subsistence has long been consumed. The poor inhabitants are kept from perishing by the contributions of the British officers; this division daily feeds above 300."

The officers, says Lord Londonderry, passed the time in hunting, shooting, and fishing; but the time hung heavy on the men, and there were still wine-cellars in the villages. One of these had been pillaged by soldiers, who got gloriously drunk. Next Sunday at church parade Picton preached them a sermon. An anonymous writer gives a vivid description of the scene and the man.

> I could not deny that I felt a prejudice against him (Picton), and his countenance did not do it away, for it had a stern, gloomy expression, which, added to a very dark complexion, made it no way prepossessing; but when he opened his mouth and began to pour forth a torrent of abuse on us for our conduct, and his dark eye flashed with indignation,
>
> *Hope withering fled and Mercy sigh'd farewell.*

While the allies were amply supplied from Lisbon and the fleet, Masséna was starving. Reluctantly he withdrew to Santarem, and after standing at bay there for months, devastating all the country behind him, resigned himself to retreat. He retired in vengeful mood, giving a free hand to his licentious soldiery. Followed closely by Wellington, famine dogged the heels of both hosts. In the swiftness of the retreat and pursuit the British divisions outstripped their commissariat trains; the biscuits in the haversacks were prematurely devoured, and when cattle were forthcoming the hungry stomachs loathed the continual meat diet, as the Israelites sickened of quails in the wilderness.

The Light and 3rd Divisions pressed hard on the French: position after position was forced, or more often outflanked. Ney was in command of Masséna's rear-guard, and though he once made a dangerous mistake, he distinguished himself as when covering the retreat from Moscow. Picton wrote of him:

> All his movements afforded a perfect lesson in that kind of warfare. Moving at all times upon his flank, I had an opportunity of seeing everything he did; and I must be dull in the extreme if I have not derived some practical knowledge from such an example.

Masséna had arrived at Guarda, and taken post on the mountain with 20,000 men. He had hoped to maintain that virtually impregnable position, that he might join hands with Soult and fall back on the valley of the Tagus. The return to Ciudad Rodrigo, whence he had marched in the full assurance of victory, seemed too humiliating. But circumstances and the insubordination of his generals proved too strong for him. Guarda was outflanked and evacuated, to the agreeable surprise of the allies, and no one was more surprised than Picton. He understood it better when informed afterwards that his dogged antagonist Ney had been superseded. Masséna had been outmanoeuvred, but there was one sanguinary struggle, when the leading brigade of "The fighting 3rd" was engaged under Major-General Colville.

The ardour of the half-famished combatants was unabated, as if they had been living on full rations and moving by easy marches. In the heat of the fight, said a subaltern, Picton rode up with his stick over his shoulder, exposed to the heavy fire, as composed as if he had been in perfect safety. "'Steady, my lads,' said he; 'don't throw away your fire until I give you the word of command.' And not a shot was fired until within a few yards of the enemy's right." Rather different fighting in those days, from these of smokeless powder, long-range guns, straight-shooting and penetrating rifles, with shells that shatter rocks into scattering projectiles and search out trenches with suffocating fumes!

The stick Picton flourished was as much a known appendage of him as Gordon's switch or Craufurd's cob.

He often carried it into action, and when the fighting commenced he began beating a tattoo on his horse's neck: when the fighting grew hot he rapped the harder; and then, with mind abstracted in what was going on, he sat his plunging charger like a centaur. Absolutely fearless, he had thrown himself with his whole heart into the war, and, unlike Craufurd or Hill, he had no domestic ties to make him homesick. He was a confirmed bachelor and of opinion that a soldier had no business with a wife. Wellington told Lord Stanhope rather a characteristic story. Picton was present when Sir Lowry Cole announced his approaching marriage, adding that he did not think he was doing an imprudent thing, as the lady was not very young. There was no great liking between the generals, and Picton broke in:

> Well, when I marry I shall do a d—d imprudent thing, for I mean to marry the youngest tit I can find.

Not that he was incapable of deep feeling. In the following winter he lost the uncle who had befriended him before the law courts, bailing him for the enormous sum of £40,000. The death had made him affluent, but that he regarded little. An officer on his staff, who observed him closely and liked him well, declares that though he repressed all emotion with Spartan fortitude, no man ever suffered more severely from the loss of a friend.

> There was no outlet, no confidence; but, locked up in the very centre of his heart, it preyed there with a strength which in any other person would have burst forth with unutterable, inconsolable grief: it produced want of repose and even ill-health, but nothing could have offended him more than hinting it was caused by regret.

That is eminently characteristic of the impassive, self-contained man, apparently unmoved either in reverse or in the pride of victory, who taught his unflinching soldiers to pride themselves on being known as "the fighting 3rd."

In the beginning of May, Almeida was in extremity, and Masséna had set his forces in motion for the relief. As Picton remarks in a letter, "Masséna had been more frightened than hurt." In the same letter he describes his share in the action. The village of Fuentes had been fiercely disputed. The 3rd Division had taken ground among vineyards and crags overhanging the valley in which the village sheltered.

> As usual, the principal share of the fighting fell to the 3rd Division. . . . The village was defended in the most determined manner by the 71st, 24th, and 79th Regiments. The firing was kept up with great spirit, and they succeeded in keeping posses-

sion of the place for some hours against repeated attacks, supported by a tremendous cannonade. About two o'clock these regiments began to give way, when at this moment the Rangers under Colonel Wallace, and led by Major-General Mackinnon, were ordered to move up and support them. They made so overwhelming a charge through the streets that they drove the enemy from the village with immense loss. Neither did he make any fresh efforts to regain it, but contented himself with keeping up a desultory cannonade.

In claiming the hardest fighting for his division, he does injustice to Craufurd, who made the memorable and magnificent retreat across the plain. But he remarks truly that the French cavalry, with their overwhelming strength, missed a golden opportunity which was never likely to recur. Had Montbrun proved equal to his chances, Craufurd, in spite of conduct and gallantry, must have been annihilated.

We learn from *The life of a Soldier* that it was on that occasion Picton for once made that *amende honorable* in answer to rough expostulations to which we have alluded, when he welcomed back the Connaught Rangers, "the greatest blackguards in the army," from their decisive charge. And the Rangers, having received plenary absolution, forthwith ran up new records of crime.

The division was marched south to Badajoz to take part in the second siege. The siege was raised, and in the time of inactivity that followed Picton wrote a desponding letter, in which he made sundry pessimistic prophecies which were happily falsified.

> You appear everywhere to entertain sanguine expectations of our ulterior successes. I am concerned that I cannot say anything to keep up so pleasant a delusion.... We are playing a very losing game.... Portugal is a deadweight upon our hands.

But Picton inactive in quarters was a very different man from Picton exhilarated by responsibility and the prospect of fighting. He brightened up when marched back to his old positions between the Agueda and Coa, taking a much more cheerful view of the situation, for Marmont (who had superseded Masséna) and Dorsenne were drawing together for the relief of Almeida. The second letter was written in August, and, though little of a Sybarite, he indulges in a grumble.

> We have been since March in continual movement—sometimes in miserable, abandoned cottages, and as frequently with-

out any covering. I have constantly, for a whole year, made use of a bundle of straw as a bed, and I do not see any probability of a change.

There was little change till 22nd September, when Marmont and Dorsenne concentrated at Tamames to strike at the centre of Wellington's line. The centre was at El Bodon, the headquarters of the 3rd Division, when the French advanced. On the 25th came the engagement of El Bodon. Montbrun with his cavalry crossed the Agueda in force, and wheeling to the westward when he came to the junction of two roads, assailed a hill which was held by Colville. Picton's left was effectually turned, and soon afterwards columns of infantry were being pushed between his headquarters and two of his outlying regiments at Pastores, far away to his right.

With the menace of a broken line, Wellington concentrated to the support of Colville, and Picton had a peremptory summons. Meantime his regiments at Pastores were inevitably left in the rear, but after a fifteen hours' march they rejoined the main army. Before Picton could bring up his troops, as Napier says, the crisis was over. Then might have been witnessed the strange spectacle of great bodies of horse charging up the rugged hillsides, stopped by the scattering fire of a thin line of infantry, checked by mere handfuls of British cavalry, but always rallying and returning to the attack. But their numbers were overwhelming, and Wellington gave orders to Colville and Picton to fall back upon the plain.

For six miles, from those heights to Guinaldo, was a dead level, eminently favourable to the action of cavalry. Colville, stopping continually to throw his battalions into squares, descended the southern slope. There is no more vivid passage in Napier than his story of the furious charge when the whole French cavalry came thundering down upon them. Closing up in a single square, they stood the onset.

"The multitudinous squadrons, rending the skies with their shouts, and closing upon the glowing squares, like the falling edges of a burning crater, were as instantly rejected, scorched, and scattered abroad ... and with firm and even step the British regiments came forth, like the holy men from the Assyrian's furnace."

The regiments were the 5th and 77th, and it was a bitter grief to them, as an officer of the latter records, that El Bodon was never inscribed upon their colours. Then Picton joined Colville, and together they withdrew to Guinaldo. A Subaltern writes in his *Reminiscences*:

General Picton conducted himself with his accustomed coolness: he remained on the left flank of the column and repeatedly cautioned the battalions. . . . 'Your safety, my credit, and the honour of the army are at stake: all rests with you at this moment.' When the retiring columns had nearly reached the retrenched camp, Montbrun made his last despairing demonstration. The clatter of the horse hoofs and the clinking of the scabbards seemed to presage a final charge. 'Had we not better form square?' shouted a mounted officer. 'No,' answered Picton; 'it is but a ruse to frighten us, but it won't do.'

(*The Subaltern Officer of the Prince of Wales's Volunteers* by George Wood also published by Leonaur).

So closed that season's campaign, and while the rest of the army was quartered along the Coa, Picton had his headquarters at Aldea de Ponte. In January, after improvising a siege train, Wellington resolved to rush Ciudad Rodrigo before Marmont could bring relief. The story has been sketched in the notice of Craufurd.

The eleventh evening of the investment was fixed for the storm. To Picton's division was assigned the assault of the greater breach to the right. His left brigade was mastered at the Convent of Santa Cruz to the right of the batteries. Major-General Mackinnon was to lead with his brigade, and was to be supported by Colonel Campbell, commanding the left. As is frequently the case in a night attack, the carefully planned arrangements miscarried. It was partly owing to Picton's spirited appeal to the Connaught Rangers. Naturally the order of the night was to be silent, but when he said, "Rangers of Connaught, it is not my intention to expend any powder this evening; we'll do the business with the *cowld* iron," of course the response was a vociferous shout. Then he galloped off to address the soldiers of El Bodon in more measured words. He said he knew the 5th were not to be daunted by fire, and that he had equal confidence in the 77th.

The enemy had taken the alarm, but that does not explain the subsequent confusion. The most lucid account we have read is by an officer of the 77th, which was published in Maxwell's *Peninsular Sketches*. He speaks with the authority of a dispassionate eye-witness, filling in picturesque details in the background, with the massive square keep looming above the old Moorish walls, as seen by the stormers crouching beneath them for their rush. Briefly, his account is this: the 77th had groped their way down into the ditch, scaled the wall, and reached the *fausse braie*, when they found the enemy on the alert.

Under a plunging fire they crowded along to the right, where they were at the bottom of the main breach, and in place of being the supports became the stormers. They scaled the breach on the left side—"a nearly perpendicular mass of rubbish." Then they heard the shouts of their comrades who had crowned the counterscarp, and under a redoubled fire from the garrison, the Highlanders, flinging down bags of straw, dropped into the ditch and assaulted the breach on the right. The converging torrents of stormers met in the face of a shower of ball and handgrenades, on a pavement of exploding shells, and in spite of an enfilading fire from two guns that were taken, at seven o'clock the breach was carried.

The 45th and 88th, who should have led, came up in time to do good service and suffer severely. Picton had taken his stand on the edge of the *fausse braie*, and was cheering his stormers as they mounted to the attack. While standing there, the ground beneath him was shaken by the explosion of the magazine which proved fatal to his friend Mackinnon and many of his gallant followers.

Picton's letter gives a brief and modest account of the part he played. But one passage is to be noted, for it contradicts Napier's narrative. From Napier we may infer that the Light Division were first on the walls, and, by assailing the defenders' rear, relieved the 3rd from a deadlock Picton writes:

> About this time the Light Division, which was rather late in the attack, also succeeded in gaining possession of the breach they were ordered to attack.

And in another letter:

> The business was divided between the 3rd and the Light Divisions. . . . The 3rd Division had by far the most difficult attack, where the enemy were most prepared."

As to precedence, his version is certainly confirmed by the officer of the 77th:

> I have no hesitation in asserting that it was the prior success of the regiments at the main breach which shook the defenders of the little one, and caused them to yield it so easy a conquest to the Light Division.

So is authentic history written. Perhaps it has some significance that, when lamenting Mackinnon, Picton makes no allusion to the fall of Craufurd, though it must be remembered that Mackinnon was his favourite brigadier. Marmont dispersed his forces without attempting to recover the fortress. Though Soult was threatening on the side of Andalusia, Wellington snatched at an unhoped-for opportunity. The fall of Badajoz was to follow that of Ciudad Rodrigo, and again time was everything. It was no light thing to risk a third failure, in which British prestige was deeply involved, and it was known that the resourceful Phillipon had made every preparation. But in early March Wellington had his quarters at Elvas; on the 15th his pontoons were thrown over the Guadiana; the 3rd, 4th, and Light Divisions passed on the following day, and then the fortress was invested.

To Picton was entrusted the charge of the siege. The difficulties were great, for the Guadiana was in spate, and incessant rains flooded the trenches. On the 19th a daring sally was repulsed. On the night of the 20th the first parallel was pushed across the Seville road, though the ring of the pickaxes drew a heavy fire from the ramparts. On the 21st the enemy placed two field pieces beyond the river, which raked Picton's lines and were thorns in the side of the besiegers. On the night of the 25th it was decided, as an indispensable preliminary, to seize the strong outlying hill-work of the Picurina. Five hundred of the fighting 3rd were told off for the duty, and by dint of fierce fighting they forced their way, through three rows of palisades, and up a perpendicular rampart and earth slope defended by slanting poles.

Then the besiegers set to the serious business of breaching. The Picurina turned its cannon on the town, and six batteries with 28 guns were concentrating their fire on the ramparts. On the 5th April three breaches, great and small, were pronounced practicable; but on a close reconnaissance it was unfortunately decided to defer the attack. Unfortunately—because it gave the governor time to make practicable breaches virtually impregnable.

On the 6th elaborate orders were issued for a combined assault at ten that night. Nothing was overlooked that prescience could foresee. To the 3rd Division was assigned the assault on the castle. It has been asserted that it was intended merely as a feint, but there is nothing to show that in the orders. On the contrary, it is assumed that Picton will carry the place, and there are detailed instructions for his subsequent conduct. As the hour approached, suspense was at its height; for, though the town was enveloped in fog and drizzle, the French knew that their enemies were busy all around them.

The 3rd Division was mustered in silence, awaiting the signal, when a shower of fire-balls from the castle revealed their position, and every gun opened on them. An immediate advance was ordered, with the 45th Regiment in the lead. Bending to their right, they forded the little stream of the Riverillas, to be brought up by the broad wet ditch beneath the works. Beyond was the hill, 100 feet in height, surmounted by the walls of 18 to 24 feet. They saw their way with the obstacles frowning in front of them, for the air was still ablaze with fire-balls. The ditch was crossed by a narrow dam, admitting only of passage by single file, and on that pass the castle's fire converged. The leading files parted to right and left, under sustained volleys of musketry—each defender had three spare muskets by his side-awhile the cannon launched continuous discharges on the supports.

There was a shout of "Ladders to the front!" and ladders were planted in various places. As fast as they were set up they were thrown down, thrust back by poles shod with iron. Others broke under the weight of the men who crowded them, and the castle seemed unattainable as ever. With round shot and shrapnel tearing through his ranks, a weaker general might have sounded the retreat. Picton kept pressing forward his supports and cheering his *enfants perdus*, who were failing at the ladders. At last pluck and perseverance were rewarded, and the gallant Colonel Ridge of the 45th was the first man to set foot on a parapet, so narrow that it might have turned a chamois hunter dizzy. He escaped by a miracle, to fall later.

A footing once gained, other soldiers followed; the French, who had at first opposed a desperate resistance, now seemed demoralised and drew back. The ladders were swarming as with bees in hiving time, and hot-blooded soldiers poured into the place. The losses had been heavy. General Kempt, who led the advance, had been badly wounded; Picton himself had been hard hit by a spent ball early in the affair. He lay for twenty minutes insensible, but rallied in time to urge his men to fresh exertions. He begged them in broken accents not to desert him: "If we cannot win the castle, let us at least die upon its walls." But his hurt prevented his climbing the ladders, and he was compelled to give his directions from the ditch.

Wellington had seldom passed a worse quarter of an hour. The hanging fog was illuminated by a lurid glare; from all sides he heard the roar of the guns, the shrieks of the wounded, and the shouts of the hostile victors. Worse and worse news were brought by each messenger from the breaches. The fiercest courage of frenzied assailants had failed to make any impression. The sacrifice of lives was ever going on, and yet the heroic efforts were fruitless. Then a mounted officer came spurring up to the height that was illuminated by the flare of a score of flambeaux. The cheery sound of the hoofs seemed to tell of good news. "Who's that?" he asked, with mounted excitement. It was Picton's *aide-de-camp*, who replied in curt, soldierly speech: "General Picton has taken the castle, my lord."

"Then the place is ours," exclaimed Wellington, and Lieutenant Tyler was ordered back to tell his chief to hold the castle at all hazards.

Picton had tried his utmost to act upon the orders of the day. These were that if the castle was penetrated, he was to break out and clear the ramparts to the left. But the enemy had found time to barricade the ponderous gates through which they had retired. Others had been previously sealed with massive stone-work. It seems strange that gates hastily secured should not have been forced or blown open: but, fortunately for them, the exultant division for the time were close prisoners. For had they poured forth they would undoubtedly have been charged by General Walker's men, who had carried the bastion of San Vincente, when the bulk of its defenders had been withdrawn, either to reinforce their comrades at the breaches or to attempt the recovery of the castle. Now the 6th took the defenders of the breaches in rear: the assailants scrambled up unopposed over the heaps of dead and dying: Phillipon, with the wrecks of his garrison, crossed the river to San Christoval, and Badajoz was given over to sack and slaughter.

A Boy in the Peninsular War describes the carnival of crime and debauchery in the castle that night. Probably, had Picton been unhurt, the night would have passed more quietly. "The scenes were of a most deplorable and terrific nature. Murders, robberies, and every sort of debauchery were seen, notwithstanding the efforts of the officers to prevent them. For many women had taken refuge there, and all the live stock of the garrison had been driven in. The howling of dogs, the crowing of cocks, the bleating of sheep, and the bellowing of wounded oxen made the night hideous; drunkards were discharging their pieces in all directions; wines and strong liquors were flowing freely, and on the gateways the soldiers of the 6th Division were keeping up a desultory fusillade."

To Picton fell the honours of the storm. Nothing could be more generous than Wellington's tribute, for he declared in orders that "the 3rd Division had saved his honour and gained him Badajoz." If the great Duke sometimes spoke disparagingly in after years of the veterans who had won him his fame and his laurels, Picton was lavish in appreciation of the fighting qualities of the 3rd. He used to talk of them fondly and paternally as his brave ragged rascals. So long as they did their duty in the field, and it was his pride that they had never flinched, he did not worry them about buttons and pipeclay or the *minutiæ* of drill. A severe disciplinarian, be was no parade martinet, and he would even jest about petty delinquencies with which the provost-marshal must have dealt had they been brought officially to the general's notice.

He used to say that all the Light Division left in the way of plunder was sure to be picked up by those ragged rascals of his. As he lay on his sick-bed after the escalade of Badajoz, he spoke with fervent admiration of the zeal with which they had responded to his appeal. "They fell so fast and the ladders were so insecure that even the bravest began to waver. I called upon them, however, to make another effort, when they poured on and bore one another up, till the wall was gained: nothing could resist them. Yet I could hardly make myself believe that we had taken the castle."

After the stress and strain of the capture of the fortresses, the allies rested for a time between the Coa and Agueda. Napoleon was then marching on Moscow. In the middle of June active operations recommenced, when the allies had been strengthened and the enemy enfeebled. Picton, always disposed to gloom and fretted by inactivity, had written on the 24th:

> I have no hopes of being able to effect anything substantial I am perfectly tired with the continual movements and fatigue of this unceasing kind of warfare, in a country where we are exposed to every kind of privation. I mean to make my interest, as soon as I can find a favourable opportunity for someone to succeed me in command of the division.

Moreover, he had physical reasons for depression. He was still suffering from his wound, and he had been prostrated by the fever of the country. In July the operations were transferred to the Douro; then came the memorable race, within musket range, back to Salamanca, when Marmont and Wellington were sparring and feinting, before the clash of the battle which both clearly foresaw. Picton was lying in hospital in the city, cursing his hard fate and eager for each successive message. The command of his division had been transferred to Sir Edward Pakenham, and it was Pakenham who led them in the decisive battle, when they well nigh annihilated the 7th French Corps. Picton would have grudged any friend the fame he had hoped to gain, but he exclaimed with soldierly spirit, when he heard of Pakenham's appointment: "I am glad he is to lead my brave fellows: he will give them plenty of fighting."

That he undoubtedly did. It might have been Picton in place of Pakenham who, when ordered by Wellington to storm some formidable heights, laconically answered: "I will, my lord, by God!"

We feel bound to tell another well-authenticated story, though far less to Picton's credit than any we have related. His favourite *aide-de-camp* looked in on his sick-room, bringing with him, for some reason, a young subaltern. Picton gathered himself up from under the bedclothes, his wasted features being covered with an enormous nightcap. The sight struck the youth so comically that after vain efforts to repress it he exploded in a shout of laughter. It was but natural that the caged and crippled lion should echo the explosion with a tornado of oaths which whirled the offender out of the room. But the sequel showed a sullen, unforgiving temper. The volatile ensign had become a colonel and was in command of a regiment at Waterloo.

Picton rode up and there was mutual recognition. "No time for compliments now, sir," said Picton. "Take that hill." A perilous business it was, but an hour or two afterwards the colonel saluted and reported the hill taken. Picton looked him in the face and rode away without a word.

As he had missed Salamanca, he did not participate in the triumphal entry into Madrid. Still prostrated by a complication of ailments, he had intermittent attacks of bilious fever. The Walcheren agues were lurking in the system, and he was ordered back to Cheltenham, whence he had been summoned. The sea breezes and the waters did him considerable good, but the cure was interrupted by mental unrest Picton could not make himself happy in the pump-room when each bulletin brought news of skirmish or battle. Early in the spring of 1813 he was back again, returning a K.C.B. He had a triumphal reception when he rejoined his division.

If his soldiers did not love him as they loved Hill, they knew when they had a man at their head—a leader who looked to their comforts and had never failed them in the field. And, as with Hill, they spoke of him as "Father Picton." An officer of the division has told the story. He heard a whisper running through the ranks; then the men—they were not on parade—began moving off simultaneously in the same direction, and from a walk they soon broke off into a run. Following them, he saw mounted officers approaching, and then he recognised Sir Thomas. The men were crowding round his horse with enthusiastic greetings, and Picton's features had relaxed; he "smiled upon them with a look of unaffected regard." The whole shouting division had gathered round him before he reached his quarters, and he had a hand and a pleasant laugh for "the Subaltern," whose greeting he gratefully acknowledged. That is the magic of the strong general who seldom unbends.

In May the allied forces were in motion to follow up the stroke of Salamanca with Vittoria Picton's division was with Graham, whose advance through a country believed to be impracticable for armies disconcerted all the vacillating plans of King Joseph. On the 1st of June the Douro had been bridged or forded, and Wellington had brought his central columns into touch with the main body, marching under Graham. Ere the middle of the month the whole of the allied army was in motion by its left towards the seaboard and the mountain sources of the Ebro. Joseph, who had been mystified by the strategy of his great antagonist, had been constrained tardily to change his front, and as he would not give up his crown without a blow, to make his last stand before Vittoria. It was no longer a question for Wellington of bringing supplies through the Portuguese highlands from the estuary of the Tagus. He had changed his base from Portugal to the Bay of Biscay, where British transports could disembark freights and troops in the harbours reluctantly abandoned by the French.

When the allies were steadily closing in upon the south and southwest of the basin of Vittoria, the 3rd Division was in the centre under the surveillance of Wellington in person. With the 7th it was told off for the attack of the bridge of Mendoza, immediately to the north of the Zadora's sharp bend to the right. Napier says that the general advance was delayed because these divisions were not up to time, having been retarded by obstacles. Picton tells another story, and it is circumstantially confirmed by sundry of his officers in narratives with all the stamp of truth. Picton simply writes that about noon—it was an hour later according to Napier—the 3rd Division was ordered to force the passage, "which service was executed with so much rapidity that we got possession of the commanding ground before the enemy were aware of our intention."

As will be seen, he apparently runs two distinct operations into one, and dismisses with barely a casual remark what Napier describes as a critical manoeuvre, attributable to the soldierly intuition of Wellington. Picton's officers paint the man as we seem to know him. They agree that while Hill was forcing the gorge on the right, Picton, far from having loitered, was on his ground and furiously impatient. As the time dragged by, and he was left without orders to strike in, his impatience became uncontrollable, and that stick of his was drumming savagely on the neck of his unfortunate cob. "D—n it," he would exclaim, "Lord Wellington must have forgotten us." When his nervous tension was at its height, a staff officer came galloping up. "Orders at last," thought Picton, but the messenger had been merely sent to look for the 7th Division, which had really been retarded, and he asked Picton whether he had seen anything of Lord Dalhousie. "No, sir: have you any orders for me?"

"None," answered the *aide-de-camp*.

"Then, pray, what orders *do* you bring?"

"Why," said the officer, "that as soon as Lord Dalhousie shall commence an attack on that bridge, the 3rd and the 6th are to support him."

Chafed to extremity as he had been, his disgust may be imagined at hearing that any other division was to take the lead of the 3rd. The answer attributed to him is—and if not true, it sounds truthful—"You may tell Lord Wellington from me that the 3rd Division under my command shall attack the bridge and carry it; the 4th and 6th Divisions may support if they choose"—which it did forthwith; Picton shouting genially to his soldiers, as he set spurs to the cob: "Come on, you rascals! come on, you fighting villains!"

Picton passed the bridge with a single brigade, his second brigade fording simultaneously higher up. The onslaught was seasonably aided by a flanking attack by Colonel Barnard and his riflemen. The 3rd Division, established on the opposite slopes, had taken Gazan's strong frontal positions almost in reverse, and that general, threatened from either flank, was compelled to fall back. The 3rd and 7th Divisions were sharply engaged with the retiring enemy.

It was then, according to Napier, that Wellington had the idea which, if it did not decide the battle, precipitated the catastrophe. He saw that a hill, the key of the French central positions, had been almost denuded of defenders by Villatte's sudden withdrawal. Riding up, he "carried Picton and the rest of the 3rd Division in close columns of regiments at a running pace diagonally across the fronts of both armies towards that central point." The hill was taken, and then the 3rd was borne forward over the crest of the flood of war that, surging up the hollows of the ragged basin, swept the mobs of discomfited fugitives out of the streets of Vittoria.

Impartial narrators describe the splendid work done by the 3rd Division, as seen from the heights on either side, when it led the advance. Sometimes, as at the village of Arinez, it was held in check for the time, but it was never to be denied. Picton halted more than once to re-form under cover, then he pushed forward more impetuously than before. One of his staff officers declares that he thrice received orders from Wellington which had been already anticipated.

Napier, while praising that brilliant advance, says that the success was greatly owing to the master-mind which directed it, and that may be. Picton, who was never slow to claim his share of glory, protests in private letters that the *Gazette* did him indifferent justice. He writes to his brother: "The 3rd Division had again the principal share of this action, and covered itself with glory," and that there was no denying. The "butcher's bill" was exceptionally heavy. "Out of 5600 men we lost 1800 in killed and wounded."

3

When Wellington's army was ranged in battle array along the Pyrenees, the division which had suffered most severely was stationed in reserve. Picton had his quarters at Olague as a support to Hill and Cole, who held respectively the Bastan and Roncesvalles. On the 23rd of July Soult issued his spirited order for a combined attack on the passes for the relief of Pampeluna. In person he directed the operations against Roncesvalles, the nearest post of defence to Pampeluna. Fortune played him false, otherwise his admirably devised combinations might have succeeded.

As it was, Byng, who held Roncesvalles, had to yield to superior numbers, while heavy columns, gone astray in the mists among the mountains, were threatening him on either flank. He fell back upon Cole, posted twelve miles behind, when Cole in turn was forced to retire. Picton had ridden across the hills which lie between Olague and the Zubizi River, with the news that his division had also crossed, and was at the village which took its name from the river. Thus a junction of three detachments had been effected, but Soult, although he had missed his chance of attacking Cole when unsupported, was still pressing resolutely forward with ever-increasing forces. Consequently Picton had nothing for it but to continue the retreat.

Napier says that when it was commenced on the 27th "it was

without the hope or intention of covering Pampeluna." He adds that by a sudden inspiration Picton changed his mind, to take a position on the ridges which screen Pampeluna. Indeed, these rugged heights protect the city so obviously that it is hard to believe that the fighting general, who knew the ground well, had ever any other idea but that of occupying them. Be that as it may, scarcely had his dispositions been made when Wellington was on the spot. Taking the shortest road from Hill's quarters in the Bastan, he had so narrowly escaped Clausel, at the village of Sauroren, that, as his *aide-de-camp*, Lord Fitzroy Somerset, rode out of the street at one end with a pencilled message, the French Light Cavalry were galloping in at the other.

As he hurried forward, he had been sending orders to his other divisions, who came wheeling in precisely as they were needed behind the bold front shown by Cole to attacks which were concentrated and driven home in a narrow ravine between two rivers. In the two days of desperate hand-to-hand fighting known as the battles of Sauroren, Picton bore no active part. With his division he was covering the left flank of the allies against the half of Reille's corps and a division of cavalry which were watching for a chance of breaking in to the fortress. As Soult failed against the centre, Picton was never assailed. When Drouet had been beaten back by Hill, Soult made one of his masterly retreats to the Bidassoa, though only accident saved him from a fatal catastrophe, and in the first week of August he had resumed his former positions.

The war languished; inactivity weighed upon Picton and he applied for leave. His health enjoined a visit to Cheltenham, and according to the political fashions of the day, the electors of Carnarvon had shown their appreciation of his services by choosing him as their representative. In November he took his seat in the House, when his modesty was tried by having to acknowledge a grateful resolution conveyed to him by the Speaker in a fervid eulogy. As preface to the recital of his deeds he was told that, "wherever the history of the Peninsular War shall be related, your name will be found among the foremost in that race of glory." Picton, for once, was overcome by emotion. He began his reply in stammering accents, and a sympathetic onlooker remarked that it was pitiful to see a man who had been unshaken in the field of battle unnerved and utterly overcome by his feelings.

Nevertheless, he pulled himself together to make a brief and soldierly reply, in which he generously attributed the chief part of the merit to the officers and soldiers who had never flinched from the foe.

His sojourn in England was of the shortest. Loath to miss any fighting, early in December he turned his back on his constituents, and before the end of the month had rejoined Wellington.

When Hill had refused it, he was offered the command in Catalonia. In straightforward fashion he asked the commander-in-chief whether there was a chance of gaining glory there. Wellington could not honestly say there was, so Picton begged to be replaced at the head of his old division. Again, from headquarters at St. Jean de Luz, he wrote with his habitual pessimism. Without strong reinforcements he did not believe they should do anything worthy of the Speaker s eloquence. For the Spaniards, then as always, he expressed profound contempt. They were poltroons in the field and plunderers on the march—an opinion which was endorsed by the Duke in his talks with Lord Stanhope—yet the Spaniards certainly showed no lack of courage at the passage of the Nivelle and elsewhere.

But Picton's sweeping condemnation is the more noteworthy that he invariably bestows high praise on the Portuguese. In a despatch after one of his bloodiest actions, he declares that they did better than the British regiments, and, rough disciplinarian as he was, he expressed the opinion that Beresford might have done as much with them by kindness as by severity.

The Gaves were successively passed by the allies: at the Gave d'Oloron Picton crossed at Sanveterre, when Villatte had abandoned his works and blown up the bridge. Wellington believed that Soult would continue to retire, but the marshal had decided to concentrate on Orthez and fight there. It would seem that he had intended to assume the offensive, but the swift advance of the allies disconcerted his plans, and he prepared to stand on his defence. For he had heard that Beresford and Picton had joined hands and were advancing along the northern bank of the Gave de Pau, on which the town is situated. To the south it was protected from Hill's corps by the rapid river, and all the bridges but one had been broken down.

Consequently he disposed his order of battle so as to confront Beresford and Picton. Nothing could well be more formidable than the natural defences on that side—they are described in the biographical sketch of Hill—and he awaited the attack with confidence of victory. At daybreak on the 27th February, the 3rd Division had formed up in column on the road to Peyrehorade, which runs parallel to the river from the west, and had thrown forward skirmishers to the wooded heights on the left of the French positions. The main battle was waged to the north, and fortune was favouring the French till Wellington delivered the stroke that won the victory by sending Colborne with the 52nd across the intervening marsh.

Picton, who had been ever pressing on the enemy's left, drove home his assaults with resistless impetuosity; he stormed the hostile batteries and established his own, opening a heavy enfilading fire. Soult, forced back on both flanks and at his centre from the base of an isosceles triangle, was rallying his strength at its apex on a second cluster of heights when he heard that Hill, having forded the Grave higher up, had virtually turned the town. Then his demoralised troops broke away in the panic-stricken retreat which was only brought up behind the Adour. Though Beresford bore the brunt of the fighting, Picton in a letter to his regular correspondent, Colonel Pleydell, claims a fair share of the credit in "this memorable business."

We are surprised by the statement that the loss of the 3rd had exceeded that of any other division; but he says that, when they had carried the enemy's advanced positions, for two hours they had been under the hottest cannonade he ever remembered. The close of that letter is amusingly characteristic: "My *aide de-camp* was killed close to me, while carrying my orders: I hope this will find you free from indisposition." Slight ailments at home and the deaths of the battlefield are in humorous juxtaposition.

In the fruitless battle before Toulouse, Picton added to his fighting reputation, and did his best to upset his chief's plan of battle. Wellington, at the critical moment, was without the reserves he had counted upon. Experience might have told him that his hot-blooded subordinate could never be trusted to confine himself to a feint; and after the storm of Badajoz he was less reliable than before. On that bloody and memorable Easter Sunday, his orders were to threaten the canal bridge at Tumean, while Hill menaced the suburb of St. Cyprian. Hill, as was his habit, held to his orders: Picton, also according to custom, could not bridle his ardour. His temperament was his best excuse for attempting the impracticable on this occasion.

The allied line of battle had been broken. Beresford had won the positions on his left, but the Spaniards in the centre were in headlong flight, "only likely to be brought up by the Pyrenees," as Picton remarked. The day was saved by the Light Division, but the French were bringing up supports on short inner lines, and the allied left was oppressed by numbers. It was not in Picton's nature not to strike in. He hurled his battalions forward on the bridge, and on works that had been deliberately and scientifically strengthened. Scaling-ladders he had none, and after rushing across an open space, he found himself helpless under a converging fire. He recognised the impossible and recoiled, leaving 400 men and officers behind him, and thenceforth the shattered division was paralysed. It was a melancholy, if not an inglorious end to his record of brilliant Peninsular services.

That he felt the failure keenly cannot be doubted. To him military reputation was as the breath of his nostrils, and his ambitions were identified with soldierly success. But he must have been consoled by the greeting at the close of the war, when he made his last inspection of his war-worn veterans. He was hailed with tumultuous shouts when he rode slowly down the ranks, and, as he remarked, the cheers which answered his closing address were "a gratifying proof that the regiments of 'the fighting division' would never forget their old general." Like Craufurd, the severe disciplinarian, short of speech, stern of mood, and constitutionally unable to unbend, had never been popular with his officers. But, as with Craufurd, if they did not love, they had learned to admire him.

When the division was broken up, a sum of £11,600 was subscribed to present "Old Picton" with a service of plate. The only corps that did not contribute was the Connaught Rangers. As we have seen, he had often praised their fighting qualities; but those confirmed pillagers and pilferers, who were seldom orderly save in the heat of action, had been roughly reprimanded and severely punished, not without reason. They would even swap their cartridges for spirits, replacing them with stained bits of wood—an offence which no general could overlook. But the frequent punishments and reprimands were so many reflections on the officers, and so they were resented.

When five of Wellington's distinguished lieutenants were raised to the peerage, Picton was passed over. He felt the omission deeply, nor were his feelings soothed by the well-meant condolences of his friends. No satisfactory explanation was given, but the truth seems to have been that he was unpopular with high officials. Wellington appreciated the soldier, but did not much like the man. His unbending nature, his blunt speech, and his rough manners irritated superiors with whom he was brought in contact.

Captain Gronow, whom he took with him on the Waterloo campaign as a supernumerary on the staff, remarked that when he met and accosted Wellington in the Park, the Duke seemed offended by the rough familiarity of his address, and stiffened visibly. And if he stood on little ceremony with his great chief, he was not likely to respect even the head servants of the household. There is an incident related in the *Personal Narrative of Adventures in the Peninsula*. The allied armies were in motion for the campaign of Vittoria.

Picton's plainness of speech was thought to have given offence, and he was unusually crusty of temper. He was bothered besides by the scaling-ladders and other lumber which his men had been told off to carry. His road was blocked by the headquarters baggage, which had the privilege of taking the lead, and he peremptorily ordered the way to be cleared. Wellington's consequential butler declined to obey, pleading headquarters privilege; whereupon Picton hit him over the head with the umbrella which he carried to protect his eyes from the sun-glare, and threatened moreover to have him tied up and flogged, if he did not give way to the division.

Yet for the seventh time he received the thanks of the House of Commons, expressed by the Speaker in most flattering terms. He withdrew himself to his Welsh seat, a disappointed man—like Hill, he had made up his mind to die a country gentleman. But in his case also things were otherwise ordained, for the Man of Destiny swayed the destinies of others. When the war clouds were lowering over the Flemish frontier, Picton felt sure that he would be called on to play his part; yet it was literally at the eleventh hour that he crossed the Channel. He had hesitated and made his conditions, at the first summons from the War Office. Remembering the past, he wrote the Duke of Wellington, saying that he was willing and eager to go, but that he would only act under his Grace, and declined to take orders from any other general.

The stipulation was acceded to; he promptly communicated with his old friend and *aide-de-camp* Tyler, instructing him to see to their mounts and make all other preparations. For himself, he set his worldly affairs in order, under the conviction that he was a doomed man. Taking leave of his neighbours, he remarked to one of them, as matter of certainty: "When you hear of my death you will hear of a bloody day." His friends gave him a farewell entertainment in the Fountain Hotel at Canterbury. A fortnight later, and precisely to a day, his body, when being carried to London, lay in state in that very room.

Gronow gives an amusing report of his conversation with his staff on board the packet, when he said many sensible things in unparliamentary language. As usual he took original views, and did not spare the sensibilities of his staff. He praised the French officers, and said: "If

I had fifty thousand such men as I commanded in Spain, with French officers at their head, I'm d——d if I wouldn't march from one end of Europe to the other."

One of his staff protested. "This is the first time we have heard. Sir Thomas, that French officers were superior to ours."

"What! never heard they were superior to ours? Why, d——n it, where is our military education? where our military schools and colleges? . . . Our fellows, though as brave as lions, are totally and utterly ignorant of their profession. D——n it, sir, they know nothing—we are saved by our non-commissioned officers."

If we may make a bull, we seem to hear the echo of the speeches of military reformers in the present day.

Landed at Ostend, Gronow had another surprise, when he heard his general in the purest French carrying on a flirtation with a pretty chamber-maid. For he was by no means of the look and build of a languishing lover. Gronow sketches him, a stern-looking, strong-built man, about the middle height, and considered very like the Hetman Platoff. And the Hetman, as we know from Scott, had a face seamed infinitesimally, in all directions, like Tom Purdie or Crystal Nixon. Naturally Gronow, who was particular about his clothes as Alvanley, and loved to ape D'Orsay whom he resembled *en petite* dresses his general. "He generally wore a blue frock-coat, very tightly buttoned up to the throat; a very large black silk handkerchief, showing little or no shirt collar; dark trousers, boots, and a round hat. It was in this very dress that he was attired at Quatre Bras, as he had hurried off to the scene of action before his uniform arrived."

He reached Brussels on the evening of the 15th, and was cordially welcomed by Wellington. Next morning, when he rode through the streets, he was acclaimed with cheers by admiring soldiers. Scott says that he was second in command, but we do not know that general orders were issued to that effect. He was appointed to the command of the reserve, and specially to that of the 5th Division, with Kempt and Pack and Colonel Winke of the Hanoverians for his brigadiers. The reserve was composed of Hanoverians and young British soldiers but slightly leavened by Peninsular veterans. On the 16th he was ordered to advance with the 5th Division to the support of the Prince of Orange, in expectation of the attack on Quatre Bras. The division was in motion at break of day, and as Picton rode out of the city with Wellington and the staff, he is said to have been in buoyant spirits. Never did he show himself more genial than in his greetings to the old comrades who clasped his hand and wished him "God-speed." Already they could hear the distant guns, and he pressed his division forward. He arrived on the scene of action almost simultaneously with the Black Brunswickers, led by their fated Duke. Already the approach of the fire of the skirmishers had given warning that Dutch and Belgians were being forced back; and the Prince of Orange had been looking anxiously over his shoulder for succour.

The arrival of these reinforcements restored the battle, yet it was the signal for Ney making another and a more determined attack with his overwhelming superiority of numbers. Two massive columns were hurled down on the allies: the 5th Division bore the brunt of the attack. Volley after volley was exchanged point-blank, and repeatedly the bayonets crossed. When the French infantry recoiled, came a furious charge of their cavalry. Picton's regiments, thrown rapidly into square, were enveloped on all sides, forming up as they could on ground slippery with blood, and among the bodies of their fallen comrades. The squares had hardly closed before the horse were upon them.

Everywhere he had been in the thick of the fighting, rallying his men and cheering them to the combat. According to all the rules of war, says Kincaid in his *Adventures of the Rifle Brigade*, "the division was beaten and ought to have given in." For the cavalry, though they had failed to break the squares, had passed through the intervals to form in the rear, and the French infantry were again threatening the front. "But the gallant old Picton did not choose to confine himself to rules."

Another headlong charge of French Lancers had been repulsed, when, seeing signs of wavering in his front, and regardless of the gathering horsemen behind him, he ordered a general advance. He led it in person, and Ney's battalions gave way. Again the scattered engagements were renewed, as supports were sent up, but with nightfall the marshal desisted from his attacks. Meantime, however, the Prussians had been beaten at Ligny: the line of defence had to fall back, and as the battle drew near to Brussels, French sympathisers were jubilant.

On the decisive day Picton was posted on the Wavre road. His troops were formed behind a hedge, extending from La Haye Sainte to Ter la Haye, but they had neither shelter from the hostile guns nor protection from cavalry charges. When Napoleon had failed in his attack on the allied left, he launched masses of his infantry against the left of their centre. Notwithstanding a murderous fire from Picton's guns, the French columns came up to the hedge in almost unshaken formation. Then he ordered Kempt's brigade to charge. Springing over hedge and ditch, they poured a deadly volley into the faces of the Frenchmen. As the bayonets clashed in the hand-to-hand struggle, Pack's brigade was hurried up in support. Picton led the charge, waving his hat over his head, with a "Hurrah!" that was heard above the din of the combat, and he was answered with cheers that rolled down the line. Alava said that the stern determination of that jubilant advance "appalled the enemy."

Still Picton rode in front of his line. He had realised what the Duke wrote in despatches, that "this was one of the most serious attacks made by the enemy"—that he was holding the key of a vital position. Always eager to hazard his person, now he did it with a dear conscience, for the odds against his mutilated battalions were excessive, and the French, although brought to a check, were still brimful of confidence. Moreover, with the rush from behind, their surging waves could hardly have receded had they willed it. Still the tide broke back, to left and right, under the steady British pressure on the centre, and the moment when it had been effectually stemmed saw the close of the heroic leader's career. A bullet struck him on the temple, and death was instantaneous.

So passed away that fiery spirit, with the ending he would have most earnestly desired. There was no lingering agony, as in the cases of Wolfe and Moore. Yet the death had been heralded by disregarded suffering, and a casual examination of the body that evening showed an almost unprecedented triumph of unflinching will. Two days before, he had been struck at Quatre Bras. There were broken ribs and grave internal injuries which must have caused intense pain. Yet military zeal, with the resolution not to fail his country in that supreme crisis, had borne him up, and through two bustling days, passed chiefly in the saddle, he kept his secret well. His only confidant was his valet, who roughly dressed the wound, and as he gave his orders for the day and took calm thought for the morrow, even Tyler, the watchful familiar on his staff, who followed each movement of the chief with anxious affection, had suspected nothing. Duty was ever his paramount consideration, and his standard was the highest. If he was hard upon others, he was harder on himself, and his country had lost one of her most devoted soldiers when happily his services were no longer needed.

General Gascoyne, in blunt, soldierly language, told the story of these last services in the House of Commons, when a sympathetic audience hung upon his words.

From the moment General Picton had left this country until he joined the army, he had never entered any bed—he had scarcely given himself time to take any refreshment, so eager was he in the performance of his duty. After the severe wound he had received, he would have been justified in not engaging in the action of the 18th. His body was not only blackened, but even swelled to a considerable degree: those who had seen it wondered that he could take part in the duties of the field. He had fallen gloriously at the head of his division, maintaining a position which, if it had not been kept, would have altered the fate of the day.

Wellington was not ungrateful. When he heard that the body of the hero had been conveyed to Brussels, he gave orders that a guard of honour should escort it to Ostend, and expressed a wish that it should be received in England with befitting gratitude. That appeal was needless. In England the war fever had been running high, and the crowning victory had at once relieved and excited the nation. When the coffin of Picton was landed at Deal, the fleet in the Downs was firing minute-guns. A procession of sailors and soldiers was formed on the beach to accompany it on the mournful pilgrimage to Canterbury. There, as we said, it lay in state at "The Fountain," where he had been feasted a fortnight before.

But personal charm and genial manners count for much in all careers, and although he had compelled admiration and respect, Picton had never been a general favourite. He had missed the peerage when his comrades were honoured. And now a proposal in the Commons by his friend Gascoyne, that he should find a resting-place beneath the dome of St. Paul's, fell still-born. His grave is in the little burial-ground of St. George's, Hanover Square, in the Bayswater Road, though his bust was afterwards placed in the metropolitan Valhalla, and his Welsh countrymen raised him a stately monument at Carmarthen.

Marshal Beresford

1

William Carr Beresford was born in 1768, an illegitimate son of the first Marquis of Waterford. He came of a martial stock, and was backed in his distinguished career by powerful family interest. If he survived till 1854, it was not that he did not freely expose himself in battle, and, like Sir John Hope, his tall and commanding figure—Wellington said he much resembled Soult—offered a conspicuous mark to hostile riflemen. Often to the front in personal combats, he had many hairbreadth escapes. A great organiser, who brought a disorganised rabble into disciplined battle line, he was, nevertheless, a modern type of the medieval *preux chevalier*. The bar sinister weighed lightly on him, as it was seemingly ignored by his noble kinsfolk: he married a legitimate cousin by blood, and in personal prowess he reminds us of the royal bastards of medieval France— the chivalrous knights of Orleans, of Burgundy, and of Bourbon.

Beresford had been educated at private schools, when, like other illustrious compeers of the Peninsula, he was sent to (Vance for military training. While studying at Strasbourg, he got his commission. Gazetted to the 6th in 1785—he had only passed a few months at the French college—he accompanied the regiment to Nova Scotia.

There he received his most serious wound, for he met with an ugly accident when out shooting, and lost the sight of an eye. He was promoted to a lieutenancy, changing his regiment, and in 1791 was gazetted to a company in the 69th. Orders for the West Indies were countermanded on the declaration of war with France. Captain Beresford, with two companies, shipped as marines, under the flag of Vice-Admiral Hotham, second in command of the Mediterranean fleet. The admiral, with the flagship, was in Toulon harbour during the siege and at the calamitous evacuation. Beresford was favourably mentioned in despatches, but won no special distinction.

His first opportunity came soon afterwards in Corsica, when he headed the storming party which carried the tower of Martello—the tower which became the cause of much wasteful expenditure on the circular fortalices fringing the southern coasts, which could be held by a sergeant's party and blockaded by a boat's crew. For that piece of good service he was rewarded with his brevet majority. He continued to serve under Moore and with Nelson at the capture of the strong places of Corsica, and in 1794 he returned to England to be promoted lieutenant-colonel. It was a time when patriotism was at fever heat, and local magnates, like Lynedoch, vied with each other in levying corps of their dependants.

A regiment had been raised on the Waterford estates, and Beresford was naturally placed in command. But the regiment was scarcely mustered when it was disbanded, and then he was transferred to the command of the Connaught Rangers. Colonel of the fighting Tipperary boys, with the war in full blast, it might have been supposed that the course of honour lay clear before him. But his hopes were baffled by a series of disappointments, and for a time, though always on active service, like Picton he was tantalisingly out of the running.

The 88th was intended to form part of Abercromby's expedition for the recovery of the West Indies. Winds and waves fought against the fleet, and Beresford's regiment was scattered with the ships. Two companies only arrived in Jamaica; another had drifted through the Straits of Gibraltar; the rest were beaten back upon the English coast. Slowly the regiment gathered again like a scattered covey of partridges, to be quartered for a couple of years in the Channel Islands. In 1790 Lord Mornington, an Irishman himself, made a special request that it should be sent to his help in the impending struggle with Tippoo Saib. But Beresford only landed at Bombay to hear of the fall of Seringapatam. He had barely time to tire of life in cantonments when he learned that he was to be a brigadier under Sir David Baird, ordered to Egypt to co-operate with Abercromby.

With such a chief, bound on such an enterprise, there was every prospect of glory. But again he was doomed to disappointment; when the expedition reached Kosseir, on the Red Sea, the war was already over, and his brigade only marched into Alexandria to assist at the surrender of Menou. Nevertheless, he had the fortune to lead the way on the long march through the waterless wilderness between the Red Sea and the Nile. It was the first experience of British soldiers

LORD BERESFORD

in desert campaigning, when guides were unreliable and water scarce. Beresford's severity, which made an effective force of the Portuguese, served him well when the column was wavering and soldiers were falling out of the ranks. He gained at least as much credit as he deserved, for popular imagination exaggerated the horrors of the march. Yet the sufferings were real enough.

Long confinement on shipboard, with rations of salt provisions, had been followed by hunger and thirst, with almost super-human exertions under a blazing sun; and when the weary soldiers bivouacked under the palms on the Nile, a violent epidemic had broken out. It was as the skeleton of its former strength that the brigade marched into Alexandria. One remarkable incident of their descent of the Nile is noted by Eliot Warburton in *The Crescent and the Cross*. The Indian troops were so impressed by the ruins of Dendera, though they must have seen the stupendous remains of Carnak, that simultaneously they sunk to their knees in prayer before the temple.

With the conclusion of peace in 1802, Baird went back to India, but Beresford remained in Egypt with the 88th until the following year, when he returned to England. There he remained till 1805, when again under his old general, and again as brigadier, he joined Baird's expedition to the Cape. Again he arrived too late. The Dutch had been beaten and their capital had surrendered before he disembarked. Baird wrote regretfully in despatches:

> Public as well as personal considerations induce me to lament the absence of Brigadier-General Beresford, from whose talents and experience I should have derived the most essential assistance.

He had speedy consolation for his latest disappointment. Baird and Admiral Popham had imagined their mad adventure on the La Plata, which takes us back to the buccaneering descents, of Drake and Morgan on the Spanish main. The means were miserably inadequate to the ends, but Beresford eagerly volunteered for the command of the land forces, and Baird was very ready to gratify him. The story of the disastrous outcome has been told in the sketch of Craufurd, but the expedition began well and even brilliantly. The Spaniards were scattered. Buenos Ayres was occupied. But they rallied from their panic, called in their outlying garrisons, raised the country, and found an able leader in Liniers.

The great city, with its feeble British garrison, was seething in sympathetic turmoil: Beresford was constrained to evacuate it: the wild weather prevented his embarking his forces, and he had no alternative but to surrender. The capitulation was inevitable and not inglorious. There had been desperate fighting in the streets before he withdrew, and for himself, he had only escaped death by a miracle. The terms granted by Liniers were repudiated by the Government, and both Beresford and Denis Pack refused to give their parole. Sent up the country as prisoners of war, already they were meditating the escape which they effected. They made their way to the banks of the La Plata, dropped down the river in an open boat, and were picked up by a British cruiser.

Much had passed in England in the meantime. Whitelocke had been sent out to command in our new dependency, which had already passed out of our hands. In the second inglorious expedition, doomed beforehand by the general's incompetency, Beresford had no share. He returned in 1807, to be promoted major-general. He sailed in the winter, in command of the troops with Hood's expedition, to take possession of Madeira and hold it in trust for Portugal. For a year he was in the island as acting governor, when he was ordered to join the army in Portugal. That brief tenure of command had no slight influence on his fortunes. It gave him considerable acquaintance with the Portuguese and their language, and strengthened his claims for the coveted appointment of disciplinarian-in-chief to the levies of the kingdom.

Again he missed a chance of distinction. When he landed, Vimiero had been fought and Junot had capitulated. But he was appointed Commandant of evacuated Lisbon: he was one of the commissioners who chaffered with Kellermann over the details of the convention, and he was charged with superintending the surrender of the southern fortress. His chief difficulty was with Elvas, for the French were loath to hand over the key of the Alemtejo, but his diplomacy arranged the business peacefully. Then Moore came to supersede Cradock, and decide on the invasion of Spain. It is needless to revert to the incidents of the retreat, for though Beresford did his duty well, he played no such romantic part as Craufurd or Paget. He did not bring up the rear with his brigades, as has been erroneously stated. They marched immediately in front of the reserves, in readiness to come to the succour of the rearguard.

But the man whose stern inflexibility broke the Portuguese to the bit kept his regiments from the excesses of their comrades, even when their sufferings were most severe, and under the temptations of the wine cellars of Rueda and Benevente. At Corunna his post was on the British left. With brigades still comparatively strong, even after the retreat and the battle, to him was confided the charge of the citadel. When the enemy was bombarding the harbour, when transports were cutting their cables and vessels were driving ashore, he still kept his men well in hand, and his battered veterans were the last to embark. If he had not done such dashing service as Craufurd, his fame had lost no lustre in the campaign, and no one of Moore's subordinates had a warmer welcome to England.

If he had been unlucky in missing hopeful opportunities, on the whole he was a favoured child of Fortune. His commanding presence imposed on the crowd: self-confidence and an almost aggressive personality won him respect at the War Office, backed up as they were by his family influence. Moreover, his merits were undeniable, and his military record unimpeachable, for if he had succumbed to stress of circumstances in Buenos Ayres, the authorities had given him plenary absolution. When the Portuguese asked for a man to reorganise their armies, we are told that there was eager competition for the post, though that is a piece of secret history, which will probably never be cleared up.

Beresford got the appointment, and undoubtedly his claims were strong. Already he had made his mark as a judicious martinet Unlike his competitors, he was a fair Portuguese scholar. He had won golden opinions as Commandant of Lisbon; he had exceptional acquaintance with the country and the people; and the result of the choice was its justification. In March 1809 he returned to Lisbon as a marshal of Portugal, with the local rank of an English lieutenant-general. His task was both difficult and invidious. But he had to work on excellent materials, although demoralised and disorganised. Essentially a martial and patriotic people, holding their own on a narrow stretch of country, between the ocean and the ever-menacing ambitions of Spain, nothing could be more efficient in theory than the Portuguese military system.

Every able-bodied man was liable to the call to arms. First came the regular army; then the militia, embodied for home service; lastly, there were the *ordinanzas*, who, like the German *landwehr*, must rally to the colours in case of emergency. But the armour had got rusty for want of use. The soldiers, with their pay ever in arrear, had broken loose from restraint. The higher posts had been filled, through political favour, by men who regularly drew pay but scrupulously neglected their duties. The mob had become the masters after much provocation. The soldiers, scattered over the country, starving and penniless, had been living at free quarters, till citizens and country folk, banding together, repressed their licence with ruthless reprisals. They had cut communications, murdered the generals, and massacred parties of foragers when they caught them red-handed. The arsenals were emptied; the ammunition lavished by England had been wasted in civil strife; and the mutinous rabble had been reinforced by British soldiers who had deserted from Moore in the retreat to Corunna.

It was then Beresford appeared on the scene, and that was the state of affairs with which he had to cope. He at once asserted a position which was not to be shaken, either by the corrupt and impecunious Government of Lisbon or by the turbulent Bishop of Oporto, who was agitating the north and urging impossible demands. The Portuguese had made him marshal, and military master he meant to be. For a time he was the most unpopular man in the country, but he held steadily to his course through stress and storm. Ere long he had his reward in the national gratitude, and the soldiers he literally lashed into obedience after many a hard-fought field became his admirers.

Yet, though they feared and respected, they never loved him, for he carried relentless severities to an excess. A stern military code was promulgated, or rather revived, and the slightest infringement was ruthlessly punished. It was well that severe examples should be made, if pillaging were to be repressed and the peasantry tranquillised. But the most trivial offences were visited with flogging or degradation. When we find even Picton censuring Beresford's severity we are inclined to condemn it: yet we may remember that there were jealousies between Wellington's lieutenants as between Napoleon's marshals, and Beresford's methods must be judged by the results.

When Wellington was advancing on the Douro, Beresford expressed distrust of his best battalion. We know how they behaved on the ridge of Busaco—a battle that was fought chiefly to blood them: and by the time the invaders had been swept out of Spain they were as dependable in action as the flower of the British regiments. Beresford was inevitably unpopular, and nothing gave rise to more irritation and intrigue than the necessity for entrusting the most important commands to his countrymen. It was unavoidable, and the choice of such men as Trant and Wilson proved invaluable in Wellington's most critical operations, yet the Portuguese naturally resented it. In that

Beresford acted with unwonted discretion. Inserting the thin edge of the wedge, he quietly drove it home as the services of those English commanders came to be generally appreciated, till at last they filled all the more important appointments.

But, great as were the special capabilities of Beresford, his counsels were not always those of wisdom. Cradock, a general whose merits have been insufficiently appreciated, wisely rejected his proposals for a premature march on Oporto. What Wellington accomplished with brilliant success would have been hazardous in the extreme under the circumstances in which Cradock had to decide. Cradock preferred to make sure of his base at Lisbon, rather than, like a knight-errant of romance, go in quest of adventure on the Douro. His wisdom was justified when Soult, who was in a very different position, had threatened an offensive movement from the north.

Then Beresford with his Portuguese was quartered between the Douro and the Mondego, and he spoke doubtfully of his men, who were still undisciplined and disposed to be mutinous. Indeed many of them, resenting his stern rule and seduced by the attractions of guerrilla warfare, left him to enlist in Trant's Irregulars. But he pursued his system inexorably: new recruits replaced the deserters, and his battalions were gradually being broken in. When Sir Arthur Wellesley had superseded Cradock and was resolved upon the recovery of Oporto, one of the reasons that chiefly influenced him was Beresford's more favourable reports of the Portuguese.

Beresford had then under his personal command 6000 fairly effective soldiers. Strengthened by two British battalions, sundry companies of riflemen, and some squadrons of cavalry, when Wellington made the movement to the north he was detached on the right to force back Loison, who had been charged by Soult to keep open the communications with Castile. Simultaneously with Hill's launching his flotilla on the Lake of Ovar, Beresford struck successfully at Loison. He drove him back from the Douro and followed him up to Amarante, which was evacuated in turn. Then Loison lost a high reputation and Soult his line of retreat. Thrown back on the mountains of the Tras-os-Montes, the marshal only saved himself by the happy interposition of the pedlar. Both his flanks had been turned, and the memorable passage of the Douro had been achieved.

The passage had been precipitated by Wellington's anxiety as to Beresford, who, having left the broad river behind him, was thrust forward in a situation of imminent peril. But with Oporto in occupation of the allies all the positions were reversed. Soult was only thinking of salvation, which he attained by the sacrifice of his artillery and stores. Then, in the opinion of Napier, had Beresford been more daring or less dilatory the retreat should have ended in humiliating disaster. Yet the rather unfriendly historian admits many reasons for Beresford's unwonted caution. He did not have the help he had expected from Silveira, and the prompt transmission of orders was impossible, when the Portuguese generals spoke no English and the British staff officers knew little of Portuguese.

The campaign had shown him the defects that were still to be remedied. He returned to Lisbon, to devote his attention to organisation and drill: and while Wellington was manoeuvring against Joseph and Victor, and winning the glorious though barren victory of Talavera, Beresford was busy with less obtrusive, but perhaps as useful work. No longer had the commander-in-chief to rely entirely on scanty and precarious reinforcements from home. Portuguese battalions were being moved up to the front, worthy of being brigaded with the British veterans. Busaco, as has been said, was in great measure fought to test the fruits of Beresford's training, though in his absences at the front discipline had retrograded, but the Portuguese had stood the test beyond the most sanguine expectations. Busaco gave him the ribbon of the Bath, and he was made a Knight of the Tower and Sword and Conde de Trancoso in the Portuguese peerage.

Masséna had been baffled before the lines: he had been starved out of Santarem: disputing the ground foot by foot, he was sullenly withdrawing to his starting-point on the frontier. During that retreat Hill had gone home on sick leave, and he was succeeded by Beresford in command of the covering army in the south-east. It is asserted that Wellington gave the appointment reluctantly, but Beresford had the claim of seniority and could not be lightly passed over. Whatever the merits of the marshal, the objections to the appointment were obvious. The troops, with unshaken confidence in Hill, put no such trust in his successor: the officers resented being under the command of a man they sneered at as a drill sergeant of Portuguese. In fairness it ought to be remembered that Beresford was heavily handicapped by those conditions. It is certain that he made mistakes and missed rare opportunities which the genius of a Wellington would have seized. Beresford, though the most hot-blooded of soldiers in battle, gave himself only too much leisure for deliberation.

Hill had been interposed between Santarem and Soult. When

Masséna drew away, Wellington followed with his whole force, hoping to fight the marshal at an advantage. He had left the Estremadura fortress to the charge of his Spanish allies, but distrustfully. As he wrote in his despatches:

> With soldiers of any other nation success is certain, but no calculation can be made of any operation in which Spanish troops are engaged.

Consequently it was disappointing but little of a surprise when he heard of Soult's successful inbreak, the annihilation of the Spanish armies, and the capture of three strong fortresses. The surrender of Badajoz, the bulwark of Portugal and the base of operations against Andalusia, was the heaviest blow. Already Beresford's corps had been detached for the relief. Now it was strengthened with the 4th Division: and his hope was that Beresford might recover the place, for he well understood Soult's embarrassments, and the anxieties that were likely to recall him to Seville. Beresford had left the northern army on the morrow of the combat at Foz d'Aronce: on the 27th of March he was at Pontalegre with 22,000 men.

Campo Mayor, which had been beleaguered, was lost already, but that the marshal did not know. Pressing forward to its succour, he came upon the French, who were evacuating it before his advance. Then occurred one of the fiercest cavalry engagements of the campaigns. Like the charge at Balaklava, it was magnificent but hardly won. The French hussars, covering the retreat, met in furious collision with the 13th Light Dragoons. Sabres clashed and crossed, though there was little time for slash and parry: many a saddle was emptied in the shock, and each regiment, piercing the files of the other, passed through to wheel and rally. Again they charged through to their respective sides, but on the third occasion the Light 13th were quicker on the swoop, and in the final charge they literally rode down the Frenchmen.

Never drawing rein, they received the fire of the infantry squares, dashed down on the flying batteries, and sabred the gunners at their guns. Forgetful or neglectful of the solid squares in their rear, with some Portuguese horse they followed the fugitives to the gates of Badajoz, till brought to a pause by the cannon of the fortress. Their reckless gallantry proved unfortunate. They had galloped out of sight, and Beresford believed, though it was not so, that he had lost them. When urged to follow up his blow, he answered that the loss of one of his few cavalry regiments was enough, and in that mistaken belief he tempered courage with unseasonable prudence. Venturesome to an extreme in the field, he was always hesitating in council

There was a proof of that immediately afterwards, when by excess of caution he again missed an unexampled chance. Soult had weakened the corps occupying Estremadura: Latour Maubourg had barely 10,000 men to oppose to more than double the number of the allies. Napier argues with good reason that, had Beresford taken a bolder course, Badajoz must have been regained without a regular siege, and Wellington's campaigns for the deliverance of the Peninsula been shortened by at least a year. Speculations of the sort have only academical interest. In modern warfare we may have gone into the opposite extreme from the time-honoured practice of giving armies an annual rest in winter quarters, and are rather inclined to work soldiers off their legs.

Beresford said that his troops were exhausted, that the 4th Division especially was utterly fagged, and that all were literally shoeless. At all events he decided to bestow them in cantonments round Elvas, and the delay gave the enemy the opportunity he needed. Philippon, the most resourceful of practical engineers, had the time to make elaborate defensive preparations; and Latour Maubourg, with very inferior forces, was left undisturbed to live at free quarters in a fertile country which had only been partially devastated. It was fortunate for Beresford that, when he bestirred himself again, the French general paid little attention to his operations. Beresford bridged the Guadiana at Jerumenha, on the great road leading from Badajoz to Elvas, with rough and ready appliances improvised by an ingenious engineer. Passing his detachments leisurely across, he took no precautions for their safety. But, when Latour Maubourg was roused to action, it came too late, and, as Napier sums up, "it is not easy to see which general acted with most imprudence—the one in neglecting, the other in unnecessarily tempting fortune."

That Soult would return was certain. Wellington had come to Beresford's headquarters to discuss the situation and survey the ground, and with his infallible glance had selected the ridge of Albuera as the spot on which the allies must concentrate for a stand. It would have been well could the commander-in-chief have remained to arrange the order of the battle, but the menacing movements of Masséna hurried him back to the Agueda. Beresford was left to do his best, which was bad: and he would have come out of the campaign with greatly diminished reputation had he not been singularly fortunate in his generals of division and his brigadiers.

Such men as Cole, Colborne, and Hardinge did much to redeem errors in strategy or blundering in tactics. And, after all, if his soldiers had slight faith in the genius of their commander, they admired the courage of the *preux chevalier* who in many a personal encounter would have merited a Victoria Cross.

His instructions were to attempt the recovery of Badajoz, but the means were miserably inadequate. The Portuguese had broken their fair promises: he had some zealous officers of engineers, but no corps of sappers, and the defence was conducted by able scientists and directed by a commandant of rare capacity. While he had been reposing his troops, Philippon had been strengthening his works, sweeping herds of cattle into the place, and replenishing its exhausted granaries. And as Soult, having had time to tide over the troubles in Andalusia, would infallibly return, failure was foredoomed. Soult did advance, gathering in his detached brigades, bringing 5000 horse with him and numerous field batteries.

When he met Latour Maubourg, who took over the command of the cavalry, his corps, complete in all their parts, consisted of 23,000 seasoned soldiers, with 80 guns. His march was swift, but Beresford's engineers urged him still to press the siege of the fortress, promising him its fall within three days. It was an idle dream, and their promises would have proved as fallacious as those of the Portuguese authorities which had made the siege a mockery. Napier, for once, gives Beresford generous credit for firmly rejecting their sanguine counsels. Leaving Cole to keep up the pretence of an investment, he prepared to offer battle at Albuera—an unfortunate decision in the opinion of the best military writers, for a doubtful victory would endanger Wellington's grand plan by the fruitless sacrifice of soldiers, and defeat might have led to the abandonment of the war.

Yet, as Wellington told Lord Stanhope, the situation could only be judged on the spot, and Beresford had free leave to fight if he deemed it advisable. Much allowance must be made for a general of high martial spirit, occupying an impregnable position, with superior forces to defend it. Wellington, at least, did not judge him severely. But he had under-rated the activity of his formidable antagonist, and with all his experience, counted with unreasonable confidence on Blake and his Spaniards being punctual to their engagements. When the best part of his troops had taken post on the ridge, he did not improve the hours by strengthening the positions with spade and pick-axe. And, as his strategy was short-sighted and defective, so he scarcely controlled the subsequent tactics.

On the 14th May it was known that Soult was within eight *leagues* of Albuera. The day before Beresford had met the Spanish generals and arranged that a battle was to be offered there. Blake had pledged himself to bring his troop into line before noon on the 15th. In that expectation the dispositions were made, and orders were issued to brigades in the rear to hurry forward by converging roads. It was a question of time, depending on fine calculations, and had Soult struck more quickly the defeat of the allies had been assured. We said that Beresford's strategy was short-sighted. His one idea seems to have been to repel a frontal attack, and to make sure of his only line of retreat by securing what he considered the key of his position. The key slipped through his fingers when Soult struck at his ill-guarded right.

That line of retreat was by the royal road leading to the bridge at Jerumenha, and the road traversed the centre of the ridge. The hills sloped gently down to the Albuera River, and the road was carried over a bridge beyond the village of the same name, till lost to sight among the wooded eminences on the opposite bank. The bridge was commanded by a battery, and the village was held by Alten's Germans. The heights above and immediately to the right were crowned by the British infantry: those to the left and bending towards Badajoz were confided to the Portuguese. The extreme right of the ridge, more precipitous in its front and breaking back above in a broader *plateau*, was to be left in charge of the Spaniards: it was a formidable position, and Beresford felt little anxiety, believing that Blake had only to counter any possible turning movement. He forgot to reckon with the insight of an adversary who was quick to hit any blot in the game.

On the afternoon of the 15th May 1811 nothing was to be seen of the Spanish auxiliaries. But what Beresford did see was his own cavalry, who had been scouting in advance, hurrying back through the woodlands beyond the river with French horsemen in hot pursuit. The initial error was that these woodlands had been abandoned, leaving Soult to mask his movements under their cover. Beresford rapidly extended his line to guard the unoccupied heights, and he sent gallopers to hasten Blake's advance, but it was midnight before the Spaniards straggled on to the ground.

Weary and hungry, they woke up in the morning in poor condition to face the tempest that was unexpectedly to burst on them. For on the previous afternoon Soult had been active. Surveying the allied positions, he understood their strength and their weakness. He penetrated Beresford's plan, which indeed was obvious. In front of the British ran the Albuera rivulet; behind them was a deep and rugged ravine. He saw that by storming these southern heights he could roll them up between ravine and river, while wheeling round in heavy masses he could grasp the road to the Guadiana and have the shattered battalions at his mercy.

A conspicuous blaze of colours on the crest of the ridge—Portuguese blue to the left, British red in the centre, Spanish yellow on the right—disclosed each position and every movement. The very privates saw that their leader would have done well to withdraw them some paces to the rear, behind the sheltering cover of the crest. During the night he had shifted two-thirds of his army to confront the weakest wing of the allies. Under the friendly cover of the woods his columns formed and waited: there were 15,000 men with 40 guns, and Beresford was absolutely unsuspicious of that terrible development.

The day began, as he had expected, with an attack on the bridge. For a time his attention was fully occupied; Godinot's brigade was crowding down to the passage; ten guns had opened from the woods behind, and light cavalry were showing from under the cover. But Beresford had a soldier's eye and instinct: he saw that the supports were coming slowly forward, and felt assured that his centre was not seriously threatened The danger must be to the right, and thither he hastened, having previously hurried down reserves to Alten and directed the Portuguese in his second line to be ready to move whenever they were ordered. Already he had sent urgent messages to Blake, warning him of his danger and asking him to change his front and form at right angles to his present positions.

The Spaniard's answer was a rough refusal, nor was he more amenable at first when the marshal met him. He only yielded to the unanswerable logic of the appearance of the enemy's columns beneath his unprotected flank. His evolution was slow, and before it was effected the rush of the French stormers had shivered his ranks. Already Godinot's supports were hastening to the scene of action; already his light cavalry had forded the stream, and galloping along a road on the north bank, and wheeling round the storming columns, had joined Latour Maubourg with his heavy horsemen.

The whole of the French horse were on the rear of the Spaniards, and confronting Lumley with his cavalry and the three regiments of his reserve. The French columns were huddled together on the heights: fortunately they had neither time nor room to deploy; but their fire riddled the ranks of the Spaniards, still changing their front and in wild confusion. Soult, believing the battle was won, was still pushing forward his columns; his reserves were pressing up behind; and his batteries were being rapidly brought into position.

The arrival of General Stewart with Colborne's brigade of the 2nd Division should have changed the face of affairs. But Stewart, of a boiling temperament and flurried by the noise and turmoil on the hill, turned a deaf ear to the advice of his cooler brigadier. Pushing the heights in columns of companies, he had no time given him to extend his battalions, as they struggled on to the summit. Enveloped in smoke and driving rain, seeing little or nothing of what was passing, he was charged from the rear by four regiments of light cavalry, and three-fourths of his brigade were cut to pieces. These light horsemen were careering everywhere: nothing but the mist saved the handful of British survivors, and the stalwart marshal was in the thick of the fighting.

A shift of the wind cleared the scene for a moment, and then Lumley sent some of his squadrons to the rescue. All the time the Spaniards had stood their ground and kept blindly firing alike on French and British. Beresford, after shouting himself hoarse in vain exhortations to advance, seized one of the ensigns with the colours and bore him bodily forward. But no one followed, and when the lad was dropped he ran back to his comrades. Yet the darkness, which had been the destruction of good part of Stewart's first brigade, had on the whole befriended the allies. It blinded Soult to an opportunity which would have been decisive had he seized it. Colborne still held the height with the surviving battalion.

Stewart, who had escaped death by a miracle, had hurried down to bring up his second brigade. The British guns had come into action, and as the mist lifted a deadly fire was rained upon the close heads of Soult's columns. The battle ebbed and flowed: the cannon were exchanging grape at short range, but it was the French who suffered most severely, thanks to their closer formation. The thin British line pressed them so hard that they had never time to open. But human strength and courage have their limits, and things seemed desperate. Some of the leaders were down, others were sorely wounded; a single regiment—the 57th—had lost its colonel, 22 of its officers, and two-thirds of the rank and file.

It is averred that Beresford was losing heart and hope: he seems to have ordered up Portuguese battalions and cavalry with a view of protecting his retreat, though it is said that he had issued no positive order. Undoubtedly he was hesitating when some of his staff urged that the day might still be retrieved by calling up the 4th Division. It had been left with Cole to mount guard before Badajoz, and had been the last to approach the scene of action. Then a subordinate took the decision out of the marshal's hands, and Colonel Hardinge, deputy quartermaster of the Portuguese army, may claim the honours of the day. He ordered Cole to bring up his division—half British, half Portuguese. He rode on to give a similar order to Abercromby, who commanded the remaining brigade of the 2nd Division.

The summons was eagerly obeyed by men who had been chafing in fierce impatience. Beresford saw the fresh regiments hurling themselves into the fight, and was powerless to check the rush had he wished it. When they came to the rescue, Houghton's stubborn line had thinned, according to one of his officers, to an extended chain of skirmishers; on the smooth green slopes, slippery with blood and bestrewed with corpses, the jubilant French Lancers were careering around six of our captured guns; below them, and in front of Houghton's line, one of our regiments, blinded by the smoke, was exchanging volleys with the Spaniards.

The startling change in the circumstances was felt before it was seen. Cole scattered the lancers, recovered the guns, and wheeling to the right of Houghton's shattered brigade, emerged from the dimness in "solid oblique line" on the massive French columns, always being crowded up and urged forward from behind. In vain they endeavoured to extend their front, tormented by searching volleys of musketry. In vain the storm of grape from their forty guns, sweeping over their heads, tore through the serried ranks of the allies. Cole and three of his colonels went down wounded; but the close of that bloody tragedy can only be told in the words of Napier. It is described in passages of glowing eloquence that must fire the blood of soldier or civilian.

> The fusilier battalions, struck by the iron tempest, reeled and staggered like sinking ships. Suddenly and sternly recovering, they closed on their terrible enemies, and then was seen with what a strength and majesty the British soldier fights. In vain did Soult, by word and gesture, animate his Frenchmen; in vain did the hardiest veterans, extricating themselves from the crowded columns, sacrifice their lives to gain time for the mass to open out on such a fair field; in vain did the mass itself bear up, and,

fiercely striving, fire indiscriminately upon friends and foes ... Nothing could stop that astonishing infantry. No sudden burst of undisciplined valour, no nervous enthusiasm weakened the stability of their order; their flashing eyes were bent on the dark columns in their front; their measured tread shook the ground; their dreadful volleys swept away the head of every formation; their dreadful shouts overpowered the dissonant cries that broke from all parts of the tumultuous crowd, as foot by foot, and with a horrid carnage, it was driven by the incessant vigour of the attack to the farthest verge of the hill.

In vain did the French reserves, joining with the struggling multitude, endeavour to sustain the fight; their efforts only increased the irremediable confusion, and the mighty mass, giving way like a loosened cliff, went headlong down the ascent. The rain flowed after in streams discoloured with blood, and 1500 unwounded men, the remnant of 6000 unconquerable British soldiers, stood triumphant on the fatal hill.

An officer of the 29th gives some melancholy details of the musters when the victors reckoned up their losses. In that regiment only 96 men, two captains, and a few subalterns remained; in Houghton's brigade every one of the field officers had been killed or wounded, and it was left in command of a captain, who, strange to say, was a French *emigré*. A few days after the battle, five of the broken regiments were brigaded into a single battalion. The cries of the wounded were piteous, and the survivors could give little help. When the pickets had been set for the night, few idlers were left, and these for the most part could not be roused from the sleep of mortal exhaustion. Like La Lapeña at Barossa, Blake absolutely refused to lend his allies any assistance.

Napier blames Soult for not renewing the attack next day: he had still 15,000 foot, and his cavalry and artillery had suffered little. But he could not have known how terribly the British had been cut up, and it is noteworthy that the officer of the 29th makes a similar reproach as to Beresford. It might have been fancied that he and his comrades had had their fill of fighting, but all the reminiscences of these Peninsular veterans show that they were intoxicated with the mad joy of battle. Even on the retreats from Sabugal or Salamanca, the beat of an enemy's drum or the flourish of a trumpet sufficed to give legs to the lame and galvanise the despairing into heroism.

The anonymous author of *Recollections of the Peninsula* gives a horrible account of the state of the field hospitals for days after the battle, though the wounded, so far as possible, had been sent to Valverde. On the 20th he saw the chapel at Albuera

> .... filled with French wounded, great numbers of whom had suffered amputation, and who lay on the hard stones without even straw ... we had nothing to give them on the spot, and they were forced to wait till our own people had been carried to the rear.

As he walked over the scenes of the carnage, he noted a touching attention of the Spaniards—though their generals were backward enough in giving more substantial assistance—which we have never seen mentioned elsewhere.

> The hands of vast numbers of the British corpses had been clasped together in the attitude of prayer, and placed by the Spaniards in the manner they superstitiously imagine it important to lay out their dead.

Fifteen months afterwards, when he revisited the chapel, he was struck by an epigrammatic inscription in charcoal.

> *La guerre en Espagne est la Fortane dee Généraux, L'Ennui des Officiers et le Tombeau des Soldats,*

rather neatly summed up the situation.

Wellington was at Elvas when Albuera was fought. He told Lord Stanhope that Beresford had written in a desponding tone, saying "that he could not stand the slaughter and vast responsibility."

"I said directly," added the Duke, "'This won't do: write me down a victory.' The despatch was altered accordingly."

Therefore the Duke must be held responsible for the elaborate report, in which the marshal actually falsified the action. He gave exaggerated praise to the Spaniards, who failed in the first crisis, though they fought respectably afterwards. From his warm commendation of Stewart, it would never be suspected that the general's hot-headed courage had sacrificed a brigade, and above all, and it must be said to his lasting discredit, he gives no honour where all honour was due. After flattering notices of officers of all ranks, who may have well deserved the distinction, Hardinge is dismissed at the end of the despatch with a cold tribute to "his talents and exertions."

It seems impossible to acquit the marshal of a paltry jealousy, unworthy of his high place and chivalrous character. But the silence or reserve is the surest confirmation of the master-stroke by which

Beresford's quartermaster won a decisive battle of the war. We need not enter on the envenomed controversy, provoked by the sharp strictures in the *Peninsular War*. Some of the pamphlets in defence, though anonymous, were confidently attributed to Beresford himself, and the imputation was never denied. Yet we are inclined to agree in all seriousness with the ironical suggestion of Napier, that they could not possibly have been written by the marshal, since the veriest egoist could scarcely have indulged in such fulsome self-eulogy.

That they were inspired by Beresford seems certain, nor did they make out a bad case. But the more the light was thrown upon facts in dispute, the more apparent was it that the great organiser was no great general. Nevertheless, the glorious victory was vociferously acclaimed in Parliament when the vote of thanks to Beresford and his forces was proposed by Perceval and seconded by Castlereagh.

He followed Soult in the retreat, when General Lumley closed the campaign at Llerena in a brilliant affair with the French rearguard. Wellington was on the ridge of Albuera a day or two after the battle, and Hill returned immediately afterwards, amid general rejoicing, to take over the command of his army of the south.

2

In any case, imperious considerations had recalled Beresford to Lisbon to resume the work for which he was exceptionally fitted. Wellington formed the second leaguer of Badajoz, and Beresford's only concern with it—be was present at the third and final siege—was that his Portuguese gunners had been trained so well that they manned some of the breaching batteries when stiffened by Englishmen. At Lisbon he found himself invested with arbitrary authority. Confusion had been coming to a head: corruption reigned supreme, when Wellington, putting irresistible pressure on the Prince Royal in the Brazils, had obtained a new commission for the marshal, giving him absolute power in all departments of the army. He saw that things had been slipping back in his absence, and again he took a resolute line of his own, in face of very real difficulties and persistent obstruction.

The British subsidies were being squandered or embezzled; Portugal was crushed under a load of taxation; the country had been desolated by the contending armies; in the general conscription that was sternly enforced, the bread-winners were torn from their starving families. Beresford was charged with the salvation of the State, and he was no seeker of popularity. He resorted to measures of extreme severity: probably nothing less would have served. Edicts were issued to lay an embargo on the ports, where men of family embarking for the Brazils sought to evade military service. Rewards were offered for the arrest of deserters; when caught, they were condemned to hard labour, or shot in batches *pour encourager les autres*. No excuses were admitted: there was no hope of pardon or reprieve.

Nor was greater consideration shown to rank, and one high-born colonel was degraded and stripped of his epaulettes in the great square of Lisbon. Gradually, as the drill sergeants did their work, the *morale* improved, for the Portuguese were patriotic and were alive to the emergency. As battalions were successively sent to the front, emulation awakened their martial pride, and when Wellington undertook the campaign of Salamanca, 24,000 of them were brigaded with the British. Thenceforward, in the fighting from the Tormes to the Garonne, Beresford's recruits proved themselves worthy of their comrades. It was the more to the credit of the men and the marshal that there was neither money in their pockets nor in the military chest. He wrote in the summer of 1812:

> The arrears of the army are getting to an alarming pitch, and if it is suffered to increase we cannot go on: we have barely bread for the day, and the commissary has not a farthing of money.

Always travelling between Lisbon and his regiments in the field, he was present at the storms of Ciudad Rodrigo and Badajoz, though he played no active part in either operation. He was with Wellington through most of the manoeuvring against Marmont, and after Marmont's passage of the Douro, with Wellington he had a very narrow escape. It was one of the most dramatic incidents of the war, and might have been the most eventful. Cotton was skilfully holding his own in advanced positions behind the Trabancos. As it was drawing towards dusk, Wellington and Beresford had ridden up to reconnoitre. They saw some squadrons of French horse bursting out from behind cover of the hills that concealed the enemy. So heedless and desperate seemed the charge that it was believed they were deserting.

On they came upon the flank of Cotton's right wing, driving his mounted skirmishers before them, to be surrounded by his reserves. But a band broke through, and, with Berserker fury, charged down a hollow between the wings, at the very moment when the two generals topped the crest of the opposite slope. At sight of an interposing British squadron they drew rein, but only for a moment Resuming the gallop, they scattered our light horsemen, driving them in mad confusion through a battery behind; the generals were caught in the rush, and could scarcely extricate themselves. At that moment the stroke of a trooper's sabre might have changed the fortunes of the war.

At Salamanca Beresford again distinguished himself by his daring, but showed once more that he had neither the eye nor intuition of a great commander. The day before the battle it was reported that the enemy was moving detachments towards the twin Arapiles, the key of the position to the south of the Tormes. Beresford paid no heed to the information, but, when it reached Wellington, he promptly gave orders to reverse his whole order of battle. Next day, when Pakenham had driven Thomières back, the fight towards the centre was raging fiercely around those precipitous rocks. Pack's Portuguese, sent to assail an impossibly slippery incline, had been hurled down by the avalanche launched from above.

Then the fighting was transferred to the hollow beneath, and it flowed and ebbed as supports were alternately sent up to the stubborn combatants. Cole and Leith successively went down, severely wounded; and then came the turn of Beresford, who had brought up another of his Portuguese brigades. Dropping to a body shot—and no one doubted it was fatal—he was borne to the rear. Never did the brave soldier show to more advantage than when he believed his last hour was at hand, and we have a vivid picture of Spartan fortitude and generous self-suppression in the graphic narrative of the surgeon who tended him on the field. This Englishman on the Portuguese medical staff was busy among the wounded when an officer came galloping from the front, shouting, "A surgeon! a British surgeon!"

It was one of the marshal's *aides-de-camp*, and the doctor, following him into the zone of fire, was led up to a covered waggon. There he saw Beresford lying side by side with a sergeant. His chest was bare, "and below the left breast was a spot of blood, bright and defined as a star of knighthood." The doctor made sure the wound was mortal, but proceeded to examine. While he was probing, "not a muscle moved, not a sound was uttered." It proved that the ball, in place of penetrating, had made the circuit of the chest; and the surgeon, speaking for the first time, said, "General, your wound is not mortal."

Without taking the slightest notice of the reassuring intelligence, like Wolfe on the Heights of Abraham, he looked up and asked, "How does the day go?"

"Well," said the doctor; " the enemy has begun to give way."

"Ha!" rejoined the marshal, "it has been a bloody day."

Then the Portuguese sergeant began to call on Our Lady and the doctor for help. The doctor bade him be silent, telling him his general was lying by his side. Whereupon Beresford, who could shoot soldiers by the half-dozen for breaches of duty, "turning his head with a reproving look, said to me, 'Sir, if the poor fellow's wounds require dressing more than mine, dress him first.'" But the sergeant was past help, and the surgeon gave his attention to the marshal.

When he seemed to hesitate, he was told to cut deeply: "I never fainted in my life." Perhaps the sequel is even more to his credit. The surgeon ordered bleeding in a few hours, and honestly avows that he would have liked to remain in charge himself with an eye to promotion. But when the marshal demanded, "Who's to do it?" he had been so impressed by Beresford's heroic bearing that he adds, with equal honesty, he thought he should serve his interests better by asking permission to look after the other sufferers. And he judged rightly, for he was not forgotten.

The marshal recovered from his wounds, to be repeatedly recalled from active service to Lisbon. Whenever his back was turned, things were going wrong at headquarters. There were constant quarrels with the Regency as to subsidies; discontent was fomented by faction in high places; and at one time the army he had painfully organised seemed on the point of dissolution. But Ciudad Rodrigo, Badajoz, and Salamanca had raised the spirit of the troops in the field, and when he had a sudden summons to the rear during the siege of Burgos, again his presence and personality worked wonders. Before the decisive battle of Vittoria, the Portuguese were once more in a thoroughly efficient condition. He had filled up the depleted regiments from the militia; he embodied all the garrison artillery, giving the fortresses in charge to men of the reserve, and disbanding some of the worst cavalry corps, he drafted the good men into others.

Those sweeping measures provoked bitter hostility, but more formidable was the underhand opposition he had to face from the corrupt court of Rio de Janeiro. Through family influence or courtly favour, impecunious nobles were permitted to enter the army, simply that they might retire with their pay and allowances—and at a time when the pay of the troops was more than a year in arrear. Careless of unpopularity, Beresford checked these abuses with a firm hand and gained the lasting gratitude of Wellington. The estimation in which he was held by the commander-in-chief was strikingly shown at this critical time. When Wellington was created a marquis, it was intended to raise Sir Stapleton Cotton—he had been second in command at Salamanca—to the peerage. Wellington would have deemed the honour well bestowed, nevertheless he begged Lord Bathurst to reconsider the matter. He said that if Cotton got a title Beresford would resign. And he added:

> All I can tell you is that the ablest man I have seen with the army, and that one having the largest views, is Beresford. . . . I am quite certain that he is the only person capable of conducting a large concern.

And, whatever may have been Wellington's private opinion of the conduct of Albuera, he evinced his unshaken confidence by continuing the marshal in important commands during the campaigns in France. Undoubtedly Beresford did more for the regeneration of Portuguese manhood, and therefore, indirectly, for the expulsion of the French from the Peninsula, than any man except Wellington himself. But he had admirable material to work with in the lower orders, and the patriotism of the rank and file was beyond praise. There was a striking example when some of their regiments were brigaded on the Tormes before Vittoria. They were on the verge of mutiny, with good reason. In rags and shoeless, their pay was a year in arrear, and the time of many of them, who had enlisted for a limited period, had expired. These demanded their discharge, and it could not be denied them. Wellington took measures to supply their immediate needs; Beresford made a soldier-like appeal to their honour and patriotism; and with one consent they remained with the colours, to carry them forward from the Zadora to Vittoria.

Larpent, who was with Wellington at headquarters in the winter of 1812-13, mentions "one regiment of the *caçadores* that is the constant astonishment of the English. Badly paid, no new clothes for the last two years, in rags nearly this winter, and yet scarcely a man has been sick." He says that in soldierly appearance they showed to disadvantage with the Spaniards, but their broad, slouching shoulders were suggestive of their strong *physique*, and they kept up their strength on slender rations. Indeed they had been so hardly treated, and the commissariat was so bad, that towards the end of May, in a burst of temper, Beresford threatened he would send them to the rear if matters were not mended.

That was a few days after Beresford had the place of honour at a banquet to celebrate the anniversary of Albuera. Castaños sat next to Wellington on the left. "We had Mr. Joe Kelly of the Life Guards, a famous singer, and he gave us some good songs; and we hip, hip, hipped, &c., to the *grandees*. I was entertained at the display of etiquette between the marshal and General Castaños, who should go into the tent first: at last they went in side by side, as other great men before have determined that knotty point."

The marshal and the commander-in-chief were constantly seen in company when together at headquarters. Larpent describes a characteristic scene at Villa Diego in June 1813.

> Lord Wellington and the Marshal Beresford are walking up and down the street, and the military secretary is writing under a wall, upon his knees, while his servants are pitching his tent. In a little field, where General Alava is about to encamp, there are just now the military secretary, Colonel Sewell, the commander of the Police Corps, Fitzclarence, General Alava, the Spanish *aide-de-camp*, Colonel Waters, the Prince of Orange, and your humble servant, all lying upon the ground together, round a cold ham and bread, some brandy, and a bottle of champagne. The Prince and Lord Fitzroy, like two boys, were playing together all the time.

Beresford was present at the decisive battle of Vittoria, with no special command, and was also in the field, though in the background, through the fighting in the Pyrenees. Again in October he had a call to Lisbon, to find confusion again confounded. Forjas, whom, by the way, Wellington described as one of the ablest men in Portugal, was intriguing for the disorganisation of Beresford's new army, of which he desired to obtain the command. He may have been an able man, but he was notoriously no general, and, had he been appointed, the English officers would have thrown up their commissions.

Moreover, he desired to bring back the regiments brigaded with British troops, to form a *corps d'armée* apart. As to that, both Wellington and Beresford spoke out in uncompromising, though flattering terms. They bestowed well-deserved praise on the gallantry of their Portuguese allies, but said they were not yet fitted to work alone, and that an independent Portuguese army would inevitably fall to pieces. The two strong wills had their way, but the trouble upset Beresford's arrangements. He had hoped for a brief furlough, and indeed, as matter of form, he should have taken his seat in Parliament, having been returned, for the second time, as member for Watford. it has been assimed in some notices of his career that he did go home, but in fact he never left Portugal. On the contrary, he was head and ears in work at the Lisbon War Office till he returned to the French frontier to play his part in the Battle of the Nivelle.

There he commanded the right centre of the attack. On the 10th November, after sundry days of deluge, a glorious morning saw 90,000 combatants pouring down from the slopes of the Pyrenees to the storm of the detached mountains beyond, by paths that the rains had flooded into torrents. Beresford's corps was to the left of the 26,000 men who were to be launced against D'Elon's entrenched positions. These positions had been deliberatelty fortifird with a vast expenditure of labour, but the enemy was driven from his redoubts in front of the village of Sarre; his strong line of defence was shattered in the centre, and before night both his flanks had been turned. Next morning the French divisions were still falling back, and there was a general advance of the allies. Beresford pushing onward from the centre, had followed Soult from St. Pé. But the floods had made the roads impassable, and the pursuit was prematurely arrested.

During the subsequent weeks rains and floods still delayed the operations: Beresford on the 23rd November had seized the bridge of Undase on the Nive, and he held it; but it was not till the second week in December that Wellington's arrangements for the passage of the river were completed. Beresford with the 3rd and 6th Divisions was to cross at Ustaritz on pontoons. There both the bridges had been broken, but he held the island connecting them, and in the night of the 8th had brought his pontoons down to the southern bank. With daybreak a beacon fire blazing above Cambo gave the signal to him, and to Hill, who was to force the lower fords. Beresford met with slight resistance, but the heavy marching delayed his advance, when the French fell back in good order. Both generals were safely established beyond the river, but Wellington was in some anxiety lest, while they were assailed in front, the communications on his right should be threatened by General Paris swooping down from the uplands on the Spanish brigades.

Consequently Hope and Alten were instructed to divert Soult's attention by menacing the Lower Adour and the entrenched camp. Then followed the five days' fighting before Bayonne, with Hill's crowning victory of St. Pierre. But the weather was terrible even for December, and again operations were paralysed by impracticable roads and swollen rivers. Soult had lost the Nive, but he was temporarily secure behind the Upper Adour and the flooded Gaves of Pau and Oleron.

Wellington was aiming at the line of the Garonne. It was dictated to him by policy as well as strategy, for there were many royalists and malcontents in the south, and Bordeaux, in especial, was seething with discontent. His forces already outnumbered those of Soult, and the majority were of better quality. The French marshal foresaw that his own ultimate line of march must be on Toulouse and parallel to the Pyrenees. He had always looked to a junction with Suchet, and doubt as to Suchet's action was an element in Wellington's calculations which greatly increased his anxieties.

Nevertheless Soult had no mind to fall back without fighting—his soldier's pride was at stake, and the arrival of Sachet might alter everything. But when the frosts had hardened the roads, action was forced upon him, and in the second week of February he was driven to dispute the Gaves. Some fighting there was, but his left was turned near their sources by Hill's corps and the Spaniards, while Beresford with steady pressure kept his centre in check. Beset on all sides, he had the startling news that Hope had bridged the Adour below Bayonne. That intelligence decided him, yet he would not withdraw without another engagement. He concentrated at Orthez, with the resolution of taking the offensive.

But the promptitude of his adversary's movements anticipated him, and he had the disadvantage of being forced to stand on his defence. On the 23rd of February, Beresford crossed the Gave de Pau, dislodged Foy from his advanced posts, and menaced Soult's right On the following day he had pushed forward, and thrown out detachments to intercept the French communications with Dax on the Adour. That night he occupied the heights fronting the village of Berights, on the north-west face of Orthez. Wellington's intention had been to deliver his attack from above the town, where the Gave, flowing through the meadows, was more easily to be forded. He changed his plan when he heard that Beresford was already on the opposite bank, in spite of steep rocks and broken water. Picton had likewise made good his passage, and on these generals the brunt of the morrow's battle was to fall.

The course of the action has been described elsewhere Beresford, baffled repeatedly in futile attempts to deploy beyond the gorge that led down from the ridge of St. Boës, succeeded at last, when by one masterly stroke impending defeat became decisive victory. The single regiment sent over an apparently impassable swamp paralysed the whole hostile machinery when seemingly working to perfection. The firm front of the French defence was shivered; there was confusion verging upon panic; the pass of St. Boës was indifferently guarded, and Beresford, thrusting forward his divisions, deployed into line beyond. The fire of his batteries enfiladed the French: the wings of the allied attack were united, and Soult, recognising that Orthez was untenable, gave orders for one of those retreats which no one could direct more skilfully.

Throughout the operations Beresford had been in great danger, and Wellington had deliberately imperilled him, though with grave anxiety. In the first place, when the marshal passed the Gave, Soult might have met him with a heavy counterstroke, had he not fortunately overrated his enemy's strength. Again, when the armies were coming to close grips, with the river dividing the allied forces, both Beresford and Picton were in evil case had Soult struck at either suddenly and sharply. But there, as so often in similar circumstances, Wellington had reckoned with the temperament of his opponent.

When Wellington passed the Adour, Beresford was sent to seize the magazines of Mont de Marsan. Wellington had been again delayed by the weather and his wound.

With regard to the wound, which was painful if not serious, Lord William Lennox tells a pleasant story of "the Iron Duke." His old *aide-de-camp*, Lord March, had been struck in the battle and was lying between life and death.

> On the following morning Wellington was enabled to get about upon crutches, and his first walk was across the square to the house in which his former *aide-de-camp* lay (Lord March had left the staff to do duty with his regiment, the famous 52nd.) His Grace hobbled into the room where the patient lay in a most precarious state, and the surgeon . . . made a sign that the wounded man was sleeping. For a second, Wellington leant against the mantelpiece. He, the sternest of the stern where the claims of duty invoked the suppression of natural impulses, gave way to the most poignant grief. Suddenly my brother awoke, and recognising his chief, expressed a hope that he had been successful. 'I've given them a good licking,' said the great man, 'and I hope that I shall follow it up.'

For the Duke always showed fatherly affection for the officers personally attached to him. The evening of Waterloo, Sir Alexander Gordon had been laid upon his own bed. At three in the morning he was roused by the doctor, to be told that that gallant spirit had passed away. As Wellington sat up, the tears streamed down his face, and he said in a voice broken with emotion:

> Well, thank God, I don't know what it is to lose a battle, but nothing can be more painful than to gain one, with the loss of so many of one's friends.

The capture of the magazines was the crowning exploit of the sixteen days' campaign, in which Soult had been forced to abandon his camp at Bayonne and severed from communications with Bordeaux. Now, as often before, policy influenced Wellington's strategy. With a superiority both in cavalry and guns, his forces nevertheless were none too many to follow Soult in his retreat on Toulouse. But the Duke of Angoulême was in his camp, and Bordeaux demanded immediate attention. The royalists were active; the merchants were praying for peace; and it was important to open the Garonne to our transports. It would be a grand *coup* to take possession of the capital of Southwestern France. So 12,000 men he could ill afford to spare marched for Bordeaux under Beresford, although meanwhile Soult had time to rally and make leisurely arrangements.

Beresford had no military difficulties to overcome, for he found the city evacuated by its feeble garrison. He made a triumphal entry with a few hundred horse, to be welcomed by the mayor and the syndics. But he was charged with somewhat delicate negotiations, for he had to warn the revolted enthusiasts not to commit themselves irretrievably. The allies in the north were discussing terms of peace with Napoleon, and if the Emperor were to remain the ruler of France, he would certainly take vengeance on those who had played him false. Beresford was well fitted for the business of throwing a cold douche on the civic excitement. He was not a man to be swayed by sentiment, or to be hurried into saying smooth things to give him a momentary popularity. He explained the situation frankly, leaving the responsibility of action to the authorities.

The subsequent pilotage was left to Lord Dalhousie, his second in command. Having discharged his mission, he was recalled by Wellington, who wanted all the men at his disposal It became imperative to deal Soult the final blow before he could be reinforced by the army of Arragon. He had been forced back stage by stage—Hill operating steadily against his left, Wellington in person directing the attacks against his right. On the 21st of March Beresford had rejoined, and Wellington had handed over to him the leading of the left wing. On the 26th he was facing the French army, which was an the Touch, covering Toulouse. On the 3rd of April he had passed the Garonne with three divisions of infantry and as many cavalry brigades.

Soult, when informed of the passage, had again the opportunity of attacking Beresford with superior numbers, but on that score Wellington felt little uneasiness. He had divined the intentions of his enemy, who hoped to make Toulouse impregnable. On three of its sides there was no more defensible city in France, and though Wellington might have assailed it with better advantage from the south, for various reasons he found that to be impracticable. The west front was guarded by the fortified suburb of St. Cyprien, a *tête-de-pont* to the only bridge over the Garonne.

The north of the city was accessible by two great roads over open country, but when the flats were crossed the assailants were confronted by the broad Languedoc canal, within musket-shot of the ramparts, and with bridges scientifically defended, and commanded by cannon on the walls. "Here," in the words of Napier, "was a fortress and not a position." Consequently, there was no choice but to attack on the east, though there the obstacles to be overcome might have daunted the most daring commander. It is certain, indeed, that in the crisis of the battle we narrowly escaped crushing disaster, when Soult let slip a golden opportunity.

On that side Soult had triple, or rather fourfold lines of defence, where science had done everything to assist nature. First came the tower, with the massive ramparts which could carry guns of heavy calibre. Then there was the canal, which swept round from the north, with its bridges defended by formidable works. Beyond was the rugged range of the Mont Rave, with carefully planned fortifications which Soult had been labouring industriously to strengthen during the breathing space afforded by the enforced delay. The heights sunk down into a narrow belt of marshy land which had been artificially flooded; and the whole was covered by the River Ers, not to be forded anywhere, but passed at long intervals by mined bridges held by the French cavalry.

These heights extended for a couple of miles and were crowned by two fortified platforms—that of St. Sypiere on the eastern extremity of the ridge, and the Calvinet about a mile and a half to the westward. Beyond the Calvinet rose the Pugade, an entrenched eminence, looking down on the angle of the works receding from the front of the Mont Rave, and marked out by a road leading from the city to the bridge of Croix d'Orade, which spanned the Ers to the extreme north-east of the positions.

The battle began on the morning of the 10th. Hill, though forbidden to push home his attack, was to occupy the enemy on the side of St. Cyprien. His object was accomplished when he carried the outer entrenchments of the suburb. Picton with his habitual impetuosity deranged the combinations when in place of feinting he sent his soldiers to slaughter, in the vain attempt to storm the bridge of Jumeaux. These distractions were to be auxiliary to the serious attack which was directed against the eastern front, and it is with Beresford's operations we are concerned. While Picton was menacing Jumeaux, and Alten was demonstrating on Picton's left, to Freire and his Spaniards, to the left of Alten, was assigned the task of seizing the Pugade, which would then protect Beresford's flanking march in the rear of it.

The Pugade was taken, according to the programme, and thence the Portuguese batteries opened a cannonade on the Calvinet. That operation had masked the movements of Beresford, who had passed the Ers at the bridge of Croix d'Orade, which had been secured two days before by our cavalry. From the bridge, preceded by his light horse, he marched northward between the Ers and the Pugade in three columns abreast. Passing beyond the shelter of the hill and under fire of the French batteries, he found the flooded country so heavy that he was forced to leave his guns behind.

Nevertheless all might have gone comparatively well had it not been for the unsteadiness of the Spaniards, on whom so much depended. A cold fit had been preceded by a hot one. Freire had asked permission to undertake the storm of the Calvinet, but instead of holding back till Beresford had completed his march, he anticipated the hour of attack. At first the Spaniards made good their footing on the slopes, but only to be hurled down again with terrible slaughter. A second time their leaders brought them back to the attack, but scared by the sight of their slaughtered comrades and raked on all sides by a murderous fire, they scattered and fled in abject panic. To all appearance the day was lost.

Hill was at bay before the inner entrenchments of St. Cyprien; Picton, beaten back from Jumeaux, had used up the available reserves; the Portuguese guns, with the batteries Beresford had left behind, were still bombarding the Calvinet. But his flanks were unprotected from the fire of the Mont Rave, and as he forced his way forward through mud and water his columns were dragging slowly along, and many of the weaker men were falling behind. The 11,000 with whom he set out were rapidly dwindling to half their number; the heads of his columns, about to wheel under a concentrated cannonade, were in dire confusion. Wellington had not a man to send to his help, and yet it was on him that everything depended.

Soult and Wellington were alike alive to the crisis. Secured on the sides of St. Cyprien and Jumeaux, the former began to pass troops and guns across the town to reinforce the exultant defenders of the Mont Rave. The odds against Beresford's success were immense, and Wellington has been not unreasonably censured for risking so much when the issues were so momentous. Had Toulouse been a lost battle, and had the peace not been agreed upon, he might have been robbed of the fruits of his labours, when they seemed actually within his grasp. But, as was so often the case in his chequered campaigns, the situation was saved when things seemed hopeless by one of the chances of war, by chiefs of brigade, and the dauntless determination of the British private.

Taupin, whose reputation for daring promptitude was a byword, for once showed himself unready. He waited till Beresford had time to breathe his battalions and throw them into line for the assault on St. Cyprien. Even then, against masses of fresh troops, with all the advantages of the steep, shingly ground in their favour, it might have seemed an effort of despair. But there was nothing of despair or despondency in the shoats with which Lambert's veterans rushed to the storm. Their way had been cleared by a discharge of rockets, unfamiliar engines, which, as at the passage of the Adour, went far to demoralise the enemy. Those soldiers of Taupin, on whom Soult confidently relied, broke when they saw the fall of their general before the British could close in to ply the bayonet, and were hustled down the reverse slope. Meanwhile Lowry Cole had scaled the eastern heights, when the redoubts on the summit were abandoned without a shot

That capture of the heights was so far decisive. The French, so advantageously posted for offence, were now reduced to the defensive, but for the defence their positions were tremendously strong. It was 2.30 p.m. when Beresford looked along the Mont Rave from St. Sypiere to see that all was still depending upon him. Before him were the twin redoubts of Calvinet and Columbette; behind, in field-works surrounding them, crowded in the cramped enclosures, was Villatte's division, with sundry brigades; it was doubtful if the Spaniards would come again to the scratch, and still there were no supports forthcoming. If Beresford had wavered at Albuera, he did not hesitate now. Pack's brigade of Scots with Douglas' Portuguese were promptly launched against the Calvinet. Panting and staggering up that shingly steep, it seems strange that the loose onset of toil-worn men should have carried the long sweep of redoubts and breastworks, bristling with cannon and lined with muskets.

Carried they were, but the French tide had ebbed only to flow back: Harispe, a fighting general *par excellence*, threw himself into the action with the mountaineers he had brought from the Pyrenees; Beresford's rear regiments, on the other hand, were pressing into the battle, and brought effective help to Pack's Scots, who had been falling fast, till, as at Albuera, the columns so hardly beset were thinning and breaking into a line of skirmishers. Still the Spaniards brought no help; in vain the British horse strove to come to the aid of their comrades, for the cross-roads ran in impassable hollows; still the combat raged around the redoubts; the Columbette was recaptured, to be again retaken.

It might seem that the French should have triumphed by a process of attrition, but when Soult saw that the Spaniards at length had rallied and were coming forward supported by the Light Division, that Picton was again menacing Jumeaux, and that Beresford showed no signs of flinching, of a sudden the retreat was sounded. The whole ridge of the Mont Rave was cleared, and the enemy had withdrawn behind the canal. Beresford had shown no signs of flinching, for at four o'clock, when the enemy withdrew, he had been preparing for the third stage in the battle. He had paused a moment to rally his shattered battalions, and at last his guns had come up; but the Mont Rave was in his hands, the battle was ended, and in the crowning victory of the Peninsular War he had the lion's share of the glory.

3

Honours were heaped on him upon his return to England. He was created a baron; he was granted an annuity of £2000 for himself and two successors; the city of London presented a sword of honour, and he had the personal thanks of the Prince Regent. Toulouse was his last battle, and he was not present at Waterloo. It was not that Wellington did not want him in Flanders, or that his martial ardour was abated;

but he had been sent on an important mission, where his influence should have been paramount. When Napoleon's escape had plunged Europe back into war, there was natural foreboding that hostilities would be protracted. Beresford had gone to Lisbon to arrange for the co-operation of the Portuguese, but Wellington's blow was dealt so sharply that his errand was forestalled. For some years he remained in Portugal as marshal in command, but, although he drew his pay and allowances, his position was anything but enviable.

With straitened finances, the Government had always grudged the expenses of the war budget: when peace seemed finally assured, they urged a reduction of the forces. When Beresford objected, they struck and refused to pay anything at all. Moreover, the rapid growth of democratic tendencies clashed with his aristocratic prejudices; imperious and self-reliant, he was a man who loved his own way. Yet there was always an appeal to the king, who was keeping a gay court in the Brazils. Thither he had gone in 1817, when the stern soldier made himself welcome by taking the lead in putting down a popular revolt. He returned to Rio two years afterwards to plead for the redemption of pledges he had been authorised to give, and to press for his troops receiving their pay and arrears.

The king had promised all that was asked, though his power to enforce fulfilment was doubtful, and Beresford sailed back to Lisbon. Before his ship cast anchor off Belem, the democratic constitution had been proclaimed, and he was refused permission to land. He left the ungrateful country in bitter resentment. Twice afterwards, during the civil war, the Government would gladly have had him back in supreme command, and were lavish of the most tempting offers. But his anger still burned hotly, and indeed, with his wealth and position, he had no personal inducement to court another dismissal from a fickle nation, morbidly jealous of foreign interference.

In home politics he was the staunch supporter of Wellington, and Wellington's friendship stood him in good stead. A striking proof of the confidential intercourse of the old comrades is the letter from Wellington to Beresford, written a few weeks after Waterloo, in answer to one of congratulations. It came from the sale of the Beresford-Hope papers.

Paris, August 9, 1815.

My dear Beresford,—I received only last night your letter of the 8th, for which I am very much obliged to you. The battle of Waterloo was certainly the hardest that has been fought for many years, I believe, and has placed in the power of the allies the most important results. We are throwing them away, however, by the infamous conduct of some of us; and I am sorry to add our own Government also are taking up a little too much the line of their rascally newspapers: they are shifting their objects, and, having got their cake, they want both to eat it and to keep it.

As for your Portuguese concerns, I recommend to you to resign and come away immediately. It is impossible for the British Government to maintain British officers for the Portuguese army at our expense, even as trifling as it is, if the Portuguese Government are to refuse to give the service of the army in the cause of Europe in any manner. Pitch them to the devil then in the mode which will be most dignified for yourself, and that which will have the best effect in opening the prince's eyes to the conduct of his servants in Portugal; and let the matter work its own way. Depend upon it, the British Government must and will recall the Portuguese officers.

I shall hold a language here that will correspond with your actions in Portugal.

Ever yours most sincerely,
Wellington.

Field-Marshal the Lord Beresford, Q.C.B.

More and more honours were bestowed; one lucrative appointment followed another. He was already a lieutenant-general, Governor of Jersey, and colonel of a regiment. In 1822 he was made lieutenant-general of the ordnance; in the following year he was created a viscount; in 1825 he was a full general. In 1828 the Duke, as Prime Minister, appointed him master-general of the ordnance. He held the post till the formation of Earl Grey's Ministry, when he withdrew from public life. Already rich and a *bon vivant*—in the Peninsula, according to Sir Augustus Frazer, he had kept the best table in the army—he might have been content to enjoy the present, looking back complacently on the past. But the favourite of fortune was not without his worries, and he was drawn into the rancorous controversy with Napier, which stung his pride because it touched his fame. The fulsome self-eulogy in which he indulged, either directly or by inspired deputy, is a humiliating revelation of his mortification and an avowal of the weakness of his case.

Nevertheless the cup of his prosperity was not yet full. In his sixty-fifth year he married his cousin, the widow of Thomas Hope, banker, of Amsterdam, and author of *Anastasius*. It was not a romantic match, but it proved a happy one. He gave the lady his great name, and she brought him superfluity of wealth. At her picturesque seat of Bedgebury in Kent he settled down like Lord Hill, to end his days a country gentleman. He survived his wife for several years, and died at Bedgebury at the age of eighty-five. Few hard fighting soldiers who have not, like Marlborough or Wellington, attained to the first rank in virtue of exceptional genius have ever done better for themselves. Like Wellington, he died a peer of England and Portugal; and like Wellington, he had a Spanish dukedom. He was covered with grand crosses of knighthood and other decorations.

Wellington paid him a great and suggestive, though somewhat dubious compliment, when he said that in the event of his death he would recommend Beresford for the succession—not because he was a great general, but because he alone could feed an army. Indeed, apart from Albuera, we are inclined to wonder at the confidence Wellington always reposed in him, when it was neither a question of commissariat nor of disciplining raw levies. The Duke knew well how to choose his instruments, and we can only assume that the fighting and hospitable Irishman has been somewhat unfairly treated in military narrative.

Lord Lynedoch

1

Napoleon abdicated empire at forty-five, the age when Thomas Graham of Balnagowan betook himself to soldiering. His is a solitary instance of a middle-aged gentleman of quiet habits, devoted to rural pursuits, voluntarily embarking on a military career and attaining the highest honours in the service. His was a romance which began when those in most lives are matters of memory. Descended from an ancient branch of the noble family of Graham, he was the third son of a gentleman who had large property in Perthshire. The deaths of his elder brothers left him heir to the estates. He had every advantage education could give. Privately educated, as was much the custom in Scotland in those days, his tutor was Macpherson who found or forged the poems of Ossian. He had gone up to Christ Church as a gentleman commoner when the death of his father placed him in possession of a large and unencumbered rent-roll.

The fortune afterwards served him well, when promotion was assured by lavish expenditure. During the three years before he attained his majority, his guardian was the Earl of Hopetoun; for if on the father's side he was descended from the "gallant Grahams," his maternal ancestors were no less famous in Scottish history. Consequently he was first cousin to Sir John Hope of Peninsular fame, afterwards the fourth Earl of Hopetoun. At Oxford the only honours he took were in the hunting field, and after two years at the university he went abroad. His was less a grand tour than times of residence: he spent several years in France, Germany, and Italy, and moving from place to place with the best introductions, made himself not only familiar with the languages, but formed valuable friendships.

Afterwards, in course of a tour in Spain, he added Spanish to the list of his accomplishments, and his rare qualifications as a linguist recommended him later for important and confidential posts. Most of Wellington's other lieutenants were, like their master, sent to study military science in France. Graham, the civilian, without a dream of his future destinies, was graduating in languages and the knowledge of men. With the firmness masked by the suavity of a high-bred gentleman, everywhere afterwards he found himself in *pays de connaissence*, whether as commissioner at the Austrian headquarters, or when acting with foreign auxiliaries.

Topography was his special study, or rather it came to him naturally. A fearless horseman, he lived much in the saddle, and whether when travelling on horseback abroad, or in the hunting field at home—for years his favourite residence was in the Shires, and he was hand in glove with the *habitués* of Melton—his was always the surest eye for a country.

Fashionable life abroad had done nothing to demoralise him. We hear no whisper of dissipation or indiscretions. His pious mother, Lady Christian, welcomed back a son unspoiled, and saw the most domesticated of men delighted to settle down on his patrimonial estates. The round of rural pursuits found him ample occupation. A keen sportsman like Lord Hill, like him he took special interest in his kennels. A connoisseur in horse-fleshy he had his string of weight-carrying hunters for the season. He was held in high consideration by his neighbours. The travelled youth of twenty-four was invited to stand for the premier county of Scotland, and was only beaten by six votes in a close constituency of 100 by the powerful interest of the Atholl family. The wanderer seemed decided to settle quietly at home, and all he wanted to anchor him was a wife.

In 1774 he married the second daughter of Lord Cathcart, on the same day that her elder sister was wedded to the Duke of Atholl, his friend and late political opponent. For the Duke was a high Tory, and Graham held advanced Liberal opinions, though, like Burke, he was converted by the excesses of the Revolutionists into enthusiastic approval of the war in which he was to win his laurels. No union could have been more fortunate, and he enjoyed seventeen years of unclouded happiness. Then the clouds suddenly blew up, and there was a brief period of terrible anxiety, with fluctuations of hope and fear. The confidential letters to his brother-in-law, the tenth Lord Cathcart, are singularly touching.

All that man could do was done, and money was lavished on the invalid. A physician of eminence was brought from London to attend

Lord Lynedoch

her on a yacht voyage in the Mediterranean. All was done in vain, and the death left him desolate. The bringing home of the body through France is another romance in itself, but it is worth noting, because the brutal behaviour of the revolutionary mobs and of the republican Jacks-in-office must have outraged the bereaved husband to the utmost. It was not in human nature to forget them, and they can hardly have been without their influence when he was seeking for a preoccupation to distract him from his grief.

The mental attitude of the strong man, stunned and half paralysed by the shock, is a curious subject of study. On the one hand, he indulged in grief to the verge of weakness; he fondled it like an emotional woman who finds comfort in her misery. On the other, he showed that supreme form of courage in which the spirit triumphs over the nerves. He faced the situation, though exaggerating its horrors, and resolved that it should not get the mastery over him. Quiet occupations at home would not suffice; he tried them and they failed. He had gone back to Brooksby, the pleasant house in the Midlands where he had passed many happy winters: "I soon found that it would be impossible to remain there alone."

But in 1793 there was excitement enough abroad in all conscience, and, probably already with ulterior ambitions, he resolved upon change of scene. His mother, who had hoped to keep him with her for the future, not only resigned herself, but wisely encouraged him. With his family connections, with his popularity in the fashionable world, with a wide circle of influential acquaintances, once his mind was made up he was sure to find help and hospitality everywhere, ashore or afloat. He was no obscure subaltern, proud of his pair of colours, but anxiously looking out for a patron and the means of purchase. Graham could give as much as he asked, and was on friendly or familiar terms with statesmen and diplomatists, generals and admirals.

Gibraltar seemed the most promising base of operations.

> I wrote to ask General O'Hara (the governor) to give me a passage in the *Resistance*. . . . This he readily agreed to, and appointed me to meet him at Plymouth.

Lord St. Helens, the ambassador to Madrid, sailed in the same ship, and war was declared by France while they were wind-bound in the Channel. He heard with great satisfaction that a fleet was to rendezvous at the Rock and proceed up the Mediterranean under command of Lord Hood. The leisurely voyage gave him time to think out his plans, and "I resolved to ask my friend Captain Elphinstone" (afterwards Lord Keith) "to receive me on board his ship, and so to take my chance of such adventures as might come in my way." Longing to assist at a naval action, but disappointed, he passed months on board the fleet blockading Toulon. Then the news came of the royal rising: the loyal citizens, led by French naval officers who had joined them—with few exceptions, these officers were aristocrats by birth and sympathies—had expelled the republican garrison and hoisted the white standard.

Graham was one of the first to land, and immediately had a flattering note from Lord Mulgrave, asking him to be one of his *aides-de-camp*. From the first, he went heart and soul into the work, welcoming an unhoped-for opportunity to learn the practice of war. Seldom has a raw *aide-de-camp* exercised such high influence, and in a few weeks the middle-aged volunteer was writing to Sir William Hamilton, our minister at Naples, urging him to hurry forward Neapolitan supports. The disembarkation was a daring venture, where the risks were great and the responsibilities greater. The defence was directed by divided counsels, and carried on with mixed forces of which the most were unreliable. The British and Piedmontese were the backbone of a mongrel garrison. The Republicans had only withdrawn to close in upon the fortress, and Graham was at once in the thick of the fighting.

For the first sortie in which he took part he could find no horse, and chartered a *cabriolet*. He tells with humour how a panic-stricken National Guard, galloping from the scene of action, shouted, "*Place! Place! Sacré Dieu! On ne fait pas la guerre en cabriolet*" The French engineers had left a long extent of unfinished works, which the allies with inadequate strength were compelled to occupy. A reconnoitring expedition in force gave Graham an opportunity for showing his qualities and the regard in which he was held. The military chiefs had pronounced a certain ridge impracticable to the besiegers. Graham proved the contrary by slipping behind, descending and scaling it again, in face of the staff. As he remarked, "I was more accustomed to mountains."

The result proved the wisdom of his warnings. Guarded as it was, the ridge was carried, and had to be retaken. When the combined movement was going forward, again he volunteered advice which was accepted, and there he showed that the courage which he never displayed unnecessarily was equal to his coolness and judgment. In a letter to his brother-in-law, he modestly narrates an exploit which would have won him the Victoria Cross. He says that, having waited an opportunity of distinguishing himself, he had felt bound as a volunteer to make himself conspicuous and place himself at the head of the column. The column under heavy fire had broken and sought shelter among the rocks, but some had scattered to the front, intercepting the fire of the others.

> I ran forward and brought them all back. A man received a shot which disabled him. I assisted him back into shelter and took his musket and cartridges. Soon after in the advance I was myself wounded in the right arm and dropped the musket; but, finding that the bone was not broken, I picked it up and carried it in my left hand, being fully aware that the advance under so heavy a fire required all the encouragement of good example.

In the advance he found leisure to philosophise, and learned that

> . . . . the interest created by such a scene totally absorbed all idea of personal danger, which was pretty well for a man with a mutilated arm. And that day's experiences decided his vocation.

He resolved to follow the advice of his friend Lord Mulgrave and become a soldier, taking an early opportunity of raising a regiment. So the English column not only won the disputed redoubt, but secured the services of the hero of Barossa. He was already in his forty-sixth year, and that fact might have discouraged most men, but he had weighed his chances deliberately.

> I am satisfied that by the experience of this day I might not unreasonably hope, even at an unusually advanced period of life for entering on a new profession, to be able to serve with credit and distinction, having ascertained that the natural turn for accurate observation of ground, fostered by a constant enjoyment of field sports, would give me advantages which many who had entered the service early could never possess.

Toulon was evacuated: Graham was in Leicestershire again, and Lord Winchilsea wrote a letter of congratulation, hoping to see him often out with his hounds. But the sportsman had entered as a soldier and hurried north to Scotland. He not only searched the Scottish counties for recruits, but the manufacturing towns in Northern England. Soon he had 800 men under the colours, and had secured his friend Rowland Hill as major of the corps. Various new levies were being made, and one had already been enrolled as the 89th Regiment. Graham was eager that his own corps should rank as the 90th. Lord

Adam Gordon, the commander in Scotland, had reviewed it at Perth, and the inspection was followed by a dinner. Graham begged Lord Adam for a few lines to Lord Amherst, then commanding in chief, expressing approval of his exertions. The lines were scribbled, Graham charged his major with entertaining the company, threw himself into his carriage, and "I went to London as fast as four horses could carry me." He was in time to have his regiment enrolled as the 90th.

To a man of his aspiring spirit and irrepressible energy, starting late in the race for fame, the delays interposed must have been aggravating and depressing. His regiment was ordered for the expedition in aid of the luckless Quiberon descent. The next year it made one of four under General Doyle, sent on a fruitless errand to an island off the Breton coast, to give aid and comfort to Charette and his *chasseurs*. Quartered at Portsmouth and elsewhere, he had civil distractions which interested him but little. Like others of Wellington's lieutenants, he had his seat in Parliament.

Once rejected for Perthshire, on a second attempt he had been successful, and from time to time he ran up to Westminster to sit out a debate or record a vote. What concerned him much more nearly was his military standing. When he got his regiment together, he had been given the temporary rank of colonel. In 1794 he had doubled his claims on the War Office by raising a second battalion, which, as he remarks, was a very serious business. His abiding desire was to have the temporary commission changed into substantive rank. Those were times when interest went far—and Graham's interest was strong—when there were short cuts to promotion, and steps were bartered freely for recruits.

Graham was over-confident; he seems to have believed that his exceptional efforts assured his exceptional claims. His staunch friend Lord Mulgrave had wisely warned him that he should stoop to begin as comet in the Blues, when he would be rapidly pushed up the ladder. He turned a deaf ear till too late, and then he bitterly repented. The most powerful interest was made with the Duke of York: Dundas declared that he had pushed his appeals to the point of a quarrel, but the Duke, though courteous, was firm, and refused to override the rule of the service. So Graham was doomed to nurse for years what in those days he considered an intolerable grievance.

He was ordered to Gibraltar, but, tiring of the monotony of garrison duty, he applied to join the Austrian armies as military *attaché*. At a time when England was financing Austria, an envoy so influentially connected as Graham was assured of something more than a friendly reception. After an interview with the Archduke Charles on the Rhine, he joined Beaulieu in Italy. He had gone to study the art of war, and he looked on at a succession of blunders which showed how war should not be conducted. More than once he was tempted to interpose and advise, but refrained when he recollected that he was there as "a volunteer."

In the passes leading down from the mountains to the lakes, the Austrian generals were entangling and committing themselves. The young Corsican artilleryman who had found the way to retake Toulon had restored discipline and confidence to a disorderly mob of tatterdemalions. At the head of the army of Italy, he was violating all the rules of war, and continually organising disaster for his enemies. Wurmser, who had superseded Beaulieu and Alvizi, made his crowning mistake when he shut himself up in Mantua in place of seeking safety in Styria. His was a gallant defence, but Arcola and Rivoli dissipated all hopes of relief. Graham had so far followed his fortunes, but fever was raging, horse-flesh was running short, and as the marshes, which were the best safeguard of the fortress, were freezing, capitulation was imminent, and Graham had no mind to see the inside of a French prison.

He planned and executed a most audacious scheme of escape which might furnish materials for a sensational novel. As originally arranged, the companion of his flight was to be his friend Radetzky, the future field-marshal, who was to carry letters from Wurmser to Vienna, but on second thoughts Wurmser thought the venture too desperate, and refused to risk an officer of his own. The stubborn Scot he could not control, though he went so far in the way of deterring him as to publish news of impending relief, which changed exultation in the garrison to despair when he had tacitly to plead guilty to the deception. The hardening of the marshes made Graham's attempt possible. He was attended by a faithful courier and guided by a lad of the locality. He wore his English uniform, like the daring Peninsular officer who brought Wellington accurate intelligence from districts occupied by the French.

But the lake and the river were lined by French pickets, and sentries were to be eluded. He was landed on the river bank from a boat in charge of an Austrian sergeant, and they repeatedly heard the French sentinels interchanging challenges. He lay hidden in peasant huts and in farm-houses; and it is remarkable that the Italians, whom the French came to liberate, seemed all in sympathy with the Austrians. Once he paused with only a wall between him and a picket, and looked over at the soldiers lying around the watch-fire, which reminds us of a similar scene in "Waverley." At last he was afloat on the Po, in a boat manned by Italians he had hired. Then an unforeseen difficulty presented itself, for they had to pass the chains and pontoons of a succession of flying bridges, all guarded by the enemy. But he carried pistols, and assured the rowers that if they surrendered to a challenge he should certainly shoot.

Finally he breathed freely when they set him ashore within the confines of the Venetian Republic, when he richly rewarded the boatmen and bought their boat, which would have led to their conviction and execution had they taken it back. He declares that he could scarcely have supported the exposure had not Wurmser given him some flasks of imperial Tokay. From dull duty in the Irish bogs he was sent to the Balearic Isles with Stewart to take Minorca from the Spaniards. The Spaniards, though nominally in alliance with France, were actually in sympathy with England. When the fortress of Ciudadella surrendered, 1000 Swiss were made prisoners. Captured by Buonaparte in Italy, they "had been sold to Spain at two dollars a head."

Graham recognised the tattered uniforms with which he had been familiar, and there were men in the ranks who claimed his acquaintance. He remarks drily in a letter to Lord Cathcart: " As I command here, I think it probable some of these honest fellows will find their way out of the gate this morning: at least I shall not bring any of the Highlanders on guard to trial if they let them pass."

With the local rank of brigadier he was transferred to the command of Messina. When there he lost the mother to whom he was deeply attached, and it is characteristic of the man that, with all his ambition and his enthusiasm for his new career, he had repeatedly entreated her to let him resign that he might attend her in her declining years. But Lady Christian had the spirit of a Spartan mother, and would not hear of the sacrifice. To the last she zealously forwarded his prospects and watched over his interests at home.

At that time, when communications were slow and precarious, commanders of outlying stations had a tolerably free hand. Pressure was brought on Graham from important quarters to assist in the siege of Malta as if he had been master of his own actions. On the contrary, he had peremptory orders from Erskine, commanding in the Mediterranean, not to move a man. But the capture of Malta was the darling object of Nelson, and from Messina there was frequent interchange of letters with the admiral and with Lady Hamilton. Lady Hamilton writes on 22nd December 1798 from the *Vanguard*:

> Five nights I have not been to bed, for I cannot get the dear, suffering queen to bed, all her children weeping about her. We are going to Palermo; God knows how we shall be received.

A strange scene: the mistress of one Hamilton, the wife of his uncle, the notorious *chère amie* of Nelson, consoling in the intimacy of a cabin the daughter of Maria Theresa and the sister of Marie Antoinette! Nelson's frequent letters were confidential and familiar. They were full of Malta. At last his influence prevailed, and Graham was ordered thither with a couple of regiments to direct the siege. But no money was forthcoming, and General Fox hesitated about furnishing it Nelson had the matter so much at heart, that he offered to mortgage Bronté, or even if necessary to sell it.

Graham landed on the island to find operations slowly dragging on. Even with the reinforcements he brought, the besiegers were inferior in numbers to the besieged. With the long, thin chain of encircling posts, there was perpetual danger from sorties in force, for Vaubois was not content to confine himself to passive defence. Fortunately, as Graham wrote, each field and garden was an entrenchment, and mounting fresh batteries, with his soldiers and marines he pressed the siege with vigour. The Maltese detested the French, and again he raised a regiment—the Maltese Fencibles. The garrison was straitened for provisions, though an occasional vessel ran the blockade. But scarcity told upon both sides, for the swarming population was on short commons, now that their seaport was blockaded.

Graham waged war by "barbarous methods." When Vaubois thrust out the Maltese who had remained in the town, Graham compelled him to take them back again. He said that war was war, and as these Maltese had chosen to cast in their lot with the French, they must abide by their decision. The consequence was that the town was starved out, and the garrison compelled to treat for capitulation. But at the eleventh hour, Graham was superseded by Abercromby, and General Pigot, who had come as Sir Ralph's second in command, had the honour of receiving the keys of the historical fortress. It is but fair to say that Pigot did full justice to Graham.

He had heard with fatherly pride of the laurels his own regiment had been gaining under Hill in Egypt He sailed for Alexandria to join it, but when he landed, it was to hear of the French capitulation. He travelled through Turkey, returning by the Balkans, to learn to his disgust that the disbanding of his 90th was in contemplation. The Ministers, willingly optimistic, preferred to believe in the reality of a peace. Happily they procrastinated over the policy of redaction, till the First Consul was again showing his hand. Graham was again for some time quartered in Ireland, acting on the staff of his brother-in-law, Lord Cathcart.

But our fleets had been shutting up the French in their harbours; the fears of a descent upon Ireland passed away, and the 90th was sent to the West Indies. Graham was set on accompanying it, but was dissuaded by his friends. They pointed out that he had already done more than enough to enforce his claims to substantive rank; and reluctantly he resigned himself to expectation in inaction. He bowed his pride to repeated appeals to the Duke of York, always rejected with the same courteous firmness. When Lord Cathcart went on a special mission to Vienna, he urged his brother-in-law to accompany him as Secretary to the mission. Graham declined; he had chosen his career, and was not to be diverted into diplomacy.

On the contrary, when Sir John Moore, in the spring of 1808, was charged with the mad expedition to assist the mad King of Sweden, he applied for the post of *aide-de-camp* and readily obtained it. That expedition, ill-conceived and ill-timed, was in its way as hopeless a fiasco as Walcheren, though through no fault of the commander, but it had opened to Graham a door which led to the Peninsula and the highest honours. Moore on his return was ordered to Portugal as third in command. He obeyed, protesting against "this unworthy treatment," and Graham again accompanied him. Graham then began the habit of keeping brief diaries, recording all the events which concerned him during his service in the Peninsula.

With Moore he had missed Roliça and Vimiero, but he was with the troops at the march on Lisbon, and concerned with the evacuation of the French fortresses. Thence he was sent into Spain to communicate with the Spanish generals, and was in constant and most confidential correspondence with Lord William Bentinck and Moore; for on the nth October, in a private note from Lisbon, Moore had written:

My dear Graham, . . . They have given me, *bon gré mal gré,* the greatest command that any English general has had this century. I hope I may be able to acquit myself as becomes me. . . . My object is to get on the Portuguese frontier before the rains, and I shall do it, and I hope to show you a good army.

Graham had been with Castaños and Palafox in Arragon. He joined Moore's army in the advance to Sahagun, after sundry perilous adventures and some hair-breadth escapes. At one town he had been stoned as a foreigner; at another he had cut his way, sword in hand, through an infuriated mob. Madrid was in a tumult, and there he was arrested as a Frenchman and taken before Sir Charles Stuart. At Sahagun the retreat was decided on. Blake had been beaten at Espinosa and Gamonal, Castaños and Palafox at Tudela, and the wrecks of the army of Arragon were retiring on La Mancha under Lapeña, with whom he was to be subsequently associated to his sorrow. Graham understood that Moore's retreat was inevitable, but entered in his diary;

> There is not a man in the whole army who will not feel mortified and disappointed.

The honorary *aide-de-camp* and volunteer was but a spectator of the march to Corunna. He had none of the opportunities of winning distinction which fell to Craufurd and Paget, though the demoralisation, the disorders, and the individual feats of gallantry were all briefly recorded in the diary; but in the dramatic climax of the general's death scene he was a foremost figure. "I was sent," he writes, "on business messages, and on my return I always found him" (Moore) "in the hottest fire."

> The general remained stationary at the cross-roads. The enemy, whose artillery all day had been directed with much precision against groups of mounted officers, continued firing at this spot, when at last a fatal ball took the general under the left arm. He fell at my horse's feet, but such was the invincible firmness of his mind, such the consciousness of his rectitude, that he bore this pain without an altered feature. I scarcely thought him wounded till I saw the state of his arm.... At night we removed his body to my quarters in the citadel; there it remained till morning, and fatigue had so far overcome me, that I slept for some hours near the corpse of my friend, as if I had been insensible of the blow.

He was interred without a coffin. The funeral was in the grey light of the winter morning, and "*the lanterns dimly burning*" was a poetic exaggeration. The only officers present were Anderson, Colborne, and Stanhope. Graham, to his regret, was absent, being with Napier on duty with General Hope's staff.

2

The fallen hero had been Graham's fast friend, and he left him as a priceless legacy the position so long coveted and so obdurately refused. The death of Moore was the making of Graham. When assured that the victory was won, Moore calmly prepared for his end, and the most pressing consideration was the future of his most distinguished followers. With his dying breath he charged his *aide-de-camp*, Colonel Anderson, with messages to the king, in favour of Colonel Graham among others. The appeal was not to be resisted, and soon after his arrival in England he had formal intimation from the Duke of York, that in consideration of his services his Majesty had directed that the established rule of the army would be departed from, and that he was to be promoted to the rank of major-general, with the position he would have held had the lieutenant-colonelcy of 1794 been a permanent commission.

Few men were more personally beloved than Frederick of York, and it is clear that throughout he had acted on principle. He bore Graham no ill-will for a persistence that must have seemed like persecution, and subsequently when he was appointed to command at Cadiz, the Duke expressed himself in cordial terms, regretting that he had missed an opportunity of making the general's acquaintance.

Graham went to Walcheren and came back sound in health but thoroughly disgusted. In February 1810, he was sent to Cadiz to command the British garrison. There was some question whether he was independent or under the orders of Wellington; it signified little, for they worked in perfect amity. Wellington recognised his worth from the first; he left everything to Graham's discretion, and made his suggestions subject to the other's superior local knowledge. At Cadiz he had to face the usual difficulties arising from Spanish divisions, dilatoriness, and vainglory. Perhaps, in his desire for harmony, he carried complaisance to an extreme.

On one occasion when Blake was proposing an attack upon Victor's lines which he disapproved, he went so far as to "place himself at his orders." It was a similar feeling which subsequently led him to resign the command to Lapeña, and nearly resulted in a catastrophe at Barossa. But of Blake, at that time, he had no mean opinion; he believed both in his honesty and his talents, though Blake's Asturian campaign should have disabused him on the latter point. Objecting to any sortie from the city as imprudent, it was he who suggested the propriety of a demonstration from Gibraltar against the French marshal's camp at Chiclana. Wellington, with his comprehensive grasp of the campaign in all its aspects, hesitated. He pointed out that if the siege of Cadiz were raised, Victor would join Regnier by the passes of the Morena and press on the British right in Portugal. Graham urged that not only would the garrison of Cadiz be set free, but that the demonstration would rouse the mountaineers of the Sierras, and that in Spain, with the slightest success, such a rising must certainly spread.

Be that as it may, Wellington, as well as Ministers at home, at that time gave him an extraordinary proof of the estimation in which he was held. Wellington wrote on the 3rd May 1810 that he had intended and hoped that Graham should succeed Sherbrooke in command of a division. "But," he added, " however desirable it might be to me that you should be in Portugal, I cannot but think it would be most advantageous to the public interests that you should remain at Cadiz as long as that place is seriously threatened by the enemy."

Still more noteworthy were passages in a letter of next month, from Lord Liverpool to Wellington.

> As to the question of second in command in Portugal, it has been most seriously considered by the Cabinet. Graham was intended for that service, but we were all of opinion that the service at Cadiz was of such a critical nature that it could not be entrusted to any person so well as to him.... He is certainly to be considered as second in command in the Peninsula. If anything should happen to you, he should succeed to the command of the army.

Strange indeed! that the veteran of sixty-two who had found a new vocation in middle-life; the young soldier of sixteen years' service, who had held no higher rank in the field than local brigadier, should have been selected from all Wellington's lieutenants to replace the leader, if it were his fate to fall.

When Soult marched from Seville to the relief of beleaguered Badajoz, the chief objection to an assault on the entrenched camp at Chiclana from Algeciras was removed. A comparatively small force under Lacy had been already partially successful in calling the mountaineers of the sierras to arms. Graham had still set his face against any frontal attack from the Isle of Cadiz, but now he consented to take part in a more formidable operation, elaborately planned. On the 21st of February, 10,000 foot and 600 horse were embarked. Then he made that initial mistake in disobeying the instructions which forbade him to act under a Spanish general. As he was in no way subject to Spanish authority, his expressions in a letter to Lord Liverpool sound strange:

> 'I did not hesitate to determine to go, as otherwise it might have been considered as a peevish objection arising *from, the command having been withdrawn from me.*

The italics are mine. It is stranger still, that he should have consented to take the second place, knowing, as he must have known, the notorious incompetency of Lapeña, a creature of the Duchess of Orsuna, and as weak of head as of heart. But if he erred, his error was amply redeemed by his subsequent conduct and heroism. From the first he was crossed, almost ostentatiously, and his counsels were ignored or overruled. Victor looked out upon the Mediterranean from the heights of Chiclana, and could see all that went on. Gales and head winds delayed the convoy, and Graham urged the British admiral to persuade Lapeña to put back. Lapeña refused, and fortune favoured the disembarkation, which was quickly effected.

Then the promised rations were not forthcoming, nor the carts which were to transport the ammunition. Nevertheless the march began; Graham had stipulated that it was to be done by easy stages, that the troops might meet the enemy fresh and confident, for now it was no question of a surprise. Lapeña promised and broke his promises. It was really a piece of good fortune that at the beginning the advance was retarded by impracticable roads. The guides misled the column, and it counter-marched to where a flooded causeway crossed a rapid river. "I set the example of going into the water, which was followed by Lacy, Prince Aglona, and others."

À*propos* of that, Larpent wrote in the spring of 1813, when Graham with "all the *grandees*" was at a grand review:

> I fear General Graham is too old for this work; at least he must not act as he did at Barossa. Before the battle, I am told, he stood up to his middle in water for an hour and more, encouraging the troops to get on, English and Spanish; jumped off his horse, on purpose for the example. It is added, some of the men said: 'Come, old corporal, do go and take care of yourself, and get out of our way.' It is characteristic of the cool yet romantic Scot, that in such anxious circumstances, he pauses in the brief diary to dilate on the picturesque situation of Vejer.

After the river passage, and contrary to his express pledges, Lapeña pressed forward through the night. Again the guides went wrong; the English column followed the Spaniards, and Graham galloping to the front found the Spanish staff in abject confusion. "I could not help exclaiming rather improperly: '*Voila ce que c'est que le marches de nuit.*'" With the dawn their leading cavalry were on the heights of Barossa.

Barossa, more commonly called by the Spaniards the Cerro de Puerco—the Hog's Back—is a ridge with the Atlantic cliffs to the south, and the forest of Chiclana on the north. It looks down on the Almanza Creek, and beyond are the Santi Petri River and the Isla de Leon. Immediately beneath is a lesser eminence, the Torre de Bermeja. The battle began with what Graham describes to Lord Liverpool as a well-directed attack by the Spanish vanguard, which repulsed the French outposts on the Almanza and opened communications with the Isla. Then as he sat on the Barossa ridge, "I received General Lapeña's directions to move down on the Torre de Bermeja."

Hitherto Victor had been silent, unseen, and watchful. Graham moved downwards, and when marching through the forest received news that the French were out in force upon the plain and advancing towards the heights of Barossa. He had never doubted that Lapeña with his main body was occupying that position, but as he knew it to command the situation, he countermarched to his support. So rapid was his movement that his rear ranks took the lead, and the whole force, hurrying and stumbling over the tree-roots, got mixed in inextricable confusion. Emerging from the wood, he saw to his consternation that two broken Spanish regiments were rushing down the steep, on one side, while Victor's left was rapidly ascending on the other. Lapeña had left baggage train and commissariat mules, crowded together on the key of the position, to the charge of a slender escort.

Not a moment was to be lost if the day was to be saved. The French left was before them; the French right within gunshot of the leading British stragglers. The word was forward and upward, and there was no time to close up. Guards, linesmen, and Portuguese rushed forward promiscuously in loose formation; but Duncan's battery of ten guns unlimbering, belched out a steady fire from a solid centre, which tore furrows through the serried files of the enemy. To right and left the British onset was irresistible; again and again the French rallied and returned, only to be again and again hurled back. The gallant Ruffin and Rousseau went down; eagles and guns were taken; the whole business was over in an hour and a half, and a bloody business it was.

Well might Graham write:

> No expressions of mine could do justice to the conduct of the troops throughout. Nothing less than the almost unparalleled exertions of every officer, the invincible bravery of every soldier could have achieved such a brilliant success against such a formidable enemy so posted.

Marvellous it was, when it is remembered that Graham's soldiers were leg weary, starving, and sleepless, as it is admitted that the French never fought more valiantly. When they were falling back on Chiclana in slow and sullen retreat, Lapeña was content to look on from behind his unbroken battalions; 800 Spanish horse, and they were led by an Englishman, never unsheathed a sabre to change the retreat into a rout. Graham remained with his wounded on the blood-soaked hill he had won so dearly, and held so well. Lapeña refused him food and even help to bury his dead.

His official despatch to Lord Liverpool is a model of correct reticence as to Spanish misdeeds and shortcomings. The Hon. Henry Wellesley, our envoy at Cadiz, urged him in a private note to speak out, and then he did tell the truth in confidential despatches. The result was a special order from the king himself, through the commander-in-chief, never to act again in any circumstances under a Spaniard; although a private note accompanying it still left him wide discretion.

Barossa covered Graham with glory, and honours were heaped upon him in profusion. What he valued most was the approval of Wellington. His lordship made no allusion to his neglect of instructions in subjecting himself to the orders of an imbecile. He said that his gallantly had saved the allied armies, as it would have raised the siege of Cadiz had Lapeña played his part. Lapeña shamelessly claimed the honours of the day, charging Graham with saving the French from a catastrophe by withdrawing prematurely into the Isla. The simple answer was that the soldiers were starving; that no help had been sent to his wounded, and that he had decided never again to risk his brave fellows with such an ally.

Even Lacy, whom he had regarded as a friend, set his name to most mendacious statements, but he was ignominiously compelled to eat his words when the fiery veteran demanded explanation or satisfaction. Truly might Napier remark of him, when the expedition was starting from Algeciras, that it was under a daring old soldier and a hard fighter. The calumnies were scarcely accepted, even by credulous

Spaniards, and the Regency had the grace to offer him a grandeeship as Duke of Cerro de Puerco, but Graham courteously declined to take rank as Duke of the Pig's Hill.

Congratulations flowed in upon him from home—from friends and acquaintances, peers and commoners. None were more cordial than those from the Premier, and from Lord Mulgrave, who may be said to have discovered him, and had given him his fortunate start at Toulon. That circumstance was eloquently alluded to in the glowing eulogy pronounced by Sheridan, when the Commons voted him the thanks of the House.

> Lord Mulgrave found an English gentleman of the name of Graham, who though not a military man led on the British forces through the heights and labyrinths surrounding the' fortress to success and victory.

For he received the thanks of both Houses, transmitted from the Commons by Mr. Abbott, the Speaker, and from the Lords by the Chancellor, Lord Eldon. Both Speaker and Chancellor added their warm personal appreciation of his great services. The city of London was equally enthusiastic. So far as we know, the only discordant note was struck by Southey in one of his letters. Graham in acknowledging those flattering tributes, often couched in the most high-flown language, modestly ascribed anything he had done to the valour and discipline of his soldiers. Possibly, the most gratifying of all was a despatch from the postmaster of Perth. Mr. Sidey wrote that when they heard of the sailing of the expedition for Algeciras, the general's constituents and tenants immediately prepared to celebrate the assured victory.

"The happy tidings" arrived, Mr. Sandeman of Luncarty rode up at the moment, and immediately gave the postmaster his mare to carry the news to Balnagowan. Forthwith bonfires were blazing on the hills, and that night there was "plenty of whisky and porter for a more numerous company than you had soldiers to fight the battle with." The festivities wound up with tossing the whisky casks into the fire with the hogsheads that had been emptied of porter. "General," the letter goes on, "I never lost sight of your orders, and only wish you may get the sheep and salmon safe, to entertain the Cortes and *grandees* of Spain."

Summoned by Wellington to join his army, Graham left Cadiz in the midsummer of 1811. At Lisbon he visited the *quinta* which he had occupied with Moore only three years before as an extra *aide-de-*

camp and volunteer. What strides he had made in three eventful years! Now the volunteer was promoted lieutenant-general, and by seniority ranked second in the Peninsula to Wellington himself. Wellington had written that he need not hurry, as nothing of moment was in immediate prospect, and he dined with his chief at headquarters on the 8th August.

Yet soon afterwards the allied army narrowly escaped crushing disaster. Marmont had come down with 60,000 men to throw convoys into Ciudad Rodrigo. Wellington, on his side, still threatened Ciudad, and was determined to maintain the blockade of Almeida. His line was weak, and as Graham at once observed, perilously extended. El Bodon was fought and saved by the gallantry of the soldiers, but for a day and a half Marmont had Wellington at his mercy, had he grasped the situation. Wellington saved himself by showing a confident front, and the marshal missed such an opportunity as he was never to have again.

Through early winter the warfare languished; on the 19th January Rodrigo was stormed. Six days before Graham, by surprising a French detachment in the Convent of Santa Cruz, which had been converted into a bastion of the fortress, secured the right flank of the trenches which were being pushed forward to the walls. Wellington reported that he had been greatly indebted to Graham for his assistance, and he was rewarded with the K.C.B. He was invested with the insignia at Elvas, for now we find him in command of a *corps d'armée*, first covering the siege operations at Badajoz, and then guarding Hill from the French armies in Andalusia, when he rushed the bridge and works at Almaraz.

In June his corps was one of the three columns which crossed the Agueda on the advance to Salamanca. Covetous of honour as the veteran was, it was a bitter disappointment that he missed the great battle. But the long strain had told; his failing eyesight indicated a breaking of his health, and he was invalided. Though Wellington missed him much, he wrote to the Ministry that he never again desired to have a second in command. He set forth various strong reasons on public grounds, but his letters to Graham, expressing extreme anxiety for his return, show that those reasons had no personal application.

3

The furlough was a short one; his health was restored, and he had rejoined early in 1813, in time to take a lead in the crowning operations which drove the usurper beyond the Pyrenees. His health was restored, but he could not renew his youth. Larpent wrote on the 8th May:

> I dined at headquarters to meet General Graham. He is a very fine old man, but does not look quite fit for this country work.
> ... It is quite a pity to see such a fine old man exposed as he must and will be.

Indeed the task to be imposed upon him was as trying as it was responsible. In a letter sent to await his landing at Lisbon, Wellington had written;

> I hope we shall be able to make a good campaign of it. I propose to take the field as early as I can, and at least to put myself in Fortune's way.

All his plans had been laid on a perfect system; but success depended on the nicety with which the complex combinations were carried out. He had misled the enemy by feinting on Toledo, but the storm was to burst on the Tormes and the Esla. Graham was in command of the left wing—the bulk of the allied army. To him was assigned the duty of leading 40,000 men, with guns, munitions, and heavy commissariat transport, through the ominously named Tras-os-Montes.

His goal was fixed on the Esla, with the day on which he should reach it. Some of his troops had to march a distance of 250 miles. For a week it was his fate to contend with physical difficulties so great, that the French had left that route unguarded and even unwatched. Sterile and rugged hills alternated with romantic valleys, which Kincaid of the Rifles describes with alternate horror and enthusiasm. The hills were seamed with profound chasms, through which streams in spate foamed down to the Douro. Defiles were threaded which could have been made good by a handful of men; the guns were lowered by ropes and pulleys over precipices, or let down into flooded watercourses where a squadron could have barred the fords.

Graham was to have passed the Esla on the 29th; in spite of floods and unforeseen obstacles he was scarcely belated. Nor was the slight delay of much moment. Joseph was mystified as to the allied movements, and altogether unsuspicious of Graham's line of march. As often elsewhere, the strength of a country had proved the ruin instead of the security of its defenders. Not till he was ready to burst down on the basin of Vittoria did Graham's scouting squadrons feel the feeble outposts of the French.

On the day of Vittoria Joseph had reformed his order of battle, and the French were ranged in three lines behind the Zadora. To the west of the great basin the river flows directly south, and to the west of the town Graham, advancing on the high-road from Bilboa, found himself confronted by adversaries worthy of him. Reille and Maucune held the bridges of Gamara, Mayor, and Ariaga, and on their constancy depended the security of the French communications with France. If Graham could force the bridges, their flank and rear were turned. Twenty thousand men with eighteen cannons were told off for the attack.

Hill had forced the Pass of Puebla and stormed the heights; all the bridges elsewhere on the river had been taken; the resolute defence had elsewhere collapsed, and pursuers and pursued in inextricable confusion were hurrying along the plain to the city. But with panic and hopeless disorder behind him, at six Reille was still making good his defence. It was only when the French right had made its last stand and failed, when the tremendous fire of their concentrated batteries had slackened, and Joseph had issued orders for the retreat on Pampeluna, that Reille gave thought to the safety of his own men. His position had become dangerous in the extreme, for the roads to Durango and Bayonne were lost; the battle was drifting into Vittoria, and the allied light cavalry riding out of the streets, were hovering around his rear. Napier says that, assailed on all sides, he nevertheless covered the retreat in some degree of order. Graham's despatch gives a somewhat different impression.

> Being in possession of Vittoria, the enemy fled from every point, and so rapidly that it was impossible for any of the troops of the left column to come up with them, having all to file over narrow bridges.

Graham pressed the pursuit to Tolosa. Joseph's flying hosts, abandoning guns, stores, and booty, and refused admission into Pampeluna, saved themselves at last beyond the Bidassoa. With one insignificant exception, the French only kept their hold on north-western Spain by the strong places of Pampeluna and San Sebastian. Pampeluna was the Jerusalem of the hill country of Navarre; San Sebastian was the Gibraltar of the north-western seaboard. The immediate reduction of the latter place was decided upon; Graham returning from Tolosa, was given the 5th Division and charged with the duty. The task was formidable enough from the natural strength of the fortress. Approached by a narrow isthmus, guarded on one side by the harbour, on the other by the tidal Urumea, a heavily armed citadel crowning Mount Orgallo towered above the houses of the town.

The commandant was the gallant veteran. General Rey; the sea blockade was inefficient, and before the beginning of the siege he had nearly 4000 men with sufficient guns to man his works, and ample ammunition. Whereas Wellington, as at Badajoz and Burgos, was only supplied with scratch batteries. His reiterated appeals to England had been ignored, and Graham made shift with supplementary iron guns from the fleet, mounted on wooden carriages which collapsed at the first cannonade. On the main front the town was crossed by three lines of defence. Graham had the advice of two engineers of genius—of Smith who had defended Tarifa, and of Fletcher, the Vauban of the allied armies. Unfortunately he did not follow their counsels. Prompt and determined in action, he seems to have been flexible in council, lending a willing ear to the specious proposals of those who were around him at the moment.

Napier, in a somewhat unintelligible passage, says that "Sir Thomas Graham, one of England's best soldiers, appears to have been endowed with a genius for war, intuitive rather than reflective," and adds that his modesty and easiness of temper caused him at times to abandon his own correct conceptions for less judicious counsels. It is certain that in the first attack he departed from the plan devised by Smith and approved by Wellington; that, moreover, he ran counter to Wellington's orders, by attacking at night instead of by day. On the 19th July, after some sharp fighting, the important suburb of San Bartomoleo was won.

In arranging for that assault as for the subsequent one. Smith was again overruled as to details. Graham insisted on beginning by breaching; Smith would have had the flanking works shattered beforehand. That second attack which ended in sanguinary repulse, was but a rehearsal of the successful storm in August, with none of the favours of fortune which attended the latter. Wellington's instructions were that it should be brought off "in fair daylight"; it was undertaken in the darkness, over slippery shingle, between the flooded estuary and the unbattered defences. It had been delayed besides for the opening of a minor breach, and as Smith had foretold, that breach was useless. The slaughter was great, the discouragement greater, and the loss of five of the few engineer officers was irreparable.

Wellington would have immediately renewed the attack, but the ammunition had given out, and he had to wait on the caprices of the War Office, the winds and the waves. Accordingly he removed his heavy guns and went to fight the battles of the Pyrenees. The siege was turned into a blockade, and we can conceive the chagrin and impatience of Graham when, smarting from a failure mainly his own fault, he had to sit down and possess his soul in patience. All the time he was looking on helplessly while Rey was repairing damages and adding to the strength of his works; and all the time, thanks to the negligence of the British cruisers, French ships with supplies and ammunition were continually running the blockade. Wellington shared his feelings to the full, and wrote with unwonted passion:

> Since Great Britain had been a naval Power a British Army had never before been left in such a situation at such an important moment.

The battles of the Pyrenees had been won, the heavy guns were brought back, other batteries from England had been landed, and on the 5th August the siege recommenced. By the way, the first use made of the breaching batteries was to fire a salute of twenty-four guns in honour of these battles. The garrison, fall of bravado, or as Larpent puts it, "very impudent," retorted with a discharge of double the number—rather a happy stroke of military repartee. Nor was their confidence altogether misplaced, as for fifty-two days Rey had been toiling indefatigably and doing everything that engineering skill could suggest.

A sustained and tremendous bombardment was the preliminary of the impending storm. Batteries were pushed forward on the isthmus; batteries were erected on the Chofré sandhills to the east of the Urumea, which kept up a continuous fire on the weakest face of the fortress. One of these was mounted in a cemetery where coffins and rotting corpses were built into the parapet. But still Graham, listening to his generals in preference to his engineers, persisted in the system of breaching without wrecking the flanking works. The stormers of the 31st were hurled into elaborately prepared death-traps, from which nothing but Providence or Fortune could have snatched the victory.

Wellington had realised the difficulties, and had done his utmost to surmount them by raising emulation to an acme. Believing that the ardour of the 5th Division had been damped by repulse, he appealed for volunteers to each of fifteen regiments in the lines of the Bidassoa. The appeal was injurious and almost insulting, for he asked for "men who could show other men how to mount a breach." It was eagerly answered, and 750 fiery soldiers marched from Behobia into the trenches at San Sebastian. Naturally, it was bitterly resented by the chivalrous Leith, who had just resumed command of the 5th Division, and who relegated the new arrivals to trench duty, and, as naturally, the slur was keenly felt by every soldier in the 5th, and the excitement rose to fever-heat.

The drama was played out on the exact lines of the rehearsal, but this time the trenches on the isthmus were nearer to the eastern front. Again the stormers stumbled in the darkness between the river and the walls, over rocks shivered into splinters by showers of shot and shell They scrambled up the debris of the main breach to find themselves crowded before the crest of the curtain, and those who struggled up to it found themselves confronted by a sheer drop of twenty feet into the town, and enfiladed by a galling fire from the loopholed houses. From either flank came grape and canister, and between the roar of the guns and cannonades was the incessant rattle of musketry. Supports kept pressing forward, till reserves were exhausted, and only one or two companies were left in the trenches. The 750 from the Bidassoa were no longer to be restrained; they slipped their leashes and tore forward to the front to claim their share in the carnage.

Graham had crossed the river and had been looking on as a spectator from the Chofré batteries. His mind had been made up to see the matter through, yet his stern determination must have been sorely tried, and failure seemed inevitable with the annihilation of his forces. On the opposite bank, his men were ever hurrying forward to death, but the enemy's cannon-fire had never been quelled and the discharges of musketry had never slackened. Then he had one of those inspirations which come of the intuition of genius. He ordered all the Chofré batteries to open on the opposing curtain, though the shot passed within a few feet of the heads of his stormers and occasionally touched their ranks. He knew his men, or he would never have given the order.

Few but British gunners could have been trusted to shoot straight and low over their comrades' heads. His veterans quailed and shrank when they first heard the storm of shot from behind, but soon they understood, and responding with a cheer, rushed wildly forward. A regiment of Portuguese, permitted rather than ordered to try the venture, forded the river waist-deep and pressed forward to the lesser breach. Now the curtain was swept by the British shot, and the French musketry fire sensibly weakened. Yet even then the attack would probably have been repelled, had it not been for two providential incidents. The tower dominating the main breach had been mined with great store of powder, but a shot had cut the sausage and so the mine was never exploded. More important still, and at the critical moment, a pile of powder and combustibles blew up, filling the air with fragments of corpses and spreading destruction on all sides. Before the panic had subsided or the smoke cleared away, the stormers had burst through the traverses and swept the defenders from the summit of the wall.

The fighting raged forward through the town, Rey obstinately disputing each street and lane till forced back into the citadel. The shouts of the combatants were drowned in a tremendous storm from the mountains which burst over the fated city. Powder casks were fired by the flashes of lightning; houses were fired by the infuriated soldiers, who had broken loose from all restraint. Hell seemed to have broken loose simultaneously above and below. Officers who sought to interpose were shot down, and the excesses of Rodrigo and Badajoz were surpassed. The general could do as little to control them as Canute when seated before the advancing tide. Had he had his troops in hand, he might have rushed the Orgallo, but Rey held the citadel to the 9th September, when he hung out the white flag.

2500 men of the allies had been killed or wounded during the sieges. Standing behind the Chofré trenches with set lips, Graham had sworn that he would send his last soldier forward, rather than fail again. The fall of the fortress was indispensable, and the necessary sacrifices must be consummated. Nor was censure mixed with Wellington's commendations—success had condoned any mistakes that had been made, and as after the failure at Bergen-op-Zoom, the Prince Regent wrote that though the losses were to be deplored, he offered his warm congratulations to the commander. But as after Barossa, Graham was again the victim of mendacity and calumny. He was actually accused by Spaniards in office of having encouraged the excesses and burned the town, because the citizens had French sympathies and a flourishing trade with France. He despised these slanders, yet they stung him deeply.

Soult had fought a battle for the relief of the fortress and failed. Then for weeks he and Wellington were watching each other on opposing lines from the passes before St. Jean Pied de Port to the *embouchure* of the Bidassoa. Moral and political motives overrode strategical considerations and impelled the British general to a descent on France. His advance had been projected for the middle of September, but the rains flooding the rivers compelled him to defer it. The passes might be forced and the Great Rhune stormed by the gallantry of the soldiers; but all depended on the successful passage of the lower river, and that passage was at the mercy of tides and currents. Soult, confident as on the Douro, never dreamed of danger below the broken bridge of Behobia, but Spanish fishermen, under pretence of their fishing, had been plumbing forgotten fords, and patriotically kept the invaluable secrets they might have sold at a great price.

For the 7th October all was in readiness; the river had gone down, and the tides were favourable. Soult had still no suspicion, and was with d'Erlon in his camp at Espalette. On the night of the 6th, one of the terrific Guipuzcoa storms rolled down from the Pyrenees and burst with concentrated violence on the French side of the river. Drenched by the rain and deafened by the thunder peals, the French pickets heard nothing of heavy guns being dragged up to the ridge of San Marcial. When the morning broke, from a veil of vapour and the embankments and sandhills behind which they had been concealed seven columns were emerging simultaneously. Four were directed upon the upper fords, three upon the fords in the tidal estuary.

Led by Graham, the 1st and 5th Divisions, with some unattached brigades, were rapidly crossing the sands to plunge into the water. Reille was with the divisions on the opposite bank, holding double parallels traversing the sandhills, and Maucune was in command of the advanced line. Both were wary and experienced soldiers, yet they were so little prepared for the surprise that Maucune's guns only opened when the allies were well through the river. That was the signal for sustained salvos from the allied artillery on the crest of San Marcial. Soult was passing d'Erlon's men in review, when the dying echoes of the thunder were succeeded by the roar of the guns. Making one mistake as to the direction, he had galloped to the sound, to come up too, late.

Maucune had retreated upon Reille, and Reille was being forced backward. Confiding in the impracticable estuary in front, the French advanced works had been scarcely completed, and the key of the entrenched position was at the Croiz des Bosquets behind. Thither men and guns were hurried up from all sides, and there the battle was fought out fiercely. But the determination of the allies was not to be denied, and Reille was driven in upon St. Jean de Luz. Graham had known well, if his soldiers did not, that the alternatives were victory or death or surrender. For the return of the tide was cutting the retreat, and Soult could have concentrated on his left with overwhelming strength in both men and artillery.

4

Even while the Siege of San Sebastian was going on, Graham had intimated his intention of retiring. He had been persuaded to remain for a little longer, and had added to his glories. But both eyes and health had failed again; and now handing over his division to his cousin, Sir John Hope, he bade, as he believed, a final farewell to the army. He returned home to receive again the thanks of the Lords, and to be elected Lord Rector of Glasgow University. But he had hardly enjoyed a few months of repose when he was surprised by a letter from the War Minister. The flood of invasion had poured into France and Flanders. When Napoleon was fencing in masterly fashion with the overpowering forces of the allies, the Netherlands had taken heart of grace and shaken off the foreign yoke.

Lord Bathurst urged Graham to take command of a scratch corps of some 6000 men to co-operate with the Prussians and Russians, who were advancing on Antwerp and on the other Dutch and Flemish fortresses which were still in the hands of the French. Graham reluctantly yielded to a strong appeal to his patriotism and soldierly spirit. What the veteran had dreaded most was that he might be suspected of malingering when he resigned his command in Wellington's army. He landed with his 6000 on the Isle of Tholen, and immediately put himself in communication with General Bulow. They began the bombardment of Antwerp, and probably it would have surrendered, had not Carnot, "the organiser of victory," thrown himself into the place.

The old republican, always a bitter opponent of Napoleon, had come to the aid of *la patrie* in the hour of its despair, and Napoleon, to his honour, had given him a free hand. Bulow raised the siege, and Graham withdrew to cantonments between Antwerp and Bergen-op-Zoom. Bulow and the Russian general seem to have been absolutely their own masters; and both were anxious to rejoin their comrades for the triumphal entry into Paris. Graham was to be left to fight single-handed, or with the doubtful assistance of raw Dutch levies, for the Prince of Orange was in his camp. Nor was that all, for there came a letter from Lord Bathurst, intimating that it was in contemplation to break up his force, sending the Guards to Wellington and some of the regiments to America.

That seems to have decided him on one of the most audacious *coups* ever attempted in modern war. Bergen-op-Zoom, the frontier fortress of Holland on the side of the Netherlands, was practically one of the strongest places in Europe. The masterwork of Cohorn, little to look at by the unpractised eye, its immense strength lay in the levels surrounding it. Labyrinths of scarps and counterscarps, ravelins, bastions, and horn-works had been scientifically devised so as to command and enfilade one another; they were encircled by ditches which could be inundated from the sea, and were surrounded by a system of mines and galleries. Had the place been adequately manned, it was absolutely impregnable.

But instead of the minimum garrison of 12,000 men, General Bezanet had barely a third of that number, and in the depth of a severe winter the ditches were frozen, though the ice on such brackish water is never strong. Graham had good secret intelligence, for many of the citizens were sympathetic; and a Dutch officer of his own, a native of the town, had actually ventured into it the day before the assault. But he was unwittingly misled. He understood that the bulk of the garrisons were unwilling recruits or war-worn veterans; in reality they were excellent soldiers, and they showed the temper of their metal. Graham won the place, though only to lose it; and his combinations gained him the admiration of Europe, and the praise of such strategists as Wellington and Napoleon.

The ramparts enclosed two parts, called respectively the town and the port. The attack was delivered by 3300 men in four columns. The assault by three of the columns was serious; the fourth was to be a feint on one of the gates, and accordingly it was repulsed. A column, led by Skerett of Tarifa fame, and by Gore, stole silently round to the month of the harbour, waded the ebbing sea channels, forced the water gate, and sending off detachments to right and left, found the ramparts undefended. Then the garrison, taking the alarm, hurried its reserves to the bastions, and there Colonel Carleton was driven back. Meantime the second column, under Maurice, crossing the ice, had reached the counterscarps near the Breda gate, but only to be fended off by the garrison.

Simultaneously, however, the works between the Antwerp and water gates were carried by the first column—the Guards, under Lord Proby. Maurice's column, repulsed at its own point of attack, and feeling its way carefully over the treacherous ice, mounted by Proby's scaling ladders to range itself at the side of the Guards. There were 2200 men on the ramparts, and the place was taken. Friends and foes were alike agreed as to that. The column that had delivered the feigned attack had gone quietly back to cantonments, and an advancing brigade of Germans, on hearing the happy news, immediately countermarched. The French garrison withdrew to the market-place, huddled together like partridges under the stoop of the hawk, and an *aide-de-camp* was despatched to treat for surrender. The *aide-de-camp* was shot accidentally, and the garrison waited. There were changes in course of the night.

The British soldiers, chilled and dispirited, broke into the spirit-shops, and many got hopelessly drunk. No reinforcements had arrived to their assistance. The French, realising the condition of the enemy, rallied and attacked them in detail. Skerett's detachment, under a raking fire of guns turned upon it from the ramparts, was driven down into the town and compelled to surrender. There was a bloody combat with the 1500 near the Antwerp gate under General Cooke, who commanded in chief, but they had likewise to resign themselves and lay down their arms. Bezanet was again master of the situation; 900 of the assailants were killed or wounded, and 1800 were prisoners in his hands.

There have been few stranger incidents in the history of war. The fortress deemed almost impregnable, and standing on its guard—for Bezanet had twelve hours' notice of Graham's intention—was stormed, without preparations, by a force scarcely stronger than the garrison. After the place was virtually occupied and with the ramparts secured, the assailants were compelled to surrender to an equal number of the enemy they had demoralised. As Wellington remarked, he wondered how they got into the place, but still more, having got in, how the devil they were kicked out. The only possible explanation is, that Graham's foresight was at fault. He seems to have reckoned either on prompt success or the immediate failure of his *coup*. With barely half his forces engaged, he had neither supports nor reserves in readiness. That fever fit of audacity was succeeded by paralysis, and thenceforth the impotent British operations were confined to observation of Bergen and Antwerp.

Graham was Liberal in politics, almost a Radical. When Brougham moved the Bill for Scottish Reform—and the abuses of the old electoral system were scandalous—he had supported it with all his influence and with his pen as well. That may have had something to do with his reluctance to accept a peerage, though the old man had no heirs of his body and his estates were to pass to a collateral branch. But while still in Holland the peerage was forced upon him. When Wellington's chief lieutenants were ennobled, Graham's kinsman, General Hope, took the matter into his own hands. He wrote his cousin, "Exclusion from such a list would have hurt your name forever." Moreover, he chose the title, "Lyndoch," oddly enough misspelling the name, a mistake which was subsequently rectified. Graham's pride inclined him to refuse the accompanying pension, but his Scottish prudence constrained him to accept it.

He resigned the command in Holland after twenty years of uninterrupted service. With something of the age, he had much of the youthful vigour of the patriarchs, and was in his maturity when feebler men were being superannuated. Returned to England, he was the originator of a memorial to his memory which is likely to survive him long. He was the founder of the Senior United Service Club, as Croker almost simultaneously started the Athenæum opposite. It seems to us now to have been an admirable and most unobjectionable scheme, but strangely enough it met with violent opposition. Lord Liverpool and Mr. Huskisson were strongly against it, and Lord St. Vincent even pronounced it "unconstitutional." But Graham was backed up by Hill and Sir Thomas Troubridge; sound sense prevailed, and the Club was founded.

On the foundation-stone, laid in 1817, is an inscription giving Graham the credit he deserved, and he was afterwards asked to sit for the portrait which hangs in the dining-room over the western chimney-piece. There is little to be added. The country gentleman came back, somewhat late in life, to indulge in the sports in which he delighted, and of which he had been deprived for twenty years. A letter to his nephew, written from the Coa, in which he had been describing the operations of Marmont, ends with emphatic instructions as to the education of a litter of pointer puppies at Lynedoch. The puppies must have been past work long before he retired; but now he rented a hunting lodge in the shires, and at seventy-three was showing younger men the way over ox-fences and through rasping bullfinches.

For twenty years afterwards he was always on the move, paying visits to friends in Britain or travelling abroad. He went to St. Petersburg and Moscow; he inspected Napoleon's roads over the Alps; he paid a visit in Lombardy to his old friend Radetzky, and then he presented the field-marshal with a valuable Arab. Twice at least he revisited the familiar scenes in Spain and Southern France, though at San Sebastian he was warned to walk the streets *incognito*, lest the inhabitants should rise and stone him. He betook himself to training horses for the turf, and the hero of Barossa was a proud man when a filly he had bred himself carried off some stakes at Newmarket. But one of the greatest compliments ever paid an old soldier was when he was invited in his eighty-sixth year to take the command in Portugal of the forces of the young queen. He professed to treat the proposal as a joke, but it was made in all seriousness.

His latest honour was when King William wrote with his own hand to give him the colonelcy of the Royal Regiment. The act was the more gracious that he had been no courtier or time-server. When he left England for Spain before the siege of San Sebastian, the Duke of Clarence had made personal application in a most friendly letter for the appointment of one of his sons to the general's staff. Graham's answer had been a courteous but decisive refusal; he had already several extra *aides-de-camp*, and had pledged himself beyond any probable vacancies.

The old man passed away painlessly in his ninety-sixth year.

The Earl of Hopetoun

1

The equestrian statue of the fourth Earl of Hopetoun stands before the Royal Bank in St. Andrew Square in Edinburgh. The rider looks across to Lord Melville on his lofty column; and though Lord Melville fell upon evil times and paid a heavy penalty for constitutional carelessness, the memories of both are equally dear to their countrymen. John Hope, after distinguishing himself in arms and diplomacy, died the head of his house, in possession of its great estates. He was beloved by his friends and neighbours as a magnificent host, and adored by his tenants as a model landlord.

A younger son by a second marriage, he had no prospect of succeeding to the ancestral domains. He looked forward to a military career, and as a boy of fourteen enrolled himself a volunteer. Privately educated, he went the grand tour under the charge of Gillies, the historiographer royal, and it was not till 1784 that he entered the army as cornet in the 16th Light Dragoons. His rise was slow, considering his family influence, for he had been nine years in the service before he was gazetted lieutenant-colonel. Almost immediately he went out to the West Indies, as adjutant-general to Sir Ralph Abercromby, and there he served with credit for four years.

Of Abercromby he had made a fast friend, and the veteran attached him to his staff in North Holland, as afterwards in Egypt. In that disastrous descent on the Texel he was fortunate, for he was wounded in the disembarkation and incapacitated for further duty. Abercromby did well in exceptionally difficult circumstances; but in the fighting between the sand dunes, the dykes, and the sea-creeks, there was great responsibility to be accepted by his subordinates and little glory to be gained. Three years before, his family interest had returned Hope as member for the county of Linlithgow, but of all Wellington's lieutenants who were seated in Parliament, perhaps no one was less efficient, which is saying much.

In 1800 he was Abercromby's adjutant-general in the army of the Mediterranean, ranking as a brigadier-general. Returning to Minorca after the surrender of Malta, Abercromby found that with reinforcements from England he had 10,000 troops at his disposal He found also despatches from Melas, in command of the Austrians in Italy, and from Lord William Bentinck, urging him to land with his troops at Leghorn and raise the Tuscans against the French. The cautious old Scotchman awaited instructions from home, and meantime despatched his adjutant-general to the Austrian headquarters to report on the situation. Hope discharged the delicate duty so well, that Abercromby held him in higher estimation than before. As adjutant-general he accompanied the expedition to Egypt, when Abercromby, who could be resolute when he saw an opportunity, in spite of the warnings of gallant naval officers achieved a successful landing on an open beach in face of formidable preparations for resistance.

In the slow advance upon Alexandria, when he hoped to force the enemy to a decisive battle, it was Hope who surveyed the ground, and came back to report on the possibilities. He could say nothing encouraging, and on the eve of the memorable 1st of March the prospects of the army seemed dark in the extreme. Hoping, rather than believing in success, Abercromby determined to deliver an attack on the morrow; in the too probable event of failure he was to fall back upon Aboukir Bay and re-embark. Then, as with Marmont at Salamanca, his adversary made the fatal mistake of taking the initiative. Menou, beaten in the field, was shut up in Alexandria; but Abercromby early in the day received his death wound, of which he said nothing till the battle was over.

The loss seemed the more grievous, that his successor Hutchinson was hated. Something like a mutiny broke out among the superior officers, and was only quelled by the stern refusal of General Moore to supersede his senior in the command. Hutchinson had resolved to march upon Cairo, and his immediate subordinates deemed the venture desperate; but he showed unsuspected strength of will, the Turkish allies behaved with unexpected gallantry and discretion, and the result justified his decision. Belliard, who commanded in Cairo, sent to ask an armistice as a preliminary to arranging terms of capitulation. It was a singular and a delicate negotiation, for the effective strength of the capitulating garrison was more than double that of the army to

THE HON. SIR JOHN HOPE
AFTERWARDS FOURTH EARL OF HOPETOUN

which they were to surrender.

But the French were eager to be out of Egypt, and Hutchinson, from political rather than military considerations, was as anxious to make a bridge for the beaten enemy. Hope was charged with arranging the terms, which he did to Hutchinson's entire satisfaction. Seldom has there been witnessed a stranger spectacle, than when 8000 war-hardened French veterans, proud of the laurels they had won in Italy, retaining arms and ammunition, with field batteries fully horsed and cavalry admirably mounted, were escorted to the ships by a third of their numbers. General Hope then resumed command of his brigade, and remained in Egypt till he witnessed the surrender of Alexandria.

In 1802 he had the rank of major-general, and six years afterwards was lieutenant-general. In the interval he had held the command at Portsmouth, but resigned to serve with Lord Cathcart in the descent on the coasts of Hanover. He was second to Moore in the ill-considered expedition to Sweden, and on its return he accompanied his chief to the Peninsula. They arrived on the scene too late for Vimiero, but after the signing of the so-called Cintra Convention, Hope was appointed commandant of Lisbon. The city was in a ferment; the 1st Division of the detested French did not embark for several days; assassinations and outrages of all kinds were of nightly occurrence, but the commandant showed as much tact as decision, and his firm measures soon restored order. Portugal had been evacuated, with the exception of Almeida and Elvas.

The governor of the latter fortress declined to give it over without authentic intelligence, and the Spanish general refused to abandon the siege. Hope was sent with a body of troops to enforce the strong remonstrances of Sir Hew Dalrymple, and he promptly placed matters on a satisfactory footing. The garrison was marched to Lisbon under British escort, and we are told that the only trouble between prisoners and guard was a friendly rivalry in outmarching each other.

The three generals who had succeeded each other at Vimiero had been recalled for the Chelsea court-martial. Moore had his orders for the invasion of Spain; how it was to be carried out was left to his discretion. He decided for the march through the interior, by Almeida, Ciudad, and Salamanca. For the topography of a mountainous country, altogether unexplored from the military point of view, he had to depend on information obtained on the spur of the moment. Officers of his own confirmed the reports of the natives—but the roads were impracticable for artillery. He learned later that he had been misled;

but meantime he reluctantly decided to violate one of the fundamental rules of war, and detach himself from his guns and cavalry. With so much at stake, and so much against him, he was to march to a doubtful objective, in hope of recovering them before coming in contact with the masses of the French.

To Hope was confided the dangerous and responsible charge of the essentials of an army in action. He was to follow the right bank of the Tagus, by way of Talavera to gain the Escorial, and then thread the passes of the Guadarama. Baird was to disembark at Corunna, and twenty days was the calculation before the columns could be united. On all sides there were unavoidable delays. On the 26th November Baird had only reached Astorga, and Moore, who had to move his men by divisions, had as yet concentrated barely 14,000 in Salamanca. On that day the head of Hope's columns had only reached the Escorial. Though his force was somewhat short of 4000, he had been marching along river meadows or across open plains, and like the main body under his chief, it had been drawn out in scattered sections. The country had been devastated, money was scarce, and when the Spaniards had anything to supply they would only sell at exorbitant prices.

At the Escorial he had to pause to gather in bullocks to drag guns and waggons across the mountains. Before that he had ridden into Madrid for an interview with Morla, the secretary-at-war. It only convinced him of the ignorance or bad faith of the Spanish Junta. Had he listened to the treacherous counsels of Morla he would have taken his column by sections through the capital, to be crushed in detail by the concentrating French. He struggled over the mountains and descended on the northern plains, to find himself in imminent peril. Had he been acting independently he would have at once ordered a retreat, for his scouts on three sides were in touch with the enemy's cavalry. The French were already threatening his communications with the Guadarama, and menacing him in front and on flank as well But he was in charge of the guns and ammunition, and bound to press forward at all risks.

Before him was a three days' flank march with a straggling convoy and a foe known to be exceptionally strong in cavalry; yet he dare not hesitate, for delay would be fatal. Napier says that "a man of less calmness and intrepidity would have been ruined"; but marching at first by night and day, turning out strong mounted patrols to make a bold show on his right, and covering the convoy with horse and foot, he sent his artillery safely forward to Alba on the Tormes, where it met a detachment from Salamanca.

The French, though they never ceased from troubling, had been not only out-marched but out-manoeuvred, for their fourth corps, in place of pursuing, had crossed his rear in the certainty of cutting him off when compelled to retreat to the Guadarama. His promptitude and celerity of action had saved the British army. Had a Lord Chatham or even a Sir John Stuart been in his place, the transports would have waited in vain in Vigo Bay, and there would have been no victory of Corunna.

Moore had hoped to rally the Spanish armies behind the Tagus, but he reached Salamanca only to hear that they had been scattered to the winds. Nevertheless he succeeded in his grand purpose, which was to draw Napoleon away from the south, and now his object was to escape with honour from the overwhelming forces set in motion by the emperor. Hope's divisions formed part of the main body, and consequently he had no such experiences as the generals who were bringing up the rear. Yet the columns of the centre were seldom safe; their strongest positions were being always turned and could only be occupied temporarily. At night the outlying pickets were never secure from alarm. His worst trouble was at Villa Franca, where the starving soldiers forced the wine cellars and broke loose from all control.

Many of the regimental officers, though indulging in no excesses, were scarcely less demoralised, and they had lost all touch with their men. In scenes like these a general who thrust himself forward in the frenzied mobs ran more serious risks than on the battlefield, and Hope's gigantic stature and commanding presence made him a conspicuous mark when muskets were going off on no provocation. But he was absolutely fearless, and the only fault with which Wellington had to reproach him afterwards—when all the Peninsular generals were brave—was his almost insane intrepidity. He busied himself at Villa Franca in restoring order, and gave the provost-marshal ample occupation.

Napier has described in glowing language how the leader restored discipline in his disorderly hosts by offering the enemy battle before Lugo. Disappointed then, they were still full of fighting ardour when mustered at Corunna for the embarkation. To a man they were eager to strike a parting blow at the pursuers who, hunting them hard, had driven them to dire extremities. Reduced to rags, but supplied with fresh muskets and ample ammunition from the magazines, with unbroken spirit they fought the defensive battle, under every disadvantage of ground. Yet nothing could have been more depressing than the preparations for the orderly evacuation, first were exploded the great stores of powder, intended for the recovery of the Peninsula, which shook the solid earth like an earthquake and shivered many a window in the town.

Even more sad was the slaughter of the horses which had carried the cavalry and dragged the guns through the snowdrifts and over the passes, yet it saddened them rather as a sign of the time and of the enemy's virtual triumph. For Kincaid and Mercer and other gossipy annotators of the campaigns have remarked, that the British artillery drivers and the dragoons were culpably careless of their horses; whereas the German cavalryman made a friend of his charger, and always attended to its wants before seeing to his personal comforts. Mercer, who commanded Dickson's famous battery at Waterloo, tells a touching story of a German trooper who had succeeded in smuggling his favourite on board ship at Corunna, to lament him when a cannon-ball knocked him over at Waterloo. (*Journal of the Campaign of 1815* by Cavalie Mercer also published by Leonaur).

At Corunna Hope's divisions were on the extreme left. The position was the strongest, for their left flank rested on the tidal River Mero, and while the French were delivering furious assaults on our right and centre, Foy on our left pressed his onsets but feebly. The general fell, Baird was severely wounded, and then the command devolved upon Hope. When the sun was declining the day was won. Had he cared only for fame, he might have followed up the victory, changing confusion into panic, and capturing many prisoners and guns.

But there was nothing to be gained by a heavier stroke, and the chief consideration was to save the wrecks of a gallant army. He was content to carry out the wishes of the dying Moore, and when Beresford had taken to the boats on the morning of the 18th January, Hope was the last man to leave the shore. To him it fell to tell in despatches the story of the retreat and the battle. They have been praised as models of style and lucidity, and they deserve the praise. If the critic can find a fault in them, it is that they are somewhat discursive, but the writer's self-suppression is as conspicuous as were his courage and conduct in the field.

2

He came home to receive the thanks of Parliament and the Knighthood of the Bath. He served like his compeers on the unlucky Walcheren expedition, and he was commander-in-chief in Ireland when Wellington passed the Bidassoa and Graham resigned. It would seem that being Wellington's senior in rank, he had not previously volunteered for the Peninsula, but Vittoria had brought his lordship the field-marshal's baton, and now Sir John proffered his services. They were gladly accepted, and it was then that Wellington made the somewhat invidious remark, that Hope was the ablest officer in the army. As has been observed, the Duke's commendations are somewhat inconsistent He succeeded to his cousin Graham in command of the left wing, cantoned between the Bidassoa and the Nivelle, and in command of that wing he skirted the seaboard till it effected the memorable crossing of the Adour.

Delayed at first by political considerations, after the passage was decided on by the state of the weather, Wellington had been preparing to force the line of the Nivelle, and his wakeful adversary was alive to his intentions. But on the 10th November Soult was once more taken by surprise, and never were Wellington's dispositions more masterly. On the day of the 9th the rain had been descending in torrents, which may have put the marshal off his guard. The morning of the 10th was to break beautifully, but meantime under the cloud of night the allied columns had been set in motion.

Before daybreak they had stolen close to the enemy's works, nor did Soult dream that there was anything before him more formidable than the usual pickets. With the first gleams of dawn there were signal shots from the mountains, they were re-echoed by other guns along the ridges, and along seven miles of concentrated fighting, with fringes of scattered onsets on either side, the columns rushed to the assault. The battle has already been described, as it was fought to our right and on the centre. Towards the French right centre the positions were too strong to be assailed, and could only be turned. Wellington had driven in his wedge higher up, had come down in strength on either bank of the Nivelle, and turned the entrenched positions there. Meanwhile it was Hope's business on the far left to menace the French line on the low ground between the mountains and the sea.

On his flank were the British war-ships exchanging broadsides with the forts on the shore. The fire of his batteries effectively engaged the attention of Reille's divisions and Villatte's reserves, preventing them from lending assistance at the critical point, where Clausel, in sore distress, was being driven back by overpowering numbers. But Clausel made good a stubborn defence, and Villatte held firmly to his fortified camp, till Reille, retiring in good order before Hope, had withdrawn into St. Jean de Luz, breaking the bridges behind him. During the night he evacuated the town, and had formed on the heights of Bidart. On the 11th there was a simultaneous advance of the allies in order of battle. Hope forded the river and followed Reille on the road to Bidart.

Wellington could have pushed his advantage, when his troops were flushed with victory and eager to change rough campaigning and hard fare for quarters in the fertile fields of France. Provisions were at famine prices. Larpent writes of fowls rising from two to twelve shillings; turkeys, when procurable, from seven shillings to thirty; and geese from one dollar to six. At dinner, when there was a dinner, the conversation of the officers turned rather on the commissariat than on military operations. Wellington was as anxious as they to advance into a country where the population showed signs of revolt against the blood tax, and where the peasants were ready to welcome an army which paid for its requisitions in cash.

The merchants of Bordeaux were impatient of embargos on their shipping, and as it proved there were bankers, even in Bayonne, willing to discount the British bills. Having passed the Nivelle, and fought on the Nive for political reasons, he could not afford to hazard the prestige he had won by being cooped up on the Peninsula between that river and the sea. But the weather was still against him, and the state of the country made immediate movements impossible. The rains had changed fields of heavy clay into impassable swamps and quagmires; and the roads had been torn up by the wheels of the gun-carriages.

Moreover, he had weakened his forces by getting rid of the Spaniards, who had begun to revenge themselves by pillage and slaughter for the atrocities of the French invaders to the south of the Pyrenees. So, as a month went by, Soult had ample time for preparing to baulk his adversary's plans, and he was maintaining his entrenched positions on the Adour, with the Nive as an advanced line of defence. Though Hill fought the most bloody battle of the campaign at St. Pierre, when he had to repel a sortie in overwhelming force, it was on Hope that the most serious responsibilities devolved. Commanding the left wing, he was confronted by Bayonne, Soult's place of arms and *point d'appui*,

It was true that it was only a fortress of the third rank, but it was held by six divisions, which could be reinforced at will. Situated at the confluence of the Nive and Adour, it was protected on the southern side by a swamp and by meadows which could be artificially inundated. In front was the entrenched camp, commanded by the guns of the fortress. In front of that again was a network of lanes, within a labyrinth of walled gardens and orchards.

When the allies first threatened an invasion of France, the place was absolutely defenceless: the outworks had fallen into utter disrepair, and there were only three cannon on the ramparts. Now all the dilapidations had been repaired, new works were rising every day, guns had been gathered in from all quarters, and there were 120 in position. On the river below the town was a flotilla of gunboats, and it was watched besides by Reille's two divisions and Villatte's reserve. These generals, like the Spanish allies, had their revenge to take, and were unlikely to be caught napping a second time.

After the inevitable delays, on the 9th December the combined movement came off. Hill and Beresford forced the Nive, fording the river and repairing the bridges. It was Hope's business then, as on the Nivelle, to occupy the French in front of him, so that Soult might neither send support to D'Erlon nor detach troops to strengthen General Paris, who was threatening the extreme right of the allies.

Thus, while Hill and Beresford were passing the Nive, Hope and Alten were pressing the enemy on the left bank. Their charge besides was to examine the Lower Adour, in contemplation of the passage which was already meditated. Hope amply carried out his orders. With three divisions and a mere handful of horse, he gave occupation to thrice his number. With insignificant losses, he fought his way up to the camp, which it was never intended to assail He had made a night march from St. Jean de Luz: he came upon the intricate chessboard of walled enclosures at break of day, and passing in front of the little village of Barouillet, a sweep of his right wing brought it in touch with Alten, while his left was resting on the Lower Adour, where his engineers were busy taking observations.

The objects accomplished, he had orders to fall back, and consequently withdrew again to his headquarters in St. Jean de Luz. The rain had still been falling, the men had been marching ankle-deep in mud, and for four-and-twenty hours they had been fasting and under arms. After exertions so prolonged and sustained, it was dispiriting to retire, on the order "As you were." If they hoped for rest, there was none forthcoming. The French behind their entrenchments had been kept comparatively fresh, and the next day Soult dealt a heavy counter-stroke.

Hope's main body was quartered in St. Jean de Luz and Bidart, and St. Jean was several miles distant from the French works. The allied pickets and detachments were posted in advance, on a ridge with three projecting spurs overlooking the French entrenchments. In the morning the British sentries saw what seemed like some horseplay going on in the pickets opposed to them. They suspected there was more earnest than jest in the game when the players began to mass themselves in the ditches. When the heads of columns were seen emerging from the wooded cover behind, suspicions were changed to certainty. The rash from the French camp came in resistless force; some of the pickets were enveloped; others fell back on the detachments which were being promptly hurried forward.

For hours there was fierce desultory fighting along the crest of the ridge and in the intervening valleys; churches and houses were held as so many fortresses, round which the warfare surged forward and receded; but on the whole the British made good their ground and the French gained only temporary advantage. The issue might have been very different had not General Kempt taken the responsibility of disobeying an order to retire his division when he remarked disquieting signs in front of him. As it was, the attempt had well nigh succeeded, but it seems to have been Soult's original intention to deliver the attack with his whole available forces. Napier, his great admirer, does not profess to explain the reasons for changing his mind. Had he brought double the number of men to bear, as he easily might, the Light Division, scattered in loose formation along the heights, could not possibly have held its own.

Hope had a very narrow escape of the capture which was to be his lot when it was of less consequence. Chaplain-General Gleig was then the "Subaltern," and posted near the *château* of the mayor of Biarritz. Hope, attended by some *aides-de-camp* and a few orderly dragoons, went into the *château* to survey the battlefield and mounted to an upper room.

> The few skirmishers who lined the hedge in front were lying down to rest when a mass of the French infantry which had formed in a hollow road dashed forward. . . . All opposition was overcome: the house was surrounded. Instantly a cry was raised, 'Save the general! Save the general!' and a rush was made from all quarters towards the *château*, but our assistance was unnecessary. Sir John threw himself upon his horse, and at the head of his mounted attendants charged from the doorway of the courtyard. He received, indeed, three musket-balls through

his hat, and his horse was so severely wounded that its strength served only to carry him to a place of safety, but the charge was decisive.

Had the Light Division been swept away, and had the French tide overflowed the heights to right and left, Alten would have been thrown back upon the Nive, and Hope's advance would have been impossible. For, while Kempt was valiantly disputing the ground, the real battle was raging at Barouillet to the left, on the great road from St. Jean to Bayonne. Along that road Reille had broken out with his two divisions, driving the Portuguese pickets and the cavalry patrols before him. It was fortunate for us that the rain had flooded the lanes: he could only at first bring two brigades into action, moving them with difficulty along a narrow *chaussée*, on a ridge which was skirted on either side by water tanks.

Robinson's brigade was hurried forward to dispute the passage, but Hope was still far away in St. Jean, and Lord Aylmer's supporting brigade was in Bidart It was midday before the French general could deploy in order of battle—he had left Bayonne at nine—and by that time the allied supports were coming up. Reille's divisions were repulsed, but in the afternoon it was a drawn battle, for Villatte was hanging upon Hope's right, and Foy, established on the ridge running out from the *plateau* of Barouillet, was sending his skirmishers down into the plain and connecting with Reille's left. And the allies, worn out with the work of the previous day, were in no good fighting condition.

Soult had given orders to renew the battle, and his solid masses were already in motion, when a report reached him that a fresh body of British troops had appeared on the scene from the heights above Urdains on the Nive. Their appearance has nothing directly to do with Hope's story, but they induced the French marshal to countermand the attack.

On the 11th the wearied allies had hoped for a quiet day. Reille and the divisions on his left had withdrawn, and Soult had concentrated, fearing a counterstroke. But everything was veiled in dense fog, and Wellington was uneasy as to his intentions. He threw forward skirmishers to feel the French, and the French were drawn to some purpose. They came again with a rush, and the 9th Regiment was barely saved by Hope's prompt arrival at the head of a Portuguese corps. The enemy's advanced pickets were forced back, and the British resumed the posts from which they had been driven. Again, for a brief space, everything seemed tranquil. The December day was damp and cold, and the soldiers had scattered to gather firewood. But Soult, as Napier expresses it, incensed by this second insult, decided for the action over which he had been hesitating. He had 24,000 soldiers in hand, and he threw them simultaneously into the battle. Heavy columns moved along the main road and the eastern ridge, while elsewhere his troops, breaking up into groups and knots, penetrated the natural barriers opposed to them by every rift and crevice. They swept up to the house where Hope had his headquarters, they seized on outbuildings and cottages, they lined the hedgerows and filled the coppices.

For a time the combatants were intermingled in a promiscuous *mêlée*: it was a soldiers' hand-to-hand fight, where the bayonets clashed and champions met in Homeric conflict. But meantime the stragglers were forming up in companies; an unbroken regiment came forward from the rear, and flanking batteries were pouring in round shot and grape, wherever friends could be distinguished from enemies. But all are agreed that the high tide of the hostile onset was stemmed and turned by the omnipresence of the British leader.

The tale of Hope's *derring-do* on that memorable day reads like a page from *Ivanhoe*. Gigantic of stature as *Coeur de Lion,* mounted on a charger like the coal-black steed that carried "The Sluggard" in Ashby lists, he seemed to be everywhere in the thickest of the combat, dealing tremendous blows and cheering his fighters to the fray. He had a bullet in the leg and a serious contusion on the shoulder, four balls had again pierced his hat, and the black horse and another afterwards were shot under him. Nevertheless he kept the field till he had seen the enemy thrust back on all sides to their positions of midday.

In one sense it was a drawn battle, and again, as on the day before, while the French were hampered in narrow outlets, the allies had barely half their available forces engaged. Hope's generalship and foresight may have been somewhat at fault, for twice he had been taken somewhat by surprise. But it may be said that Wellington was equally deceived as to the intentions of an able opponent who could strike out on either side with superior forces. Moreover, the powers of even Peninsular veterans were limited, and these men of iron could not altogether dispense with food and rest. There are always chances in war, and in the upshot Soult was baffled. Having failed on the left bank of the Nive, he proceeded to try his fortunes to the right of the river, and turned his attention to Hill. Assuredly, if Hope was in any way to blame, he more than redeemed his reputation by his conduct.

Wellington wrote to Colonel Torrens:

> I have long entertained the highest opinion of Sir John Hope, in common, I believe, with the whole world, and every day's experience convinces me of his worth. We shall lose him, however, if he continues to expose himself to fire, as he did on the last three days. . . . He places himself among the sharpshooters, without, as they do, sheltering himself from the enemy's fire. This will not answer, and I hope his friends will give him a hint on the subject.

But on the third day's fighting there was nothing to reproach him with on that score, for the reckless exposure came of cool calculation. Whether blameworthy or no, we had been somewhat caught napping; and it was his coolness and decision in swiftly succeeding emergencies even more than his courage which saved his command from a crushing disaster.

The sequence of the left wing holding its own was the memorable passage of the lower river. Lord Wellington's prime object was to drive Soult from Bayonne, or at least to see it left with a simple garrison. The strength of an antiquated fortress was in the camp and the surrounding inundations, but that strength would be tamed to weakness with a garrison inadequate to hold the extended defences. Wellington's strategy was successful; and Soult was compelled to withdraw his army, to dispute the allied advance on the Upper Adour and its mountain tributaries. The first step in that strategy had been the passage of the Nive; it was to be followed by the passage of the Adour either below or immediately above Bayonne, for the fortress was to be invested. For various excellent reasons Wellington decided for the former course.

The chief of them was that the venture seemed so doubtful, or even desperate, that his more cautious adversary was scarce likely to forecast it, and the result proved his sagacity. Soult was again surprised. So little did he dream of the possibility that he withdrew some of his gunners from Bayonne to man the batteries and forts on the Garonne. So to Hope was confided one of the most daring and original ventures ever hazarded in war: he had to contend with conditions unprecedented; for the winds and the waves, the shoals and the tidal currents were the active allies of General Thouvenot; they lulled him, like Soult, into false security and committed him to a fatal error. Both Wellington and Hope had drawn their best encouragement from the very temerity of the enterprise, and Hope was trusting to science as much as to British pluck. The men he sent to the front were the scientific engineers and the skilled artillerists with the new-fangled Congreve rockets.

Wellington's schemes had so far succeeded. Soult, falling back on Toulouse and vainly looking over his shoulder for help from Suchet, was disputing the upper Gaves when Hope set himself to his task. He had two British and two Spanish divisions, with some Anglo-Portuguese and a brigade of cavalry. In all, but 28,000 men with twenty pieces of artillery. On the night of the 22nd February the 1st Division was in motion, with six guns and the rocket battery. The night was dark and the cross-roads were heavy as it filed in silence to the right, across the front of the entrenched camp. At daybreak the column had deployed on the sand dunes between the pine forest—familiar to riding parties from Biarritz—and the tidal estuary.

The French pickets were driven in upon their camp, the pontoons and the field guns were brought down to the river shore, and the heavy ordnance was placed in battery on the bank behind. In the meantime, frequent attacks to the south and east of the town were distracting the attention of the garrison. Hope had looked for the co-operation of gunboats and *chasse-marées*, but he had to count with the Bay of Biscay. As Moore at Corunna, he looked in vain; there were no signs of a fleet in the offing. Time was of the last importance, and he determined to attempt passing his troops across. Already the garrison must have taken the alarm, for the French flotilla and a heavily armed sloop were exchanging broadsides with his batteries. The heavier metal of the latter, with a shower of rockets, put three of the gunboats out of action and forced the squadron to withdraw out of fire.

Not a moment was lost. Sixty men of the Guards were rafted over on a pontoon, and landed in face of a French picket As at the passage of the Douro, it was the first step that cost; the picket withdrew, and the little party established itself to cover the disembarkation. Each detail had been carefully planned by Sturgeon, of Peninsular fame—the same resourceful engineer who had spanned the Tagus with a suspension bridge of cables for the passage of artillery. That forlorn hope of the Guards had taken a hawser across. The remaining pontoons were coupled into rafts and hauled over, but the process was slow, and when 600 of the Guards' comrades had landed with a rocket battery, the flow of the tide stopped operations.

News of the crossing had reached Thouvenot, and it was then he made an irretrievable mistake. He may have deemed that the venture was merely a feint to distract his attention from a frontal attack. Be that as it may, he only detached two battalions, and they recoiled before the fire from the batteries. What scared them most was the erratic play of the rockets, which demoralised alike the sailors and soldiers. Had he sent down field batteries to guard the bank, the passage could scarcely have been effected. As it was, the pontoon bridge was made fast, and all night the troops were passing over.

It was noon on the following day before the fleet was sighted. Baffled by head winds, the seamen had heard the guns, and were keen to have their share of the glory. But the bar of the Adour with its shifting sandbanks and shoaling channels is dangerous at the best of times, and only practicable for craft with light draught of water. As in internal Dutch channels, the seaways were marked out by poles, and these poles had been removed. The wind had gone down, but there was a heavy sea running, and the pilots could distinguish no smooth races to guide them through clouds of drifting spray over a turmoil of broken water. The boats of the men-of-war dashed at it all the same; the leading boat was caught up, whirled round, and engulfed.

Meanwhile the others were helplessly looking on, tossed about upon the surges in imminent peril. Then one daring officer—Cheyne of the *Woodlark*—tried his fortune, and happily hit off the right passage. It was as venturesome a feat as fell to the lot of any leader of the stormers at Badajoz or San Sebastian. The other boats and the Spanish *chasse-marées* followed in his wake; some came to utter grief, but most threaded the surges safely. The *chasse-marées* brought a welcome reinforcement, for on each was a party of sappers under an English engineer. By fall of night 8000 men were in strong positions on the northern sandhills.

The next day Hope made a circling flank march, with no interruption from the fortress. Thouvenot's immense works had to be held by inadequate forces against menaces on all the faces. Soult had gone; the tables were turned, and Bayonne was invested. Now Hope's left was on the Adour, above the town, while his right was resting on the lower river. There the floating bridge had been solidly affixed; and the bridge, with the boom protecting it from gunboats and fireships, were triumphs of military engineering.

In setting himself to the siege Hope's first step was to contract the lines of investment round the citadel, and it was not effected without severe fighting on the north. There the outworks were exceedingly strong. There the high-road to Bordeaux ran along a ridge, on which was the village of St. Etienne, loopholed for musketry, strongly entrenched and covered by the guns of the fortress. On either side the ground fell sharply into ravines, the sides of which were sprinkled with country houses of the citizens, each standing in its garden. These villas were occupied, and the garden walls were loopholed. The attack was delivered in three columns; the village was carried by the Germans, a sortie led by Thouvenot in person was repulsed with heavy loss, and the Germans entrenched themselves on the ridge within musket-shot of the enemy's works. Then Hope busied himself in collecting gabions and fascines, in preparation for the storm of the citadel.

Meantime his anxieties were great, as the investing force was divided into three bodies, separated by the rivers. A system of signals was arranged, and every precaution was taken for securing the bridge below the town. Still the communications to the north-west were at best precarious, for the low grounds on the right of the river were flooded at every tide, when the only means of passage was by the solid retaining wall, which was barely four feet in breadth.

The siege was maintained with unceasing vigilance, and preparations for the assault were approaching completion when rumours of the abdication of the Emperor reached the camp. Vague as they were, they were transmitted to Thouvenot, but Hope was in no position to make an authoritative announcement Consequently the French commandant was justified in regarding them as possibly intended to deceive, the rather that he saw no relaxation in the efforts of the besiegers. He determined to anticipate and baffle the impending assault by a vigorous blow, and though the fruitless fighting cost the lives of many brave men, he can scarcely be blamed.

The besiegers were not without warning of the projected sally. Soon after midnight on the morning of the 14th April, a deserter came over to their lines, bringing exact information. He was sent to General Hay, who commanded the outposts on the ridge. Hay could speak no French and sent him on to General Hinüber, who commanded the German reserves on the left. Even when the message was translated to him. Hay seems to have disbelieved it; he took no extra precautions, and paid the penalty of his incredulity with his life. Precisely at the time and in the way that had been foretold, Thouvenot broke out in great strength. He rolled up the pickets and posts on the ridge, and rushed the village of St. Etienne, with the single exception of a fortified house, which was obstinately held by Captain Forster of the 38th.

Having driven in the centre and severed the wings, the shouting rush of victorious assailants swerved to their left, turning the line on the right of the allied attack. Happily General Hinüber had given heed to the deserter, and had his Germans in readiness. As the fighting drifted along the hill crest towards the west, he led his battalions up the eastern slope, rallied some of the scattered soldiers of the 5th Division, and, reinforced by a Portuguese battalion, recovered the village.

Below him, to his left, the battle was still raging fiercely. In the darkness no man could tell how it was going, and the combatants intermingled in the enclosures could scarcely distinguish friend from foe. The French gun-boats dropping down the river were plying their guns on the flanks of the columns supposed to be moving along the right bank. The guns of the citadel were firing at random, guided by the flashes of musketry beneath. Hope had hurried up at the first alarm, followed by the reserves of the right.

In any case he could have done little to restore order in the darkness, but he vanished and was seen no more. It was only afterwards his men learned how they had lost their general. It appeared that with his slender escort and *aides-de-camp* he had struck into a hollow way leading to St. Etienne behind his pickets. The pickets had been forced back and the French were on both banks of the road. They had opened fire on the party, when Hope gave the order to turn. Thus, instead of the leading horseman, he became the last: and, as his followers struggled out of the defile, a shot struck him, while his horse rolled over, riddled with bullets. His colossal rider lay under, pinned down by the leg, and his *aides-de-camp*, on seeing his plight, dismounted to the rescue.

One was Captain Herries; the other a nephew of his old friend Sir John Moore. Both fell severely wounded while striving to release him, and all three were made prisoners. As Sir John was being carried in, he was struck again, and by an English bullet It was an unhappy climax to a scene of bootless slaughter; but he had the consolation of knowing that his work was done, for both siege and war were over. With break of day the allies formed up in loose order, and, rushing in upon the French on three sides with vengeful fury, drove them back into their entrenchments. Had it not been for the circumspection of the German Hinüber, the series of Wellington's victorious campaigns would have closed with a brilliant success for a French general.

The terms of peace had been already signed, and Hope's confinement ended with his convalescence. He came home to receive the thanks of Parliament, and, what gratified him more, to become the idol of his Scottish countrymen. He was raised to the peerage as Lord Niddry of Niddry, Niddry is the old tower in West Lothian where Queen Mary rallied her supporters before the fatal Battle of Langside. A pension of £2000 was to have accompanied the creation, but that he declined. Two years afterwards the new title merged in that of Hopetoun, when he succeeded his half-brother. In 1819 he was gazetted full general, and in the following year, to his great gratification, had the colonelcy of the Black Watch.

When George IV. paid his visit to Scotland, the colossal figure of the Peninsular general was conspicuous among the Scottish *noblesse*. Always keeping open house at his beautiful seat of Hopetoun, he entertained his sovereign there with great magnificence. In Scott's spirited ballad of welcome to the king, "*Carle, now the King's come*," "*Being new words to an auld sang,*" Hopetoun was bracketed in a couplet with Lord Tweeddale.

Tweeddale, true as sword to sheath;
Hopetoun, fear'd on fields of death,

Whenever he appeared in the public ceremonials, he was greeted by the shouts of his admiring countrymen, and indeed he was the veritable type of the modern *preux chevalier*. Ever ready to risk his life for the humblest comrade, never neglecting an opportunity for a kindly action, he was as open of hand as he was stout of heart. When smarting from wounds and mortification, in his confinement at Bayonne, he astonished three French generals, whose sympathies he had won, by presenting each with a valuable charger from his stable. With his Herculean frame and superb constitution, he might have looked to as long a life as Hill or Lynedoch, but he died of sudden illness at Paris in his fifty-eighth year.

The Marquis of Anglesey

1

It was perhaps logical that Wellington and his most illustrious lieutenants should have been men of extraordinary vitality. All had undergone the hardships of rough campaigning, but Lord Anglesey is the most remarkable example of tenacity of life, as for many years before his death he was a martyr to *tio-douloureux*, which tried his days and broke his nights. The veteran was born the year before the birth of Wellington and Napoleon. He survived the fall of the Emperor by forty years, and stood at the head of Wellington's coffin in the Abbey, when his own great leader was laid in the dust. Henry William Paget was the eldest of six brothers, five of whom were more or less distinguished. The fourth of them was General Sir Edward, who lost an arm at the passage of the Douro, as his senior left a leg at Waterloo; who commanded the cavalry reserve in Moore's retreat; and whose brilliant career was prematurely cut short when he was taken prisoner in the other retreat from Burgos.

The heir to the title and estates was born in 1768. Lord Paget was sent from Westminster to Oxford, but though afterwards a zealous student of the art of war in his own branch of the service, he had no great love for letters and won no academical distinction. Otherwise, he was much as Macaulay describes Wyndham—a finished gentleman, an accomplished athlete, above all a daring horseman, and with a singularly handsome person, developed by all manly exercises. In common with Combermere, he delighted in gay trappings and the pomp of war, and so he shared with him the *sobriquet* of the British Marat.

Wellington always spoke well of his dandy officers, and some of Paget's most dashing exploits—at Sahagun and Benevente—were at the head of the dandy 10th, the Prince Regent's pet regiment, generally quartered at Brighton to furnish escorts to the Pavilion, and in

Marquis of Anglesey

which Brummell at one time set the fashions.

His military instincts had lain dormant, when the peace was broken and war was proclaimed with the French Republic. Patriotic gentlemen of great estate were levying regiments for foreign service, and Paget raised a corps of his father's tenantry, "the Staffordshire Volunteers," afterwards the 80th, which did gallant work with Abercromby at Aboukir. His lordship had the rank of lieutenant-colonel: he modestly declined a full colonelcy on the ground that he had seen no service in the field The regiment mustered 1000 strong when embarked in the Channel Islands to follow the Duke of York to Flanders in 1794. It arrived somewhat late, when a doubtful business at the best had become hopelessly tangled, but Paget had his baptism of fire, and distinguished himself on various occasions. Commanding Cathcart's brigade on the withdrawal from the Low Countries into Westphalia, he had his first experience of guarding a retreat, learning the lessons he put in practice between Sahagun and Corunna.

But he was cut out for a cavalryman, and, returning to England, he exchanged from his own regiment into the 7th Hussars. He was quartered at Ipswich in command of the 7th and other mounted detachments. Most men in his position, with his attractions to society and his passion for field sports, would have divided the time between the drawing-rooms and the hunting-field. But Paget was a thorough soldier at heart; he devoted himself to the training of his cavalry command, and, devising novel systems of discipline and tactics, tested them in a severe course of exercises and manoeuvres.

The work he went through then, with his patient submission to drudgery, bore fruit a dozen of years later when he landed at Corunna with his brigade, pronounced perfect alike in training and equipment. Meantime his energy had found active employment in the Duke of York's expedition to the Helder. We said that Cotton was fortunate in being wounded at the disembarkation, as there was little credit to be won. But of such credit as was going Paget had his share. The English were soon on the worst possible terms with their Russian allies. The Royal Duke, always frank to a fault and indiscreet to insanity after dinner, loudly abused the Russian generals at his table. The consequence was that the concerted operations generally resulted in failure and always in disappointment.

In the attack at Alkmaar Lord Paget was attached to the corps of the Russian commander-in-chief, D'Essen, who savagely resented the Duke's dislike, and was believed to be treacherous as well as incapable.

It was a bloody day and ended in a drawn battle. The story of Paget's concern in it is another proof of the unreliability of written history. The version in the *Historical Record* of the 15th Hussars might be supposed to be official. It gives Paget credit for a clever piece of strategy: he is said to have baited for the enemy with some apparently unprotected guns, and then charged victoriously from under cover of the sand-dunes. Sir Henry Bunbury, on the contrary, tells a different tale which has all the air of veracity, and he was almost an eyewitness. It is more picturesque and it glorifies Paget's readiness and gallantry as a dashing chief of guerrillas.

The night was falling, and the fighting was over, as all believed. The cavalry had unsaddled on the sands and the men were lighting their bivouac fires. Suddenly two squadrons of *chasseurs à cheval* charged down on the horse artillery, which had unlimbered at the head of the column. Paget and Sir Robert Wilson with some of the other officers had gathered in a group; they sprang to their horses, which were at hand; they were joined by some non-commissioned officers who were still in their saddles, and together they plunged furiously into the thick of the *chasseurs*. The rally gave their squadrons time to remount; and the chasseurs, almost to a man, were sabred or taken. Bunbury's story is all the more probable that the loss on the British side was but three *troopers and four horses*.

In the final retreat on the Helder, Paget, as before and after, was again in the rearguard. It was hard to transport the cannon over dykes and across ditches, and several pieces were abandoned. In one of those fights for the batteries, Paget with a single squadron made a desperate charge on a strong body of the enemy, and, riding through them, not only recaptured several British guns, but took five pieces from the enemy.

Again nine uneventful but not unfruitful years were spent at home. Again Paget returned to regimental duties, pursuing his military studies and indefatigably drilling his troopers. In 1802, promoted a major-general, he was removed from the command of his 7th Hussars, but the regiment, which did brilliant service under him, was always the object of his special affection. He was a lieutenant-general in 1808 when, ordered to Spain with two brigades of light cavalry, he embarked with the force under Sir David Baird. Baird joined the main army, only to receive orders to fall back upon Corunna or Vigo; but Paget, with two regiments of light horse, was in the forefront at Sahagun, when news came that Napoleon had left Madrid, and the memorable retreat was finally decided upon. Debelle with a body of heavy horse held the position in front of the British.

On the night of the 20th December, Paget with the 15th and 10th Hussars moved forward to attempt a surprise. While the 10th rode up to the village, the 15th, with Paget leading in person, turned it on the right. The surprise failed, for a patrol had given the alarm, and 400 of the 15th found themselves faced by a line of 600 horsemen. Paget charged incontinently, broke the line, and followed for some distance in hot pursuit. The affair was over in twenty minutes, but he made prize of eleven officers, with 150 of the rank and file. Always skirmishing in rear of the retreat, the next engagement of importance came off at Mayorga. He was threatened and intercepted by a body of cavalry, strongly posted on a ridge looking down upon his road The odds were all against him, but the way was to be cleared at any cost.

The ground was saturated, the hillside was slippery with sleet-drift, when two of his squadrons rode up the slopes, sabred twenty men, and took 100 more prisoners. That was an affair of pure dash and pluck, for his horsemen had gained confidence from constant successes. But at Benevente he found opportunity for a display of generalship. A halt and a rest had brought the disorderly troops into hand again; the magazines had been emptied and the town evacuated. Only Paget and his troopers were left to delay the pursuit and give time for the stragglers to gather in. Four miles to the east of the town, and the key of the position, had been the bridge of Castro Gonzalo, which Craufurd had broken down. But there were practicable fords above, and the French were already massing on those eastern heights, and the very next day Bessières was to ride through Benevente with 9000 horse.

At daybreak Lefebre Desmonettes could see nothing but pickets on the plain. He forded the river at the head of 600 *cuirassiers* of the Imperial Guard, and they passed it under the eye of their imperial master, for Napoleon was already at the front. The pickets fell back, but, when reinforced by some Germans, they charged and checked the enemy. Meantime the town was in a tumult and the plain was still covered with camp followers and baggage animals. Paget sounded to boot and saddle, forming his men up under cover of houses in the suburbs. As yet he would not show his strength, and the enemy, suspecting nothing of it, still came on.

Then, having gathered in the pickets and the German Hussars, the word was given for the onset. There was a shock; the enemy wheeled in squadrons, and in squadrons they plunged back through the Esla, turning to bay on the further bank. They seemed to threaten a second attack, but a battery of horse artillery had come up and unlimbered. Lefebre Desmonettes had taken a line of his own, and ridden for another point on the river. He was followed up, cut off, and captured, and Napoleon had the mortification of seeing one of his best cavalry generals lost to him. Needless to say that the prisoner was treated with all possible respect. When asked why he did not repass the river at once, when his flanks were turned and his retreat menaced, he replied:

> It was impossible for the Imperial Guard, who had won Austerlitz and Friedland, to retire without fighting before any enemy in any position, and in presence of their Emperor.

The answer gives an idea of what Wellington had to face at Waterloo, when, with wearied men and skeleton battalions, he had to stand the last desperate onset of the Guard.

Even in the rear, between Benevente and Corunna, though there were great hardships to be borne, there was little glory to be gained. And at Corunna Paget was ruled out of the game. Not only was the battle-ground impracticable for horse, but the troopers had been dismounted and their horses slaughtered.

Lord Paget came home in 1809 in time to be appointed to the command of a division in the Walcheren expedition. For four years he sat in Parliament for an obscure pocket borough, and in 1812, on the death of his father, he went up to the Lords as Earl of Uxbridge. He took no part in the debates and led a quiet and uneventful life, till Napoleon broke out of Elba. Then, when the armies of the allies were mustering, he was called to the command of the cavalry in the Low Countries.

Before he left for the war as Lord Uxbridge, he sat to Lawrence for his portrait, and as to that there is a well-authenticated anecdote which is at least a singular and veracious coincidence. As the hurried sittings were drawing to a close, the painter apologised for the trouble he had given, but added that he was not satisfied with the right leg and begged for one other hour. Lord Uxbridge answered that it was impossible, saying: "I must be off tomorrow morning, so the leg must wait till I come back." He came back, but he had left that leg to be buried in a garden at Waterloo, and, as he said, for he would often tell the story himself, "after all Lawrence had to paint from the cork substitute instead of the original"

In letters and memoranda sent to Captain Siborne, who was officially modelling a plan of the battle, he tells his own story of the campaign. On his arrival at Brussels the Duke said to him: "I place the *whole* of the cavalry and light artillery of the united army under your command." A few days afterwards the Duke intimated that for political reasons he desired that the Dutch cavalry should be under the immediate command of the Prince of Orange, and Uxbridge at once consented. It is undoubted that thenceforward, till the victory was won, they were working in the most harmonious relations, though a conversation of Wellington with Grenville gives a somewhat different impression. At that time all that was known was that Napoleon, by superhuman exertions, had mustered a formidable army with a powerful artillery, and had advanced in great strength to the French frontier.

It was believed that he was only weak in the cavalry arm, and that, as the event proved, was a strange delusion. But his operations were masked behind a triple line of fortresses, and Wellington had the disadvantage of standing on the defensive, in doubt as to where the attack might be delivered. He always maintained that the true line of attack should have been on his right, where Hill was on guard, far from the field of Waterloo. Yet he had to take precautions against the Emperor's actual scheme, which was to drive a wedge between Prussians and British, crushing the latter before their allies could come up.

Consequently the position of Quatre Bras, at the cross-roads, was of supreme importance. It locked the high-road from Charleroi to Brussels, and it kept open communications with the Prussians by the road leading eastwards to St Amand. On the 16th Napoleon attacked the Prussians at Ligny, while Ney had orders to drive in the allied posts at Quatre Bras and march upon Brussels by the grand *chausée*. Picton with the Brunswickers and the Guards under Maitland came up in support of the Prince of Orange; the fight was maintained with varying fortunes, but at nightfall the allies still held their positions.

With that fighting the cavalry had no concern, and Uxbridge was only a spectator. Cantoned at distances of from thirty to forty miles, they were being hurried forward to the scene of action. When Uxbridge rode into Quatre Bras in the afternoon, finding the Prince heavily engaged, he had turned back to hasten the light regiments which headed his columns. It was not till eight in the evening that the first of them arrived, to throw out pickets in advance of the positions.

By the morning of the 17th the circumstances had changed. The

Prussians had been driven back from Ligny, though still showing a dogged front, and Wellington learned the result at Quatre Bras when preparing to renew the battle. Now there was nothing for it but to retire likewise, re-forming his lines in advance of Brussels, and so keeping open his communications with Blücher's right. A strong rearguard was left in Quatre Bras to cover the withdrawal, and Uxbridge was ordered to protect it with his cavalry and guns.

The order was given at ten o'clock. It was difficult of execution, for the road ran through the street of Genappes, and in the rear was a flooded streamlet, spanned by a narrow bridge. Above and below were awkward fords, by which some of the cavalry squadrons were withdrawn. But the rains which flooded the little river had swamped the rye-fields on either side, hampering the action of the heavy French horsemen. Yet Wellington afterwards expressed his surprise that, with such an adversary as Ney behind them, the allies had been suffered to pass that Genappes defile without disturbance. As it was, according to Lord Uxbridge, the enemy made no movement till one o'clock. Then "very large masses of cavalry began to show upon our left and on the road from Namur. It was obvious they were coming on, and I therefore withdrew and sent back the infantry and the Light Dragoons that had been in front."

The enemy came on fast with horse and field batteries, the fire was hot and the onslaught vigorous, nevertheless the allies passed the river with trifling loss. Then the attack was concentrated on the *chaussée* and upon the central column. The 7th Hussars were sent forward, but those light troopers could make no impression on the solid mass of the enemy, who could hardly have fallen back with their reserves pressing forward. Uxbridge appealed to the 23rd Light Dragoons, "but my address not having been received with all the enthusiasm I expected, I ordered them to clear the *chaussée*, and said: 'The life Guards shall have the honour.'" The Life Guards came on "with right good will," and drove the French Lancers back into the town, "where they punished them severely." "The retreat was continued with perfect regularity."

Ponsonby's heavy brigade;

..... retired by alternate squadrons, skirmishing in the very best style, but finding that all the efforts of the enemy to get upon our right flank were vain, and that by manoeuvring upon the plain, which was amazingly deep and heavy from the violent storm of rain, it only uselessly exhausted the horses, I drew those regiments in upon the *chaussée* in one column, the guns falling back from position to position. We were received by the Duke of Wellington upon entering the position of Waterloo.... Thus ended the prettiest field day of cavalry and artillery I have ever witnessed.

Never again will be witnessed such hand-to-hand combats and conflicting shocks of cavalry in masses as turned from time to time the fluctuating fortunes of that battle. Horsemen were freely launched on either side, to break or support the stubborn defence of the British squares. It had been believed that Napoleon was weakest in that arm. In reality, he had there an overwhelming numerical superiority, and he had aligned on the ridge of La Belle Alliance 30,000 superb horsemen. There were the heavy squadrons of the Imperial Guard, the famed Ironsides of the *cuirassiers*, and the Poles with the long weapons that held the enemy at lance-length, remembering the proud traditions of the day when they stormed the Spanish batteries in the Somosierra. Uxbridge's brigades were far inferior in numbers, but at least as eager for the fray, and the incidents of the previous day had confirmed their confidence.

Brigades they were, for, unfortunately as it proved in the memorable charges at Waterloo, he had had no time to carry out his intention of forming them into divisions. At Waterloo they were posted in rear of the second line of the allied defence. To the extreme left, behind Picton and Kempt, were the light brigades of Vivian and Vandeleur. In support of the centre, on either side of the Charleroi road, were the heavy brigades of Ponsonby and Lord Edward Somerset. Far away to the right were the Brunswickers and Hessians.

The battle began at 11.30 with the attack on Hougoumont. Lord Anglesey—as he then was—writes that he had been visiting his posts on the extreme right, and those placed in support of the defence, when he saw large bodies of the enemy moving down upon our left, supported by simultaneous gunfire from all the opposite batteries. D'Erlon and Reille had come down on La Hale Sainte with four divisions of infantry, preceded by a cloud of *cuirassiers*. The Hanoverian sharpshooters still made good the farmhouse; the British regiments threw themselves into squares, the gunners running to them for shelter with their rammers and sponging-rods.

A Belgian battalion stationed in advance was scattered or cut to pieces, and when Picton brought up Pack's brigade the battle was going badly for the British. It was then that Anglesey galloped up, ordering the Household squadrons to form in line, and passing on from

Somerset to Ponsonby, bade him wheel into line with the other brigade. Turning back, he headed Somerset's brigade in the shock with Milhaud's *cuirassiers*. "'I led the advance,' he says: and the descent was so steep and the ground so broken that, on a very active horse, he was hard put to land safely. The ranks were naturally in confusion, but there was no time to lose, and *tant bien que mal* they hastily formed again." Forward they rode, threading their way through the intervals, round the left flank of the scattered squares. Then, forming again, they charged impetuously on the intermingled foot and horse confronting them.

Ponsonby went down, but nothing could withstand that furious onset. They took or rather rode over 40 guns; they captured two eagles; they made 3000 prisoners, who were disarmed and sent to Brussels. But when, after the overthrow of the *cuirassiers*, Uxbridge sounded the rally, his troopers were deaf to the call. Their blood was up, and moreover they were getting deeply entangled in the supports pressing forward from La Belle Alliance. So he rode back to bring up his second line, "which unhappily had not followed the movements of the heavy cavalry." The light supports were not forthcoming, and he says:

> 'Had I found only four squadrons coming steadily along at an easy trot, I feel certain that the loss the first line suffered when they were finally forced back could have been avoided.

Beyond the actual material gains, he says that tremendous charge had a great moral effect, for though the *cuirassiers* made repeated attempts on our lines, they always made them *mollement* and "as if they expected something more behind the curtain." When he regained his original position, he

> . . . . . met the Duke of Wellington, surrounded by all the *corps diplomatique militaire*. The plain appeared to be swept clean, and I never saw so joyous a group. They thought the battle was over. It is not possible to conceive greater panic and confusion than was exhibited at that moment.

The battle was far from over, but Uxbridge seems to have thought that it might have been, and severely reproaches himself for having put himself at the head of his squadrons.

> I committed a great mistake. The *carrière* once begun, the leader is no better than any other man; whereas, if I had placed myself at the head of the second line, there is no saying what advan-

tages might not have accrued from it.

It is not often that a veteran in retreat, proud of a great reputation, has the courage to be so frank, and the fact was that the second line, intended as a reserve, had pressed tumultuously forward to mix ranks with their comrades.

In the afternoon the French cavalry attacks shifted to the right of the Charleroi road, and it was then that our shattered infantry was most sorely pressed. Lord Anglesey says indeed that they never came on with a vigour which gave them "a hope of penetrating into our immovable squares," nor did they charge in a connected line. Charge in a connected line they could not, for each of the scattered squares was a little fortress sputtering fire, which they sought to outflank or break from the rear. But not even in the earlier onsets did they show more splendid or deliberate courage. Riding between those embattled squares, they were raked and riddled with ball from either side, while our guns belched shot and grape on them wherever they had a fair opening. Uxbridge had no means of interposing directly in that desperate and doubtful game; the wrecks of the heavies were not at hand to deal with the cuirassiers, and his light brigades were still far away to the left. But by a charge of Sir Colquhoun Grant's horse he silenced a battery which greatly annoyed the British right.

When the French attack was again directed on our centre, he galloped up to Vivian, sending his *aide-de-camp* to bring up Vandeleur in support The remains of the Household Brigade were formed up to the right. It was in repulsing the final attack that he received his wound. His horse was foundering, when he rode up to the major of the 23rd Dragoons and asked for a remount. The major gave him a troop horse and he spurred to the front, when a bullet struck him on the knee. "Perceiving his lordship to have fallen, and on galloping up finding it to proceed from a dangerous fracture, I ordered a small party to remove his lordship from the ground."

Sir Hussey Vivian had begged him not to expose himself, for "he had actually descended the hill previously, on foot and unattended, in hopes to be able to see under the smoke and make his own observations." But Sir Hussey says that the bold venture was made with a purpose and that it decided his conduct. He adds indeed that he mentions the circumstance to show that his lordship, though intrepid, was not incautious. Considering his ubiquity, his gallantry, his timely interpositions, and the spirit he inspired in the regiments he commanded, he may fairly claim the second honour of the fateful day. He was rewarded immediately by a marquisate, and shortly afterwards by the ribbon of the Garter.

From that precise narrative by one who was present, we may take it for granted that the familiar story about Lord Uxbridge's wound is apocryphal. It was told and believed that he was riding with Wellington when the shot shattered his leg. He quietly remarked, "By God, I am hit:" and his chief as calmly replied, "Are you, by God?" If not true, it was *ben trovato*, for the philosophic coolness of both was proverbial. There Wellington transcended all his lieutenants, and in some sense he was a fatalist When warned against solitary rides in France, or rides when only attended by an *aide-de-camp* or orderly, he said that his work was done, or if otherwise, that Providence would protect him from sharpshooters.

But perhaps the most notable instances were when he was confronting Marmont at Ciudad Rodrigo, after Fuentes d'Onore; they were told Larpent by Lord Ayimer. The situation was eminently critical. Once, when passing the French in dense fog, he found one of his divisions much exposed and the French in a village within a mile of him. He could see nothing, but on some prisoners being questioned, "they, to the dismay of everyone except Wellington, said that the whole French army were there. All he said was, quite coolly: 'Oh, they are all there, are they? Well, we must mind a little what we are about.'"

Again, soon after the battle, while holding his positions to cover the siege of Almeida, and reluctantly determined to engage superior forces rather than retire, Lord Aylmer burst in upon him while shaving, to tell him the French were away and their last cavalry mounting. The relief from prolonged tension must have been intense; but "he only took off the razor for one moment and said, 'Ay, I thought they meant to be off; very well,' and then another shave, just as before, and not another word till he was dressed."

Tranquillity had succeeded turmoil, and for ten years, without public employment of any sort. Lord Anglesey gave himself up, notwithstanding the loss of his leg, to yachting and field sports. An excellent and liberal landlord, he looked closely to the management of his estates. When Canning formed his Ministry in 1827, he was made Master-General of the Ordnance, with Cabinet rank. In the following year, when a strong man was needed for the Lord-Lieutenancy of Ireland, Anglesey was sent over. Nevertheless he had a warm welcome, for he was known to incline to liberal principles, and to be in sympathy with the claims of the Catholics. Characteristically, instead of making his entry into Dublin in a state coach, he rode in on his charger at the head of his staff.

The pageant fired popular enthusiasm, and he was followed to the castle by a shouting mob. That first vice-royalty lasted only for a year, but though O'Connell was then at the height of his power, the English Lord-Lieutenant rivalled him in popularity. When he was recalled, he rode out again as he had entered, attended to Kingstown by crowds of ragged admirers, who mingled lamentation with their farewells. An indiscreet letter to the Catholic primate had offended the Duke of Wellington and caused the recall. When the Grey Cabinet came into office, Anglesey was easily persuaded to return. His second tenure of office was less successful; the troubles had become more acute; he was constrained to strong measures of coercion, and he gave an opportunity to the agitators by exclaiming in an outburst of temper that he would control the country with a flotilla of gunboats.

His unpopularity came to a climax when after repeated warnings to O'Connell, and pelting the irrepressible demagogue with proclamations, he was finally driven to arrest him. Whatever support he may have had from ministers, he knew he had a powerful enemy at home. George IV. disliked his Liberal tendencies, and saw everything he said or did with jaundiced eyes. We have the word of the Duke of Wellington that "the king was furious with him." He said Anglesey "took upon him as King of Ireland."

The Duke added that "if there were two men the king detested they were the Duke of Cumberland and Lord Anglesey. He feared them both and dreaded their sarcasms." All things contributed to disgust him with an ungracious task; his health was shaken and his nerves overstrained; in 1833 he resigned and withdrew from active politics, though he was again for a time Master of the Ordnance. In 1842 he was gazetted to the colonelcy of the Horse Guards Blue, and four years afterwards he had the baton of field-marshal.

Lord William Lennox, in his *Celebrities I have Known*, has some pleasant recollections of his lordship. One incident especially shows his kindness of heart. A month before the Battle of Waterloo, the Duke of Richmond gave a great dinner at Brussels in the Rue de la Blarchisserie, the scene of the memorable ball. Many of the heroes of the battle were present; the room was small, and Lord William with two or three other youths were seated at a side table. Lord Uxbridge was there.

Of a noble presence, his carriage was erect, his figure betokened strength and activity, and his demeanour was dignified: in his splendid uniform, he was the *beau ideal* of a dashing Hussar. Of course, in the presence of royalty and so many other distinguished officers, we youngsters were somewhat cowed, and on our best behaviour, when during a dead silence Lord Uxbridge rose from his chair and in the blandest manner said: 'May I have the pleasure of drinking a glass of wine with the sideboard?'

A keen sportsman like Hill, and accustomed to stand fire himself, he scarcely sympathised with the susceptibilities of civilians. It is said that on one occasion he riddled the hat of a clergyman. "Don't be alarmed, my dear fellow," he said reassuringly, "I'm a perfect master of my weapon." He prided himself on his shooting, and one day, riding to his coverts—latterly he shot off a shooting pony—with Lord Lichfield and a young guest, he asked the youth whether he could shoot well. " I flatter myself I am as good as my neighbours," was the answer. "The devil you do, with Lichfield one side of you and your humble servant on the other."

Thanks to his wooden leg, he was familiarly known in military circles as "Old Peg." One day at dinner he remarked: "I hear that in my regiment"—"the Blues"—"almost every officer has a nickname. I suppose they will soon give me one."

"Why, bless you," said one of his sons, "they've called you 'Old Peg' ever since you've had the regiment."

"'Peg' I don't object to," was the comment, "but perhaps they will kindly leave out the 'Old.'"

He died in 1854. He had lived to extreme old age, but to the last the veteran, with his show of sprightly youth and his firm seat on a horse, was a familiar figure in the clubs, the Park, and the streets. When he was borne to the family vault in Lichfield Cathedral, few of his companions in arms were left to follow the coffin.

Lord Combermere

1

To the left of Lord Lynedoch's portrait in the "Senior" hangs that of Lord Combermere. There is striking contrast between the men. Lynedoch's portly figure is the sturdy Scot, with strong good sense predominating over an air of martial resolution. Combermere is a soldier of very different type: the light cavalry leader *par excellence*, the *beau sabreur*, disputing with Anglesey the *sobriquet* of the Murat of the army, delighting in the pomp and the trappings of war. He made the most of his rare chances of distinction, and though scarcely mentioned half-a-dozen times in the pages of Napier, like the Pagets he did good service on more than one battlefield, and more especially in protecting retreats.

But the cavalry were rather out of the running in the Peninsular campaigns, and had frequently to look on as spectators at combats they would gladly have shared. The cavalry was Wellington's weaker arm; he nursed it, and it may be said that he carried it in a sling; yet on occasion it could strike strong and sharp. The actions were often fought in the mountains or on broken ground; the passes in the sierras were steep and rugged; forced marches were frequent, forage was scarce, and the strain upon horseflesh was severe.

Stapleton Cotton came of a hunting family and was brought up in the saddle. He was the second son of Sir Robert Salusbury Cotton, member for Cheshire, and was born in 1778 at Llewenny Hall in Denbighshire. When Sir Robert succeeded to the title, on the death of his father, he had removed to Combermere Abbey, the chief family seat. Both he and his predecessor had done their best to dilapidate extensive estates. Unlike many of their aristocratic contemporaries, they were neither courtiers, *roués*, nor gamblers; but they never condescended to business details, and kept open house for all comers. The stables were filled with horses; there was welcome for the horses of any number of guests, and the very servants were encouraged to entertain their friends as they pleased.

Stapleton, though free-handed like his forebears, had enforced opportunities of economising in Spain, when the death of his elder brother had made him heir to the estates. At the age of eight he went to a private school and thence to Westminster. He was not a bookish boy; he must have been a thorn in the side of his teachers; but if his high spirits were always landing him in scrapes, his pleasant manners made him a general favourite.

After four years at Westminster, his father reluctantly consented to his entering the army, but would not hear of his going to one of the French military schools. For his misfortune, the boy missed the opportunity of studying the science of war and acquiring foreign languages; he was put in charge of a dull-witted Shropshire major who cared for nothing beyond buttons and pipeclay. But if he had slight advantages of education, he had nothing to complain of in the way of promotion, for on attaining his majority the fortunate youth was colonel of a crack light cavalry corps.

In 1791 he had been gazetted to the Royal Welsh Fusiliers at Dublin, and thence he was transferred to a troop in the Carabineers. The Carabineers were an Irish regiment—such a regiment as might have suggested the most rollicking scenes in *Charles O'Malley* or *Jack Hinton*. They were notorious as a hard-living and deep-drinking set—backing each other's bills with generous recklessness, and ready to "blaze" on the slightest provocation. Naturally the young captain's friends were anxious; with his buoyant spirits and careless temperament, there was cause enough for anxiety. But he showed unusual strength of will, with discretion and moral resolution that carried him safely through the ordeal. He could take occasional liberties with an iron constitution, but in that convivial age he was remarkable for sobriety.

Yet his jovial colonel, who took a great fancy to the lad, set him the worst possible example; and when the Carabineers were ordered to the Low Countries most of them modelled themselves on the general in command of the forces, who made a point of getting drunk after an early dinner. While in Flanders, in a single week Cotton figured twice in the *Gazette*, He was promoted first to a majority in a line regiment, and immediately afterwards to the lieutenant-colonelcy of the 25th Light Dragoons. He had actually left the camp for England on the morning of the 25th May 1794, when dropping shots were heard in

LORD COMBERMERE

the distance. He turned bridle and galloped back to place himself at the head of his still vacant troop and play a distinguished part in the Battle of Cateau.

The 25th was quartered at Weymouth and the young colonel, who frequently attended the king on his rides, was a special favourite. George III. liked him for his joyous humour and pleasant manners. Gay, rather handsome, and with brilliant prospects, Colonel Cotton was naturally in favour with the fair sex, but he never seems to have been much of a ladies' man, though he could love very seriously and was thrice married. At any rate, he never cared for a Capua at home when honour was to be won abroad. In 1796 his regiment was under orders for India. His mother and sisters besought him to exchange, but he declared he would rather throw up his commission than forego the opportunity for distinction in foreign service. He had no opposition to fear from his father, for old Sir Robert, though he seems to have been a henpecked husband, sympathised with his son's military ardour. The transport touched at the Cape when the Dutch were threatening a descent to recover their lost colony. Cotton landed his smart dragoons and mounted them on ragged little Boer horses, but their services were not called into requisition. They looked on, disappointed spectators, when the tables were turned at the surrender of the Dutch fleet to the future Lord Keith.

He was disappointed, too, at being disembarked at Madras instead of proceeding to Calcutta, as he had expected, for the pay and allowances in the premier presidency were higher. But he consoled himself with the hope of seeing some fighting, and his wishes were soon gratified. Tippoo Saib was preparing to make his last stand, and it must be owned that Lord Mornington's suave and provocative diplomacy had been pushing the fiery Sultan hard. Malavelly was almost a bloodless action on the British side, but the *Nizam's* soldiers and two regiments of Floyd's cavalry, commanded by Cotton, bore the brunt of the engagement, such as it was. Tippoo, with his own wild horsemen, had attempted a turning movement, when they found themselves faced by Cotton's dragoons and a native cavalry regiment. The enemy drew bridle and turned before Cotton could charge, though the fugitives were followed in hot pursuit Tippoo rallied his broken host in the fortress he deemed impregnable to any assault.

But a breach was made, and in open day Seringapatam was stormed. Tippoo died fighting gallantly at the northern gate, and there in a gloomy archway, with eyes unclosed and a scowl on his haughty features, the body of the fallen autocrat was found by the captive he had chained in his dungeons a few years before. It was a strange freak of fortune when Tippoo and Baird were brought face to face for the second time. During the campaign Cotton made the acquaintance of Colonel Wellesley, who was seven years his senior. No mutual attraction ever drew the men together, and though Lord Wellington appreciated Sir Stapleton's services in the Peninsula, he was never over liberal of praise.

In 1800 Cotton came home, to be gazetted full colonel. A matter that concerned him more nearly was his marriage. It was at once a marriage of love and of *convenance*. His wife was a very beautiful girl, but she was also the daughter of the Duchess of Newcastle, and the stepdaughter of General Craufurd's elder brother. So Cotton added to his own family influence that of the powerful house of Newcastle with its plurality of parliamentary votes. If he made friends by the match, he was soon to make a formidable enemy. Quartered at Brighton, he was a frequent guest at the Pavilion, and honoured with the intimacy of the Regent. A foolish indiscretion as to the Prince's somewhat mysterious relations with Mrs. Fitzherbert cost him the royal favour, for the Regent was vindictive over mere trivial offences.

He left the luxuries of Brighton for quarters in the Irish bogs, when the country was seething with the spirit of sedition, and he was in command of the cavalry in Dublin when Emmet's rebellion broke out. That amiable enthusiast could not control the demon of anarchy he had evoked. The venerable Lord Kilwarden was brutally murdered in his daughter's arms—a repetition of the tragedy of Magus Moor—and a colonel riding through the streets in uniform and unattended was shot down in cold blood. For that afternoon, alarmed by the popular excitement, the Lord-lieutenant had called the colonels of regiments to a council at Kilmainham. Cotton rode thither from his distant barracks and returned in safety, but he had the intelligence to skirt the sounds of the shouting and avoid the streets where the rioters were committing all manner of excesses. He had seen and heard enough to make him urge General Fox (the brother of Charles Fox) to call out the military and fire on the mob, and so the *émeute* was suppressed before the conflagration spread to the provinces.

2

The Regent might be unfriendly, but Fortune was still his friend. In 1805, at the age of twenty-seven, he was a major-general. Next year saw him seated as member for Newark, one of the Newcastle boroughs. The *amari aliquid* was then to come. The young wife to whom he seems to have been warmly attached sickened of consumption and died at Clifton. Like Graham, he sought relief in action. As it happened, he was ordered to Portugal in charge of the 14th and 16th Dragoons, brigaded together. He landed too late to take part with Moore in the advance to Sahagun. When Soult was descending on Oporto through the Tras-os-Montes, his brigade was dispersed on outpost duty, and he pushed his patrols to the Vouga.

When the conditions had changed and Wellesley dared what Cradock would not have been justified in attempting, he was with the cavalry division under Payne on the march to the Douro. On the 9th May 1809 he found himself facing Franceschi and his horse, from the southern bank of the Vouga. Hill had turned one flank of the enemy, Beresford the other, and Wellesley had devised a scheme of combination which was to surround Franceschi and crush the French centre. Napier does not mention that Cotton in the afternoon had ridden to headquarters to urge Sir Arthur to let him anticipate the hour fixed for his crossing the river, that he might surprise Franceschi with a night attack. Wellington always disliked nocturnal operations, and moreover he probably objected to any disturbance of his arrangements.

Be that as it may, when Cotton passed at midnight as prearranged, Franceschi had got wind of the allied movements. Gun carriages were breaking down in narrow defiles, and the difficult passages were obstructed. Cotton's guides misled him; when he came upon the French it was broad daylight, and they were formidably posted in superior numbers. To his mortification he could only look on while they retired, for his orders forbade him to hazard an encounter. So the cavalry had but the role of onlookers at the passage of the Douro, only two of the squadrons being sent across. Yet it seems that, had they been passed over at Avintas, they might have done good service, when Murray let the rabble of fugitives go by without firing a shot.

At Talavera the cavalry were in three brigades, and one of them was commanded by Cotton. Recalled from outpost duty, he had ridden on to the battlefield on the evening of the 26th July, anticipating Craufurd's arrival by several hours. His post was in reserve behind the great field redoubt which marked the left of the Spanish line and the right of the British. The nerves of our redoubtable allies were so highly strung that, though they knew the French were massed in front, they greeted Cotton's dragoons with a scattering volley. In the morning, on the plain below, the French brought off the surprise at Salinas; when Wellington himself was well nigh captured, Cotton was hastily called forward to help in covering the retreat. On the day of the battle he was in rear of Campbell's division, the rest of the cavalry being held in reserve on the extreme left. The battle had begun in the intense heat of a sultry noon, and through the afternoon it was raging fiercely. Hill still held to the height on the right, the key of the position, and Campbell was standing firm on the other flank.

It was then that Lapisse flung his serried columns on the allied centre. Received with a deadly discharge, shrinking from the shock of the bayonets, they were hurled back in a scattered rout. The Guards broke their ranks and rushed down in reckless pursuit. The flying masses met their supports, rallied on them, and returned. The Guards were broken, the Germans were in confusion, and the British centre was pierced. Cotton had no orders, but it was no time to wait for them, and he sounded the charge.

At that moment the orders came from the hill whence Wellington had been looking down on the *mêlée*. As the 48th Foot fell upon the flank of the triumphant French, Cotton charged them in front. The centre battle was restored and the day was won. He was afterwards thanked by the House for his deeds at Talavera, but got little credit through the general, who seems always to have been chary in praising him. Wellington indeed had thanked him personally, but did not even name him in despatches. Yet a private letter to his sister shows that it was a desperate piece of service, and Cotton, though he wrote freely to please his family, was never the man to blow his own trumpet.

> I have before experienced an equally hot fire, but never one of such duration. From ten in the forenoon of the 27th to the close of the day on the 28th (with the exception of a few hours at midnight) I was exposed to the enemy's shot.... The charge of cavalry, so much talked of in your newspapers, was led by your humble servant, at the head of two squadrons of the 23rd Light Dragoons, and so desperate was the undertaking, out of the two squadrons consisting of 160 men, all were either killed or wounded, with the exception of myself and six or seven dragoons.

The close of the day was unsatisfactory. He came back, hoping for supper and a change of clothes, to find his baggage had been pillaged by the flying Spaniards. The actual pecuniary loss must have been serious, for no general officer carried about a more costly kit When the British withdrew from the valley of the Tagus, he covered the passage at Arzobispo. When the army was in cantonments on the Guadiana, being made a local lieutenant-general, he became ineligible for the command of a brigade, but Sir Arthur gave him a lieutenant-general's command at Merida, attaching some artillery to his cavalry. He was fortunate in escaping the fever which sent many of his men into hospital; he always said that he had been saved by sobriety and his habit of taking early exercise on horseback. In the winter, having heard of his father's death, he went home on furlough.

In possession of the estates, devoted to his family, delighting in the life at Combermere, though by no means averse to the gaieties of the fashionable world, he nevertheless was not to be tempted to retire, and rejoined the army in the summer of 1810. He was given command of the whole cavalry, for now the cavalry was a separate division. But it was only occasionally, in general actions or when protecting a retreat, that the leader was personally engaged, and Cotton, although notorious for intrepidity, is said never to have crossed swords in single combat. Even as a veteran in retreat, he was not garrulous, and was seldom to be drawn as to his personal actions. Detachments of his division were in skirmishes on the Coa and Agueda.

In Craufurd's unfortunate affair of the 11th July, two squadrons of his old regiment, the 16th Light Dragoons, were very unjustly reproached with misconduct. In reality they had behaved with surpassing courage, and their gallant colonel, when charging home, had actually fallen on the enemy's bayonets. Cotton took up the matter with characteristic zeal; the mendacious calumnies were conclusively refuted, and Wellington wrote in express terms that the 16th had merited high commendation. But when mud is flung some will always cling, and the calumny has been revived in many popular histories.

Masséna descended on Portugal and Wellington withdrew to the lines. Throughout the long and harassing march, broken only by the interlude of Busaco, Cotton protected the retreating forces, nor did he lose a single baggage waggon. It is another example of how wild rumours are accepted credulously by conscientious historians, that Southey tells in his *Peninsular War* of Cotton losing six guns at Quinta del Torre. In reality his conduct of the retreat may compare with that of Ney when the tables had been turned, and he showed himself equally skilful as strategist and tactician. There were daily and nightly skirmishes between the hostile pickets and patrols. His system was to throw out light lines of skirmishers, to lure the enemy forward into traps and ambushes, where stronger reserves and supports were concealed.

Then came the counter-charge, the flight and the pursuit, for though the allied cavalry were inferior in numbers, they were much the better mounted. For himself, he was continually in the saddle, and often reconnoitring with the leader of his rearguard. A hot-tempered man, he was not to be trifled with, but on calm reflection he was inexorably just. He was a strict disciplinarian as to essentials, but, military dandy as he was, he never worried his men needlessly over details of ornamental equipment They had a rough time enough as it was, for in one of his officers' journals is the regular entry: "Rained heavily all night."

The skirmishes, in which they were almost invariably successful, gave his men a confidence which stood them in good stead, and the chief set an example of personal coolness which sometimes looked like *fanfaronade*. On one occasion he was with his rear-guard, and riding with Captain Brotherton, one of the paladins of the army. While the feeble guard was holding the enemy in check, a deep ravine dividing it from the main body, some squadrons were seen descending into the chasm to intercept it. Cotton was surveying the foe through his field-glasses, when Brotherton hinted it was high time to be off. The answer was worthy of the Iron Duke: "Why, Brotherton, what a fuss you're in!" and he "bluffed" the enemy for a little longer before wheeling round to gallop away. Brotherton (afterwards Sir Thomas) owned he was stung, "for I was one of Sir Ralph Abercromby's soldiers, and had seen some service before the Peninsula."

There was no place for horsemen on the precipitous steeps of Busaco. They held the plain behind the ridge, to the extreme left of the positions, a single heavy regiment being in reserve on the sierra. But there had been sharp fighting before that at the fords of the Mondego, and they were heavily engaged afterwards at Alcoentre and Quinta del Torre. Tompkinson, then a captain in the 16th Dragoons, gives a soldier-like but very graphic account of the affair at Alcoentre, and we take it as a representative sketch of what happened at many other places.

A narrow, hog-backed bridge spanned a yawning torrent bed, and beyond was the main street on a steep ascent, turning sharply off at right angles. The enemy brought up two regiments of cavalry, and the English picket was withdrawn behind the bridge. The supports were hurried into the village from the upper side, and were ready to charge down the street. "Colonel Elley" (the assistant adjutant-general) "was standing shaving at a window, as we came in. The confusion was complete; the street was blocked with gun carriages and ammunition waggons, with mules and oxen." The enemy sent two squadrons into the village; when they turned the sharp corner, they found themselves in face of the English; then the front ranks turned to fly, but those in the rear, knowing nothing of what was passing in front, were still pressing forward.

> They got so close that it was impossible to get at them, but we took twelve and killed six, driving them over the bridge again, and by this means allowing what remained in the town to get away. The enemy dismounted their dragoons and we retired through the town, forming on the heights on the other side.

When the army was safe within the lines of Torres Vedras, the cavalry was sent to the rear. Wellington wrote in a despatch to Lord Liverpool:

> Since the end of July they have done the duty of the outposts and the enemy has never been out of sight of them; and on every occasion their superiority has been so great that the enemy does not use his cavalry except when supported and protected by his infantry.

Again Sir Stapleton was in England, and again in April he was back with his division. Actively engaged in outpost duty and patrol work, constantly employed in keeping open communications, for a year he was necessarily kept in the background, and he did little more than look on at Fuentes d'Onore. In the end of February 1812 he had left the Agueda for the neighbourhood of Badajoz. On the 16th March that fortress was invested, and Graham was despatched towards Llerena to cover the siege operations. Cotton accompanied him in command of two cavalry brigades. Trusting in the tenacity of Philippon's defence, hoping against experience for a junction with Marmont, Soult was bringing up the army of Andalusia to the relief.

On the 8th April he learned simultaneously that Badajoz was taken and that Marmont had failed him; then he withdrew his headquarters from Llerena. Cotton was following with his cavalry, and Peyremont's horse were protecting the retreat. Then Cotton planned a daring operation, devised with remarkable skill, to surround and capture Peyremont's brigade. He had orders from Graham to make a demonstration.

Mounting a church steeple, he made his survey. He could see that Usagre, a perilous advanced post, alternately held by the French and the allies, was still occupied, while in an intervening wood were the bivouacs of Peyremont's cavalry. Behind that wood was a line of low heights upon their left. Immediately he took his measures. His light dragoons under Anson marched at midnight; the officers were called away from a ball they had been giving to the Spanish ladies.

While Anson amused Peyremont from the front, Le Marchant with the heavies was circling round to cut the road to Llerena. But Anson began his attack too soon, and the French, seeing nothing of Le Marchant, who was screened by the heights, fell back to form again in order of battle. Anson still kept the enemy in play, till Le Marchant came up to charge them in flank. There was a fierce encounter; the French horse broke and fled; in the hot pursuit many were cut down, and a considerable number of prisoners were taken. For that, as for the more important affair of Castrejon, Cotton got but cold commendation. In the despatches he was merely bracketed with Le Marchant and the soldiers under his command.

Castrejon came off in this wise. In July the warfare had shifted from the Guadiana to the Douro. Wellington was watching the river, passable by various fords and bridges. On the 17th, Marmont, after sundry feints and manoeuvres, had concentrated at Nava del Rey, to the south of it, and driven in the allied pickets on its tributary, the Trabancos. Wellington was much in the dark as to the strength and positions of his enemy. On the night of the 17th, Cotton with the right wing, composed of the 4th and Light Divisions, with Anson's cavalry, was guarding the Trabancos. His position was weak, and though he did not know it, he was opposed to the whole French army. Wellington learned at midnight that Cotton was in touch with the French—Cotton had sent the tidings by three separate messengers—and immediately threw himself into the saddle, ordering the other cavalry brigades to follow.

At daybreak Cotton's pickets were again driven back. He drew up his infantry behind the village, but the divisions were separated by a ravine. Before them his horse were posted with a troop of horse artillery, but the country in front was so broken that the enemy and their movements were effectually concealed. Cotton, seeing nothing but horse patrols, advanced his own cavalry by his right towards the river. The movement was answered by a heavy fire from musketeers and masked batteries. He sent forward a foot regiment to the support of his horse, and skirmishing went on till, at seven o'clock, Wellington and Beresford galloped on to the ground.

It was then Wellington had a more narrow escape than at Salinas before Talavera, when the incident occurred that has been described elsewhere, and when the course of European history might have been changed, had the Commander of the allies gone a prisoner to Paris. Then Cotton, by his able handling of his force, kept the enemy at bay till supports came up, and with equal skill covered the retreat to the Guarena. Wellington paid him with only verbal thanks, but Soult gave warmer praise. He wrote in despatches, that had it not been for the stand of General Cotton, Marmont would have surprised and defeated the British before Wellington could have rallied them in a defensible position.

The 21st July was the eve of Salamanca, the battle that shook Napoleon's hold on Spain and went far to win the Borodino. Yet Wellington was never in greater anxiety than when back in his old positions on San Christoval; be had been out-marched and out-manoeuvred in the race for the Tormes. He had to choose between seeing his communications with Portugal cut and abandoning Salamanca, or adopting the third alternative of risking a battle at disadvantage. He could not foresee that next day he would be vouchsafed such a crowning mercy as Cromwell at Dunbar, and that his watchful and sagacious enemy would deliver himself into his hand. Marmont had passed the fords on the Upper Tormes and was extending his left under cover down the left bank. Wellington had also passed by fords and bridges lower down, but he still kept the 3rd Division and D'Urban's cavalry on the right bank.

The darkness had deepened as Anson's brigade of horse, following the Light Division, descended the heights. It was the prelude to the bursting of one of those terrific storms which heralded so many of the Peninsular battles. The peals were deafening: the lightning was flashed back from the points of the bayonets as the columns waded the Tormes shoulder high. Anson's brigade had hardly bivouacked when the horses tore up the picket pins and stampeded. Colonel Dalbiac of the 4th Dragoons was seated with his wife in front of the brigade. "We had barely time," wrote Captain Tompkinson, "to hurry the lady for safety under a gun."

The day broke, and Wellington from the heights was watching the development of operations. The initiative was with Marmont, for he could not even continue a retreat without exposing both flank and rear. Then ensued the fighting from the twin heights of the Arapiles; but, as the day went on and operations dragged, Wellington personally withdrew from what was called the English Arapiles and waited. At three o'clock news was brought which roused him to activity. He galloped forward to a commanding headland, and saw that Marmont had given the unhoped-for opportunity.

Weary of waiting, seeing no considerable force on the right bank of the river, circling round behind the wooded screen of a forest, the French marshal had sent General Thomières forward to throw himself across the Rodrigo road. "Now I have him," was Wellington's exclamation, for the continuity of the hostile line was broken by a broad and inviting gap. The order was given, the signals were passed, and the troops massed on the English Arapiles were launched like an avalanche on the plain beneath.

It was at five according to Napier, an hour earlier according to other authorities, that Pakenham struck his tremendous blow at Thomières. The French general, emerging from the woods and gaining an isolated hill which terminated the southern heights, in place of seeing the British in full retreat, found himself faced by Pakenham and his solid columns. His own line had straggled in threading the woodlands; the irresistible shock of his adversary rolled it up. He was driven back on a host already in confusion, though desperately disputing each inch of ground. Marmont had gone down, two other generals of division had fallen, and Clausel was left in command. While Pakenham was fiercely pressing upon Thomières, Cotton with his heavy and light brigades, and Ball's troop of horse artillery, were following along the higher ground on his left rear.

Cotton had ridden forward to reconnoitre. What he saw was Thomières closing up on Clausel, Pakenham fast closing in upon the flanks of both, and the 5th Division assailing the front through a storm of ball and cannon shot Immediately beneath the hill where he stood was a division of French infantry. Riding back, he formed his men in three lines: the heavies under Le Marchant first, Anson behind, and Victor Alten in the last. When he brought them to the summit he saw that the division below had weakened, a part having been drawn off to the right battle of the French. He gave the order to charge; it is said that Le Marchant asked in what direction; that Cotton answered briefly, "To the enemy," and that high words ensued.

Naturally both those hot spirits were fired to fever heat, but it is hardly within the range of possibility that Le Marchant can have suspected that any impeachment of his courage was intended. Be that as it may, Cotton had cause to lament the outburst of temper, for those were the last words Le Marchant ever uttered. The tempest gathering on the hill burst on the French below. Le Marchant's heavies came thundering down, flanked emulously by Anson with his light cavalry. Twelve hundred Frenchmen were literally trampled down; the survivors, awed by the suddenness of the catastrophe, sought refuge in their panic in British squares.

Le Marchant had soon lost his saddle, but then Cotton and Anson took the lead. The tremendous onset was furiously continued, a second column of infantry was ridden down, and five cannon were captured. Wellington had as usual turned up where the battle was hottest and most critical. He may not have loved Cotton, but for once his feelings found vent. "By God, Cotton," he exclaimed, "I never saw anything more beautiful in my life! The day is yours!" That burst of feeling, on the spur of the moment, was worth more than any formal praise in despatches.

Le Marchant's dragoons, wearied with striking and slaughtering, were relieved by D'Urban's brigade. Anson's light cavalry still led, Cotton riding with the brigadier; D'Urban followed, and the rear was brought up by Alten's Germans. As Clausel was driven back towards Alba de Tormes, which in Wellington's belief was held by Carlos d'España, the cavalry, keeping between the retiring foe and the Tormes, made many prisoners. But Wellington had missed the full cast of the net, for the Spanish garrison had evacuated Alba and the broken battalions of the French were streaming unmolested across the river.

Cotton had escaped in the battle by a miracle, though his magnificent dress and the gorgeous trappings of the superb charger he rode made him a conspicuous mark. He had been posting his pickets towards Alba and was returning to camp, when he was fired at by a handful of Portuguese soldiers, who mistook his party for a French patrol. A bullet shattered his arm; the consequences were serious, nor did he ever altogether recover the injury. But those Peninsular heroes were men of iron, priding themselves, from the highest to the lowest, on the stoicism with which they supported pain. Recalling the experiences of the wounded commander of the cavalry, we can realise the sufferings of the subalterns and the rank and file.

Mastering his agony. Cotton rode on to the nearest village. There he found shelter in a hovel, and they made him as comfortable as possible in a pig trough. Wellington, on hearing the news, galloped thither to inquire, having picked up, a surgeon on the way. The surgeon would have amputated, but Cotton refused till the sentence was confirmed by the chief medical officer. The result was that the arm was saved, though the recovery was painful and tedious. Wellington wrote, in recommending him to Lord Bathurst for the red ribbon of the Bath:

> No cavalry could have done better than ours in the action, and I must say for Stapleton that I don't know where we could find an officer who could command our cavalry in this country as well as he does.

Sir Corbet Corbet, his uncle, was a constant correspondent, and now, when Cotton was incapacitated from writing, Sir Corbet had a letter from a lieutenant in the 16th Dragoons.

> Do not be alarmed—slightly is Sir Stapleton wounded in the arm. It could not be otherwise; he is so desperate in exposing his life. It is perhaps a fortunate thing for his family and friends that he is impeded in his glorious but too dangerous career. He never goes into action but in the richest of dresses, puts himself at the head of everything, and courts danger like a soldier of fortune whose future welfare depends upon a single dash. But Sir Stapleton's conduct is admirable, and the lowest soldier reveres him. If we lose him, the British cavalry will be in a wretched plight.

His wound laid him up for many weeks. It was fortunate that his staff surgeon was at his side to curb his impatience, but there was a tragic incident when Dr. Littledale fainted on his shoulder in their carriage, and was carried away to his deathbed. Spanish *grandees* vied in their attentions; one offered a palace at Salamanca, and another lent a coach with the team of mules. He rejoined on the retreat from Burgos, and headed some hard fighting on the 29th October. When the army withdrew to winter quarters he went home on sick leave, and Lord Wellington expressed his regrets in a letter to the military secretary at the Horse Guards. At the same time the praise was in more modified terms than the despatch sent off in the excitement of victory.

> He commands our cavalry very well—indeed I am certain much better than many who might be sent to us, and who might be supposed cleverer than he is.

The congratulations that greeted his return were not unmixed with mortifications. His services had been considerable, his position was high, and his connections were powerful. He seems confidently to have counted on a peerage, but the honour was as yet denied him. There and towards another object of his aspirations it was Beresford who blocked the way. Wellington represented that a peerage for Cotton would be a tacit slur upon the marshal, nor was he prepared to press either claim on the Ministry.

Moreover, two days after his arrival Cotton was invited to an interview with the Minister at War. His hopes were high, but if he expected that it would pass off pleasantly, he was disappointed. Beresford was Cotton's junior in the service, and in point of fact the minister wished to persuade him to waive his claims to succeeding by seniority as temporary second-in-command of the allies in the event of anything happening to Wellington. It was very natural that Cotton should refuse; it was still more natural that, in the interests of the country, ministers should hesitate as to giving the supreme command to a cavalryman.

Returning to Portugal, he hurried after the army, arriving at Vittoria, as an Irishman might say, barely in time to miss the battle. The cavalry quartered in the plains could only hear of the mountain warfare which succeeded, and even after the invasion of France there were few laurels for the horsemen to gather. After the passage of the Bidassoa they were on constant outpost duty before a vigilant and daring enemy; and then, like Craufurd on the Coa, each evening Cotton had his baggage packed and his horses saddled.

Nothing of consequence happened to him before Orthez; then when Hill was hanging over the French communications, and their retreat had degenerated into a race, Cotton charged through some covering companies, sabred several hundreds of the fugitives, and made 2000 prisoners. His work would have even been more effective had it not been for a rugged torrent bed, beyond which the bulk of the fugitives saved themselves. Nor did he do more than look on at the battle of Toulouse, though with two brigades he had followed the retreat of Soult, watching the roads by which the army of Arragon might have answered Soult's summons to the rescue.

Napoleon had abdicated; Soult had recognised the armistice; and Cotton, coming back to Toulouse, issued his farewell "order" to the cavalry. Remembering the course of events in the following year, there is pathos in the passage where he expresses a hope—it was really confident assurance—that, should they again be employed in the service of their country, he looked forward to the honour of being again at their head.

He was in England in May; this time he had his peerage, nor had he any reason to complain of the delay. It would be difficult as invidious to draw distinctions, but those associated with him in the honours were Hill and Hope, Graham and Beresford. Cotton had passed through the fires of the war, and come off with an arm slightly maimed; he was not yet forty, and had half his life before him; he was rich, handsome, and a lion in society. He had engaged himself on his previous visit, and now he was married to Miss Greville. The marriage proved ultimately unfortunate, though the causes of the disagreement have never been cleared up, but meantime he was passionately in love.

One taste the betrothed couple had in common, for both were devoted to music, and before the Portuguese bullet had splintered his arm bone. Cotton had been no mean performer on the violin. A man of middle age, he looked young for his years. With regard to that. Sir Harry Jones of the Engineers had a good story to tell. He was in a group of staff officers sitting round a bivouac fire, when apparently a young *aide-de-camp* galloped up to give some peremptory orders.

"Who is that chap?" asked Jones of the distinguished engineer, Sir Richard Fletcher.

"Don't you know?" was the answer; "why, that is Sir Stapleton."

Lord Combermere celebrated his wedding with characteristic dash. It seems to have been fixed for a particular day, when an imperative engagement clashed with it, for the city was giving the great banquet to the allied sovereigns. Lord Combermere duly dined at the Guildhall; he slipped away early, and drove to Lambeth Palace, where he was married by the primate just before midnight.

For nine months the honeymoon was prolonged, and then Napoleon had broken out of Elba. Europe was again shaking to the tread of armed hosts, and Lord Combermere was confident he could redeem the pledge he had given in orders at Toulouse. A great army was assembling in the Netherlands and Wellington was in command. Impatiently he waited for the expected summons, but no summons came. Then he lost patience and wrote the Duke to place his services at his disposal. It would appear that Wellington really wanted him, and had made application for his appointment.

It may be plausibly assumed that a grumble of the Duke to Lord Bathurst had special reference to the case of Lord Combermere. He wrote that, as he had consented to take command of a raw army, he might have been permitted to choose his own instruments. But it has been suggested that the powerful influence of the Prince Regent was thrown into the opposite scale. He had never forgotten or forgiven the indiscretion of Colonel Cotton at Brighton, so Lord Uxbridge received the coveted command, when he won some glory and lost an arm.

Lord Uxbridge had lost his arm and was invalided; the very day after Waterloo, Wellington wrote to Lord Bathurst: "We must have Lord Combermere if he will come." Covetous of fame, it was a cause of never-ceasing regret that he had missed the crowning battle of the closing campaign. With many similar passages, there is this one in a letter to an aunt: "I shall never recover the mortification and disappointment which I feel at not having been at the famous battle." But he accepted the proffered command and joined the army in Paris, to be quartered in Josephine's favourite Malmaison.

Oddly enough, the caretaker left in charge by Eugènie Beauharnais was a Cheshire woman, to whom the memory of her divorced mistress was sacred. Lord Combermere's consideration for the old lady's feelings is an engaging trait in his character. When the Duchess of Rutland was coming on a visit, he had arranged that her Grace should occupy the private apartments of the Empress. But the old housekeeper looked glum, and consequently the order was countermanded.

3

With the withdrawal of the army of occupation came a break in Cotton's career. Napoleon was an exile in the Atlantic, and there was the promise of a long European peace. It might have been supposed that he would have settled on the patrimonial estates, kept open house at Combermere, and given occasional attendance in the Lords. His income must have been ample, and moreover an annuity had just been voted him. We are puzzled to surmise why he should have accepted such an exile as had been forced upon the fallen Emperor. But in 1817 he sailed for Barbadoes as governor of that colony and commander-in-chief of the Leeward Islands.

There he remained for four years, practising hospitality in Government House, in place of his own old Abbey, oiling the wheels of diplomacy with our French neighbours by his gracious manners in an interchange of courtesies, and reducing the heavy mortality in the garrisons by attending to the sanitation of their quarters. In 1822 he was again in Ireland as commander-in-chief, after an absence of fourteen years. The country at that time was comparatively quiet, and Lord Combermere gave a lead to the gaieties of the capital, making many

Irish friends. One of his cronies, and a congenial spirit, was Lord Norbury of duelling fame— the Toler who was said to have shot himself into practice—and who, had their *rôles* been interchanged, would have revelled in heading a cavalry charge. But he was summoned of a sudden to very different scenes, and for the first time he was to have an opportunity of handling an army of all arms in the field.

There was war in Burmah, there was trouble brewing in India, and the strong fortress of Bhurtpore—the fortress which had given the name to Colonel Newcome's favourite hack—was in the hands of a daring usurper, who was bidding defiance to the British flag. It seemed likely that another expedition must be undertaken against the formidable place which had baffled Lord Lake of Laswaree. At that juncture the health of Sir Edward Paget, who was in chief command, had given way, and he expressed a wish to resign. The juncture was critical. Many of the native princes were disaffected, and if Doorjam Sal, the usurper at Bhurtpore, could hold his own, there were not a few who were ready to throw in their lot with him.

Moreover Runjeet, the old lion of the Punjaub, was not to be trusted. Professing friendship, he was waiting on events. A deputation from the directors of the company sought counsel of the Duke of Wellington, asking him to suggest a successor to Paget. He seems to have thought more highly of Lord Combermere than formerly, for he answered unhesitatingly: "You can't do better than have Combermere: he is the man to take Bhurtpore."

The deputation objected, in language which was the echo of the Duke's Peninsular despatches:

We don't consider him a man of any great genius.

"I don't care a damn about his genius," said his Grace, "I tell you he is the man to take Bhurtpore." The deputation withdrew, and Lord Combermere had the appointment

Everything happened as had been feared and foreseen: the usurper remained recalcitrant, gaining increasing confidence from the assurances he received. All the surrounding states were seething with excitement, and the eyes of their restless rulers were turned upon him. And, indeed, it appeared probable enough that the English would recoil from risking a second check. The garrison the *rajah* had gathered was largely composed of fighting Rajputs and Pathans: they were encouraged by the prestige of the former success, and, as it proved, they were men to die at their posts. Although the *rajah* had won his position by poison and the dagger, they could not have found a more gallant leader. In numbers they were scarcely inferior to the besieging force, which consisted of natives, stiffened by four English regiments and one or two batteries of artillery. With his 25,000 men Combermere was to invest a city with an *enceinte* of eight miles.

Enclosed in formidable ramparts, with many bastions which enfiladed the intervening curtains with flanking fire, those defences might be battered but could scarcely be breached. For they were built on a peculiar system of Oriental architecture, of clay and cow dung mixed with straw, and supported by balks of timbers, each layer having been baked hard in the sun-blaze before the next was laid on. The *enceinte* was encircled by a deep and broad ditch, in many places a natural torrent bed, and (the low lands beyond could be flooded by a cutting from an adjacent lake.

In the centre of the city was the citadel, commanding everything and tremendous in its strength, with wall rising over perpendicular wall, each of them flanked with semicircular towers and bastions. Lake had made a rush on the place from the west side and failed. Combermere, impetuous as he was by nature, realised the gravity of the crisis, and made his preparations with extreme deliberation. Nine days were devoted to a survey: then he decided on conducting operations from the east, and began by cutting the lake channel, so as to be free from the danger of flooding. The trenches, once opened, were pushed steadily forward, under heavy fire. It became comparatively harmless as the parallels were advanced, for the guns riveted on the ramparts could not be depressed, but then the sorties became more frequent.

Combermere had no little trouble with the *coolies*, who naturally objected to deadly exposure for small pay, and with the *sepoys*, who had taken it into their superstitious heads that they were made the subjects of experiments in hospital. In dealing with them he showed exemplary tact and patience. In many respects it was a remarkable siege, and it dragged slowly. The line of investment was weak, and at one place a body of horsemen broke through. It might be well for the *rajah* to get rid of his horse, but the rest of the garrison were staunch to his standard. The fire of the besiegers was heavy and sustained; in a single day, and scarcely an exceptional one, 1600 shot and shell were expended. Latterly, while the batteries were cannonading the ramparts, the mortars were showering shell upon the city. "A disagreeable necessity," but the end must be attained quickly, or there would infallibly be a second failure.

The reserve arsenals at Agra were nearly emptied, and no wonder. For, as the works defied ordinary breaching, the attack was carried on chiefly by mine and sap, and the consumption of powder was enormous.

The parallels were thrust forward, nearly to the foot of the ramparts; galleries were being driven under the ditch, and beyond scarp and counterscarp. Small mules were frequently exploded under the bastions to aid the guns in the breaching. There were exciting scenes in that subterranean warfare, when mine was met with countermine. Once, when there was but a thin partition of earth, the British sappers heard voices and the clink of iron. They quietly deposited some powder casks at the end of their passage, laid a sausage, lighted the train, and blew the counterminers into eternity. The guns were directed upon four points; explosives and shot had broken the ramparts, but these breaches were rather rough landslips than practicable slopes.

Moreover the besiegers learned by their spies that, wherever there was an earth-slip, the crown had been retrenched. It was of the last importance to learn how far the access was practicable, and some of the ventures made to obtain information read like episodes from an extravagant romance of knight-errantry. Once a single *havildar* crawled up in broad daylight, the mark for a thousand matchlocks. On another occasion a party led by two English officers went on a forlorn hope as desperate: they actually gained the summit and pelted the soldiers of the *rajah* with stones. Yet, in both cases, the daring adventurers came back almost unscathed. Their reports of the obstructions convinced Combermere that if the place was to be taken, it must be taken by mines.

The day was fixed for the assault. Everything had been done to keep the matter secret, but an intensified cannonade seems to have given the enemy some warning, and they were not taken altogether by surprise. Combermere had adapted his dispositions to the difficulties to be surmounted and the defence to be overpowered. The explosions were to create confusion and clear the way. There were to be no forlorn hopes as at Badajoz or San Sebastian; the attack was to be delivered by companies, and as far as possible by regiments. So every man fought shoulder to shoulder with his comrades, and under the leading of his own officers.

It was to be delivered in two columns, subdivided into six sections, and for the last time in the story of British warfare there were "grenadiers" actually handling grenades. In reality it was a confession of impotence which reminds one of the tactics of the Chinese, for, though the fusees were lighted, the grenades were not charged. The general directing the attack counted on the moral effect on the enemy, but declared that loaded grenades were most destructive to the men who carried them.

At eight o'clock in the morning the signal was given to fire the mines. There were two minor mines, and a third near the chief breach, which contained the almost unprecedented quantity of 10,000 pounds of powder. The smaller mines were sprung with deadly effect, followed by a brief interval of breathless suspense. Then came a roar and rush like the outburst of a volcano; it was succeeded by an earthquake, and the air was darkened with such clouds of dust and *débris* as overwhelmed Pompeii and Herculaneum. The troops had been prudently kept back in the third parallel, where they crouched in comparative safety. Combermere, eagerly watching, stood more exposed, and was enveloped in the falling showers of brick and timber.

One of his brigadiers had been struck down at his side, and two of his orderlies were killed behind him. But the besiegers were prepared for the shock and the beleaguered were not. Before the clouds had lifted or thinned, the heads of the attacking columns were at the foot of the works and scrambling up the landslips. They were aided by light bamboo ladders, lined with stout canvas, in the manner of fire-escapes. They gained the ramparts barely in time, turning to right and left, for the gallant defenders were already rallying. On that narrow roadway, rent across occasionally by mines discharged by the retreating garrison, and with an abyss on either side, the combat raged, the bayonets clashing with the sabres and *tulwars*. At one point there was a singularly tragical episode.

Two hundred of the enemy, forced to the verge of the rampart, were taken simultaneously in front and rear. There was no asking for quarter or thought of surrender. The strength of the onset was irresistible, and to a man they were hurled down into the ditch. To add to the horrors of the scene, muskets flashed off at close quarters had set fire to the armour of quilted cotton, and those who had fallen unhurt on the bodies of their comrades were suffering the agonies of slow cremation. Combermere, when the great mine went off, had been with difficulty restrained from heading the stormers; he had hurried forward with the supports, when the enemy, recovered from their alarm, were pouring in a deadly fire. He came up with his staff, when some of those miserables were still alive and piteously shrieking for succour.

Giving assistance was a work of extreme peril, for matchlocks and ammunition pouches were still exploding. Some scorched and blackened victims were extricated, but the rest had to be left to their fate.

The carnage was well nigh over and the town was won when Combermere emerged from the narrow streets on the glacis of the citadel It had already hung out the white flag, and the gates were reluctantly opened, though not before guns had been ordered up to blow them in. The easy surrender was probably owing to the flight of the *rajah*. At the head of a troop of horse, heavily girdled with gold *mohurs*, he had forced a picket and ridden forth into the jungle. But the skirts of the wood were guarded by our cavalry.

After lurking in hiding for two hours, the *rajah* broke out prematurely: had he had the patience to wait a little longer, he might have effected his escape, for the brigadier, believing that all was over, had already ordered his men to dismiss. The stubborn resistance of Bhurtpore may be gauged by the fact that half the garrison were killed or wounded. The treasure taken was nearly half a million, and these were golden days, for the commander-in-chief for his share got £60,000, and the shower even reached the privates, who had £4 per man.

The campaign had justified Wellington's penetration and greatly raised Combermere's reputation. He had admirably handled a force of all arms, and showed himself possessed of qualities of which he bad scarcely been suspected. He had adapted himself to trying circumstances, gone to work circumspectly, and mastered his own impetuous temperament. In his strategy he had displayed both initiative and decision; and, unlike Lynedoch at San Sebastian, where conscious of ignorance he had let himself be guided by the counsels of the professional engineers. He received the thanks of the Governor General and of both Houses of Parliament, and besides the pecuniary reward, he gained a step in the peerage.

For nine months, while Lord Amherst was invalided in the hills, Combermere was acting Governor-General. The double work was severe, but he was indefatigable in the discharge of his duties. Calcutta in the hot season might have tried any constitution, but he kept his health by early exercise, regular habits, and extreme sobriety. He breakfasted lightly and dined at four, when the *aide-de-camp* on duty was victimised to keep his chief in countenance over an ascetic meal. But seven was the regular dinner hour, when the staff assembled, and at great entertainments guests of many classes and conditions had hospitable welcome.

The host merely trifled with a little rice and some weak wine and water. Always energetic and delighting in change of scene, he made many progresses through the expanding empire. There were still a Great Mogul, with the shadow of power though the substance had departed, and a King of Oude, with feudatories of various degrees, but all with exorbitant pretensions. The progresses, being political, were pompous as the ceremonial receptions, and Combermere's letters and journals are full of picturesque description. His camps, with the attendants and interminable baggage trains, often contained 5000 souls. At the entry into Lucknow, like Marmion scattering angels on the drawbridge at Norham, the king, the commander-in-chief, and the resident were tossing handfuls of gold *mohurs* to the crowds.

At the close of the festivities the city was blazing with lights and the Jumna was illuminated with showers of fireworks. At the interview with the Mogul, though the resident, as was customary, removed his shoes, Combermere insisted that he and his staff should approach the presence in boots and spurs. But he could not escape the dress of honour, and to his disgust was invested over his uniform with a flowing robe of spangled muslin.

At Sirdanha he renewed acquaintance with that very remarkable woman, the Begum Sumroo. She had come to him in his camp before Bhurtpore, begging to be permitted to assist in the attack. The offer, which was courteously declined, was probably prompted with a view to sharing the spoils; for, although the treasure actually taken was great, there was a belief, and apparently a credible one, that fabulous riches were buried about the place. The *begum* was a famous Amazon who headed her armies in the field, and extended effective protection to the feeble descendant of Akbar when menaced in Delhi by his warlike feudatories.

Combermere and the lady were kindred spirits; regard and admiration seem to have been mutual She promised solemnly to remember him in her will—a promise she failed to keep—and persuaded him to pledge himself to act as guardian to her stepson, with whom he was to share her wealth. For the *begum* had been twice wedded, and both times to European adventurers. Her stepson and heir was the once well-known Dyce Sombre. When the youth came to England many years afterwards, plunging headlong into a career of folly, Combermere did his best) to redeem an embarrassing pledge which caused him infinite trouble and anxiety.

Possibly the missionaries and chaplains might have objected to one part of his policy. He made a point, of conciliating the Hindoo priests and falling in with, their superstitions; if he did not actually worship at their shrines, he offered sacrifices to their idols. The customary victim was a sheep: the head was severed at a blow, and it was diplomatically arranged that the gods should graciously accept the offering. So all the omens were invariably favourable when the progress moved forward on the next stage.

Then, as before, it was the familiar story; as Macaulay has put it tersely in the essay on Hastings: "Govern leniently and send more money," was the invariable refrain of the Board in Leadenhall Street. On one point Combermere gratified them, and at some sacrifice of popularity: addicted to personal display as he was, he suppressed the costly bodyguard, kept up for show. But in a more serious matter he crossed their wishes, and he protested earnestly against an edict of Lord William Bentinck, who had succeeded Lord Amherst as Governor-General. The field allowance granted to officers of the native army was to be arbitrarily reduced It was a paltry piece of false economy, for the saving was barely £20,000 a year.

The officers were thrown into a ferment of discontent, and they had the sympathy of the *sepoys*, who feared that their own pay might be cut down. Combermere laid stress on the danger of a discontented army, but the directors declined to recede from their decision, and he anticipated dismissal by handing in; his resignation.

4

After all his service in India did not help him pecuniarily, and, as his hospitalities had been profuse, he doubtless returned a poorer man. He had placed his Bhurtpore prize-money with a firm of Calcutta bankers. There were whispers as to their credit: he repeatedly desired to withdraw his funds, and was as often persuaded to delay on representations that the firm was perfectly solvent, but that the withdrawal of the commander-in-chief's confidence would be their death-blow. He had come back to England and gone down to Combermere Abbey when the news reached him that Alexanders' had failed. He and his family had been getting up a little dramatic performance: the host played his part with his accustomed serenity, and all went merry as a marriage bell. Not till the next morning at breakfast did he mention that he found himself poorer by £60,000.

In the preceding year he had been gazetted colonel of the 1st Life Guards; consequently and *ex officio* he was one of the gold-sticks in waiting. As the gold-sticks were in personal attendance on the sovereign, it had been customary to swear them in as members of the Privy Council. Lord Combermere vainly expected an intimation which did not come. He had always been on cordial terms with the Duke of Clarence, and the explanation of the delay came from the outspoken sailor-king. His Majesty said that the Duke of Wellington had objected, and that the objection had only been overcome by his own imperative order.

More than that, it had been intended to create him an earl, and in the circumstances nothing could have seemed more natural, but there again the Duke stood in the way. In fact the attitude of Wellington towards his lieutenant is almost as inexplicable as Combermere's sudden separation from his wife. The Duke was straightforward to a fault, and his actions were governed by the strictest sense of honour and duly. Yet with Cotton he seems always to be blowing hot and cold; sometimes he ignores him in despatches; sometimes he gives him moderate, and at other times unstinted praise. He created a special command for him on the Guadiana, that he might retain his services; yet in a private letter he damned him with the faintest praise, after his splendid behaviour at Castrejon and Salamanca.

In later life some of the letters were almost affectionate; and on his side, when the Duke was to be laid to rest in St. Paul's, Combermere's letter to Hardinge, begging for an invitation to assist at the funeral, is that of a bereaved friend and sincere mourner, mindful of old times and grateful for many kindnesses.

Like his Grace of Richmond—the Lord March of the Peninsula—who, as he used to say at agricultural dinners, had taken to breeding South Downs when he sheathed his sword, Combermere betook himself to rearing cattle. His herd of Ayrshires was famous; he kept his bailiffs up to the mark, and looked carefully to his farming accounts. The balance was always on the wrong side, but that was inevitable. The best of landlords and a great builder of ornamental cottages, there was an annual gathering in an adjacent village, when tenants and neighbours met to celebrate his birthday. He seldom went to town when he could help it, and his old comrade, Lord Hill, who was tied to the Horse Guards by his duties, was always ready to relieve him as gold-stick in waiting.

But he had a special summons to take leave of King William on his deathbed, and as gold-stick he attended at the young queen's coronation. The wife from whom he was separated had died, and in 1838 he married for the third time. That proved a happy union, and, though already sixty-five, he had still a long period of matrimonial felicity to look forward to. The years immediately succeeding his marriage were passed between the Abbey and travel on the Continent.

In 1852 he was somewhat mortified by being passed over for the master-generalship of the ordnance when Lord Hardinge received the appointment, but on the death of Wellington he was consoled with the constableship of the Tower. As constable and colonel of the 1st Life Guards, the veteran of eighty found ample occupation. He had commanded the regiment for thirty-five years; he had been careful in the selection of candidates for commissions; and he took a paternal interest in the officers, who had, one and all, been chosen by himself. When the Crimean War broke out, like an old war-horse he scented the battle from afar, and would gladly have taken the field again had there been a chance of his services being accepted.

After sixty-five years on the army lists, with the distinction he had gained, he felt it as a grievance that the baton of field-marshal had not been bestowed. The coveted honour came at last in the summer of 1855, when he was agreeably surprised by a graceful letter from Lord Hardinge. Men of exceptional strength and vigour are inclined to become morbidly sensitive to any indications of old age. Lord Combermere met with a mortifying contretemps at the grand volunteer review, when, ignoring his years, he appeared on horseback in the heavy uniform of the Life Guards and carrying the gold stick of office. His friends fancied they had found him a safe charger warranted to stand firing and shouting, but the horse got restive, took to plunging violently, and finally had to be led by one of the pages.

On the return of the procession he became altogether unmanageable, when his Lordship was persuaded to condescend to take a seat in one of the royal carriages. Nor was his annoyance lessened by comments in the papers next morning, with sympathetic condolences on his years and infirmities. His last public appearance was at the wedding of the Prince of Wales, when he was one of the witnesses to sign the register. For many seasons, as his friend Lord Londonderry said, he had been in the habit of "boiling himself" at Buxton, latterly passing his winters in the milder climate of Bath or Clifton.

It was at Clifton he died in 1865 in his ninety-second year: till he lay on his deathbed he had kept his faculties unimpaired, though his strength and vitality had been gradually decaying. He had outlived all his distinguished contemporaries, and when he passed away he was the last of Wellington's lieutenants. His resting-place might well have been in Westminster Abbey or St Paul's, but he was buried in the family vault in his own parish of Wrenbury.

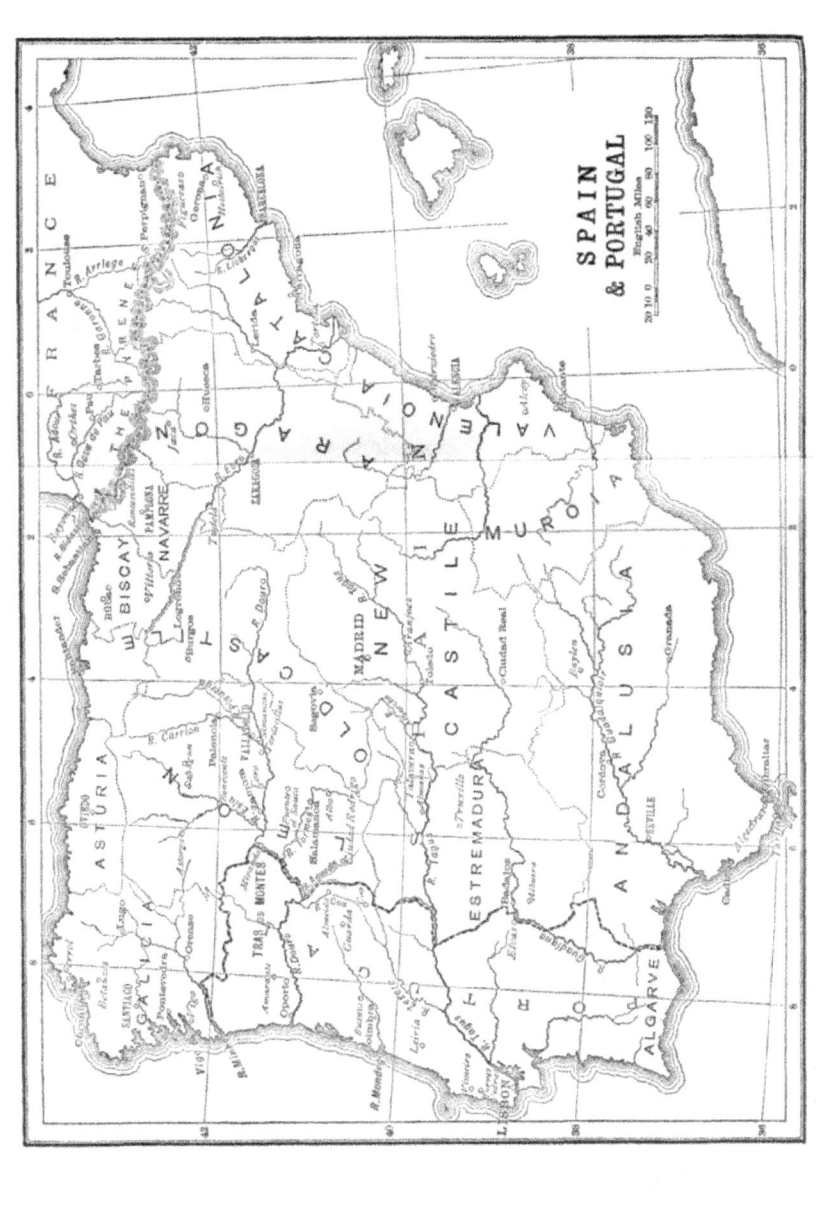

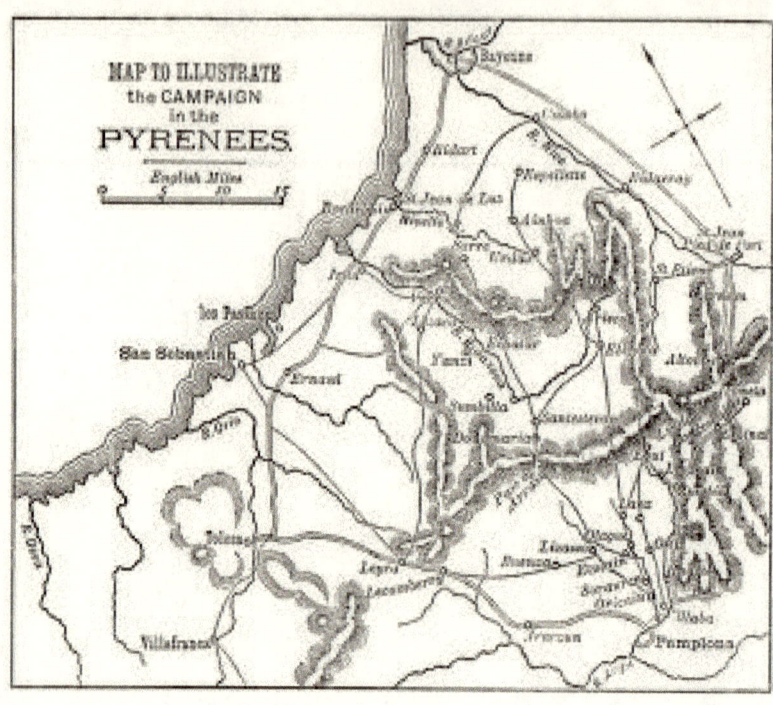
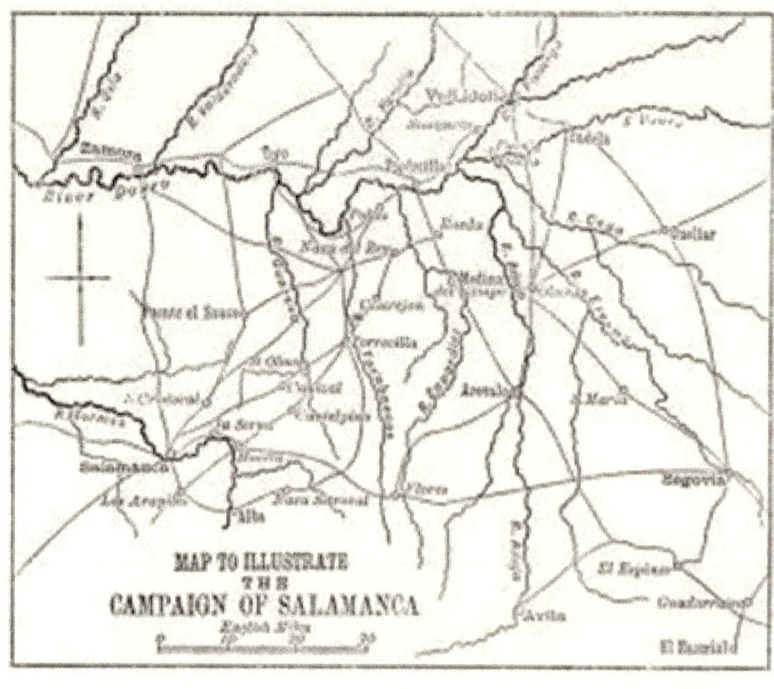

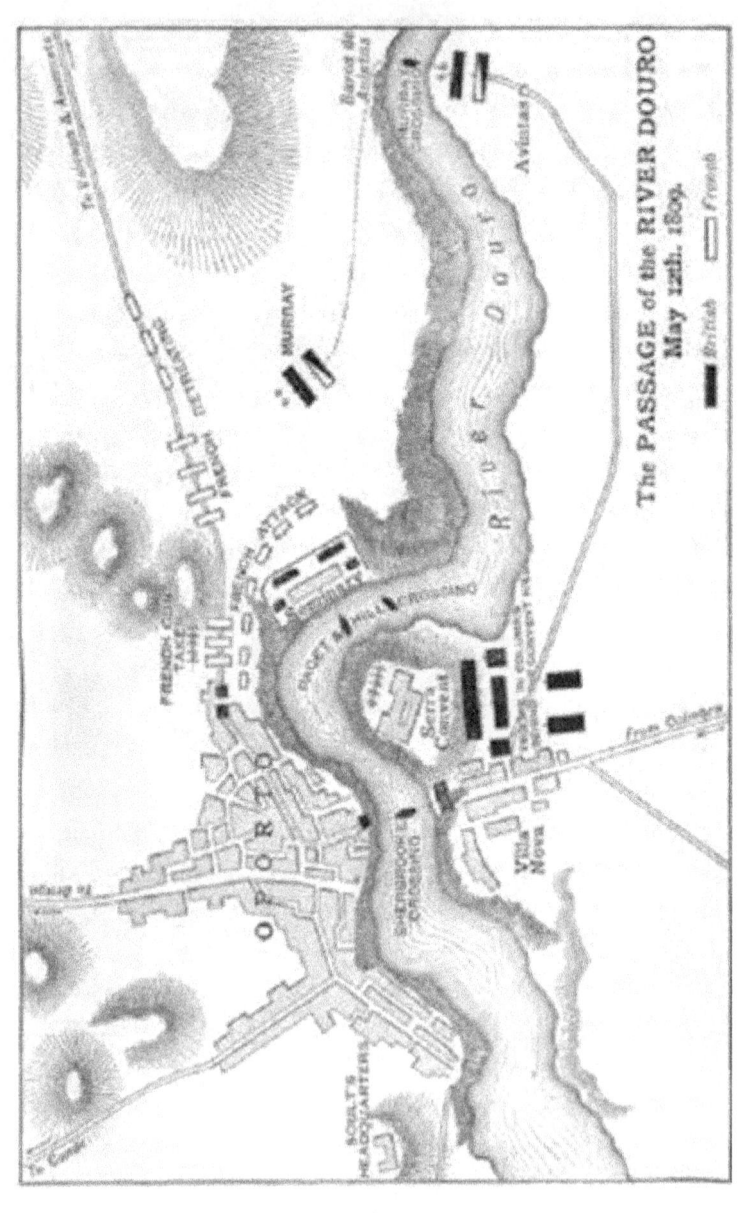

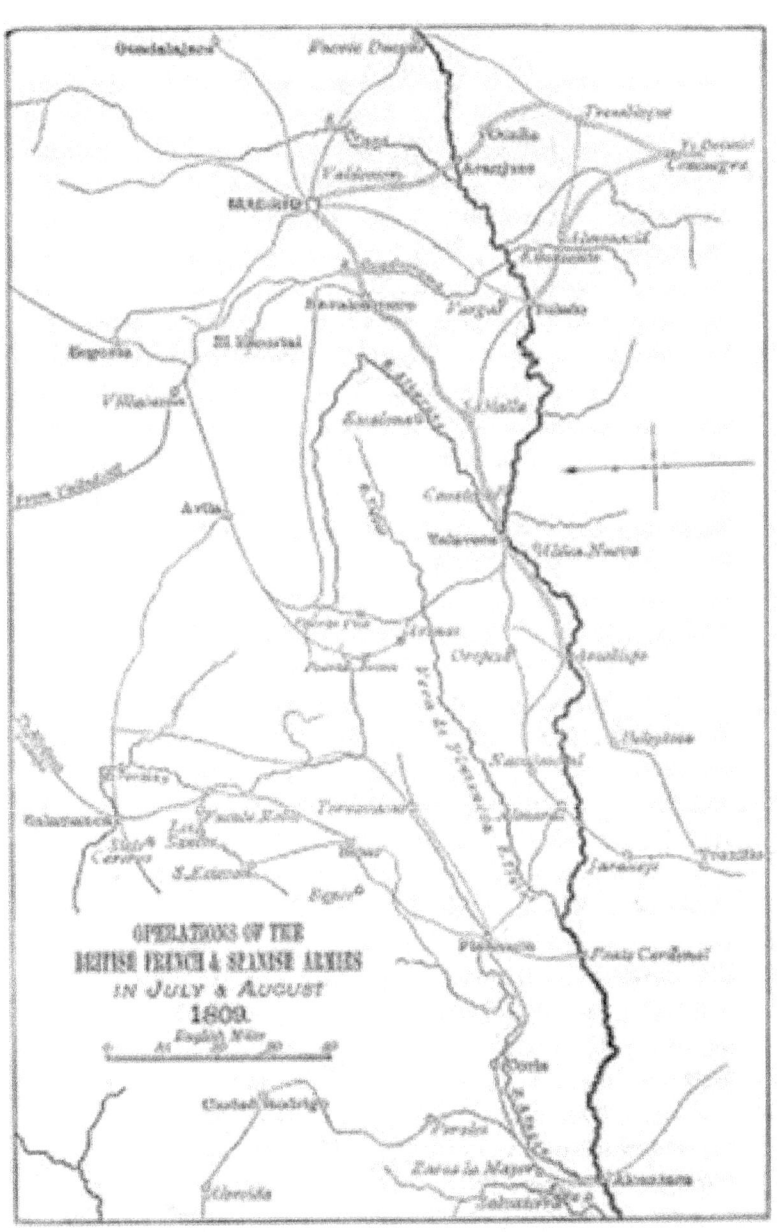

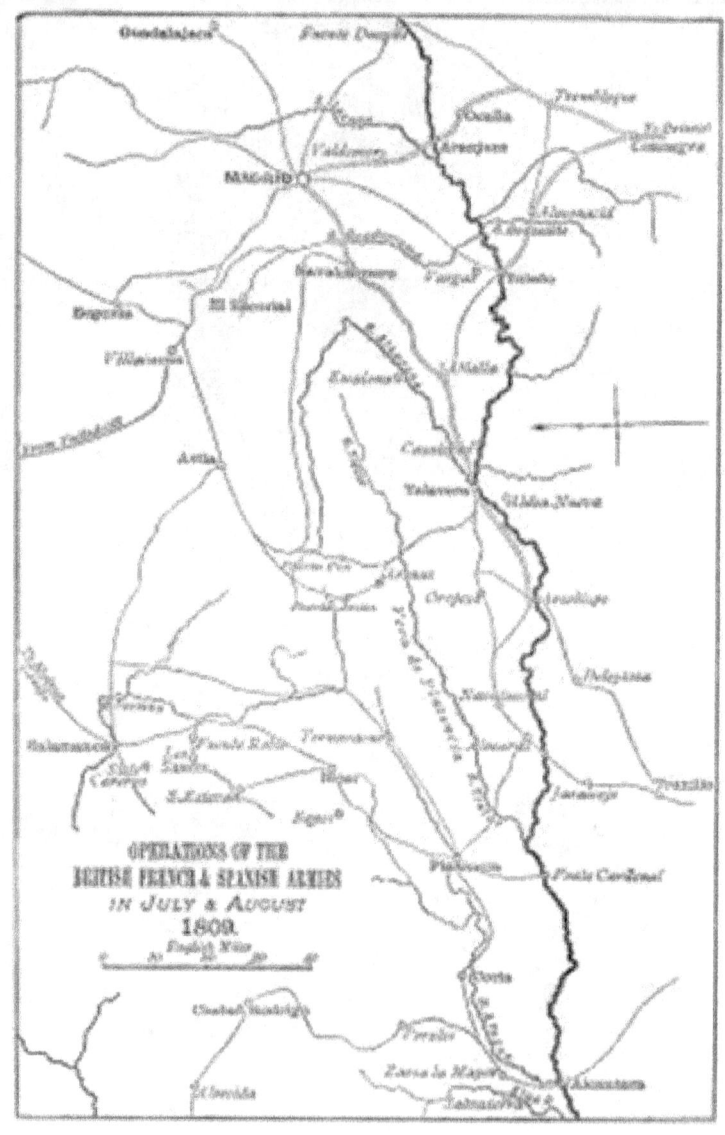

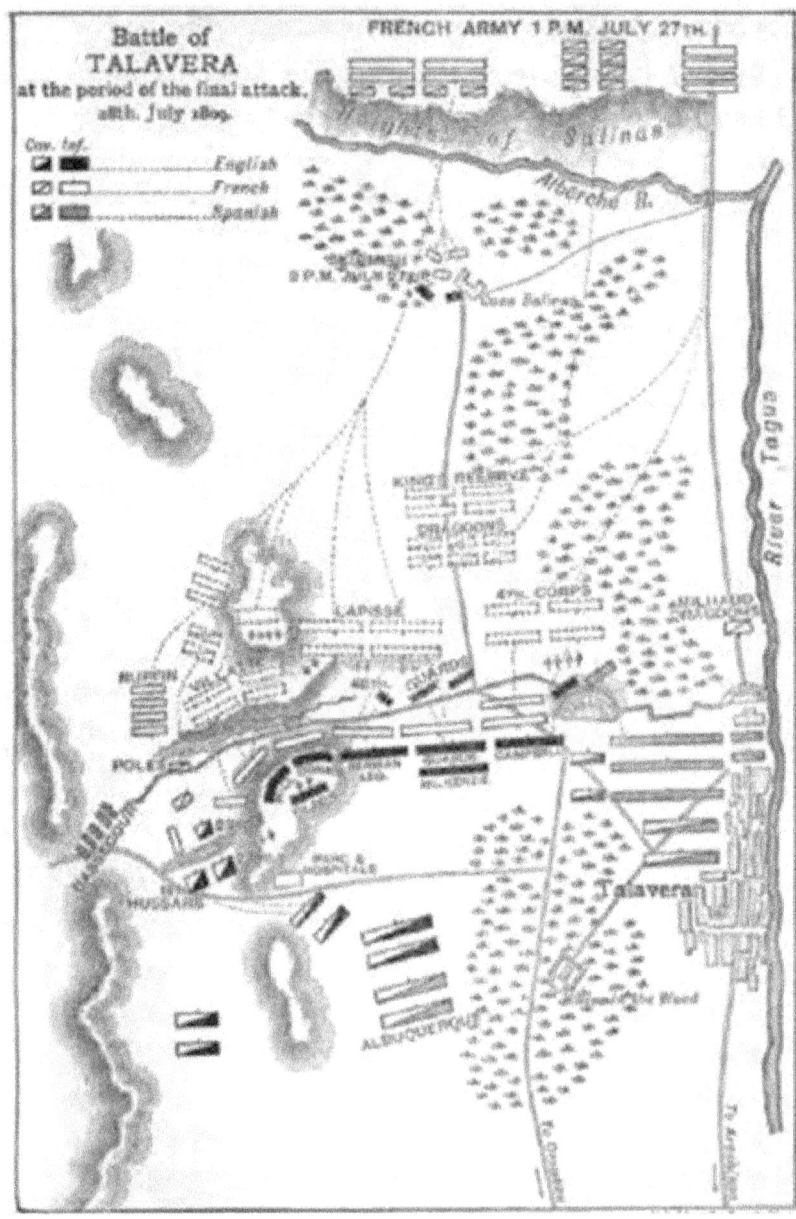

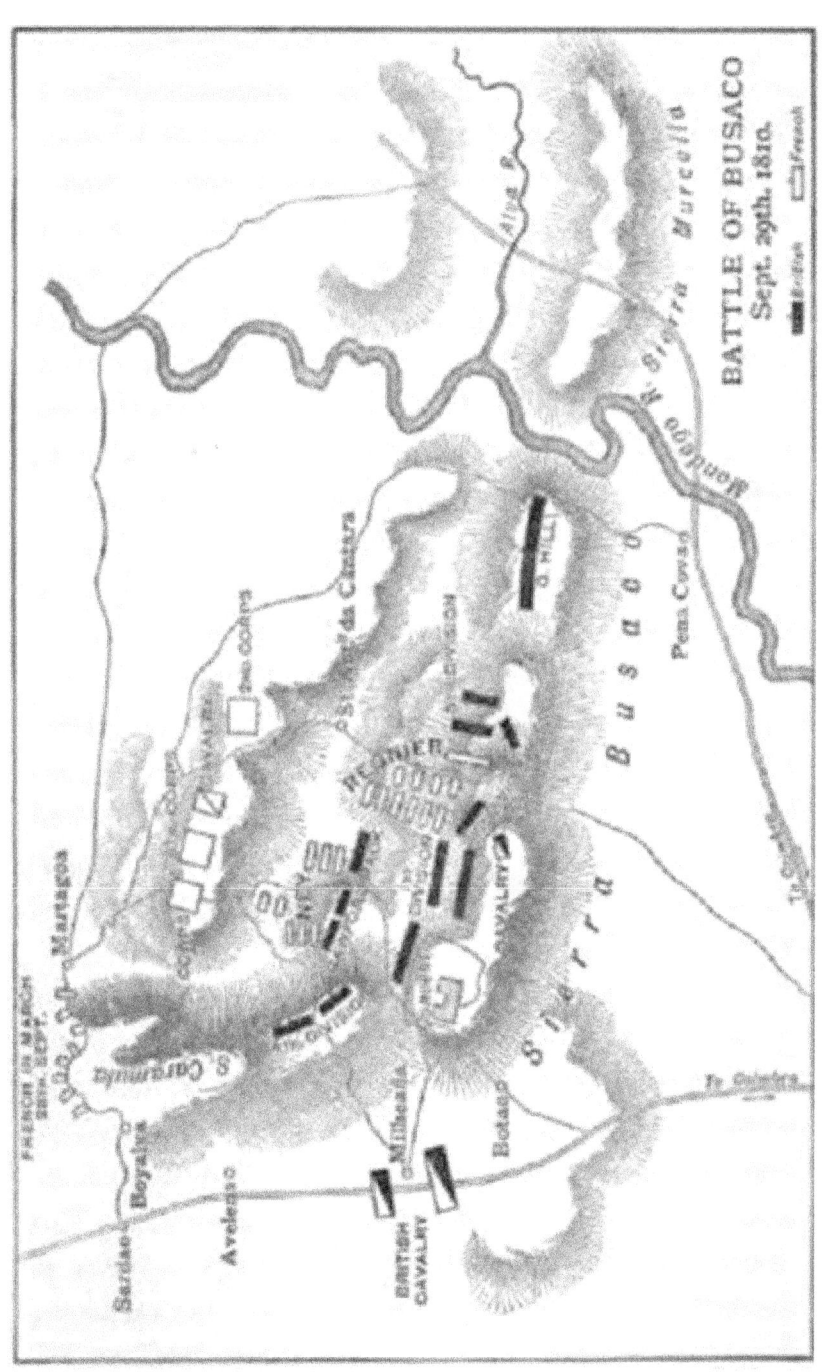

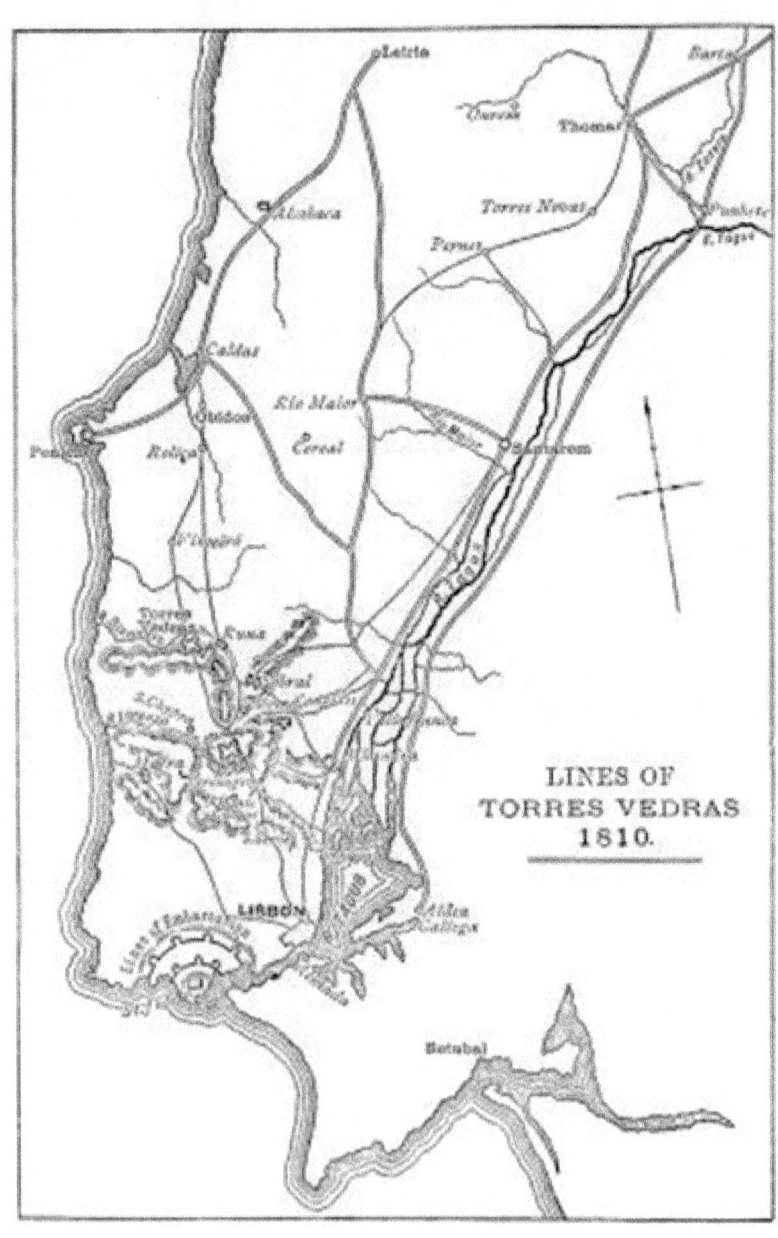

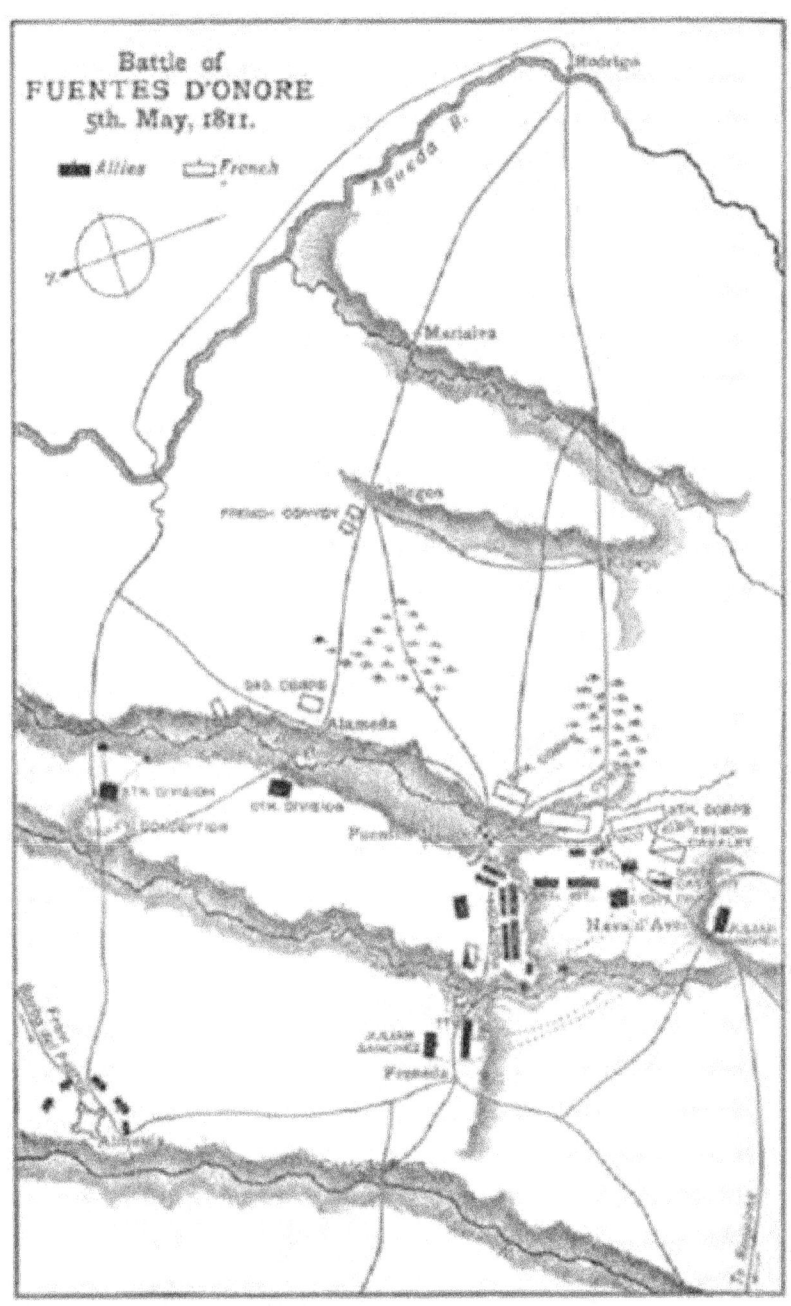

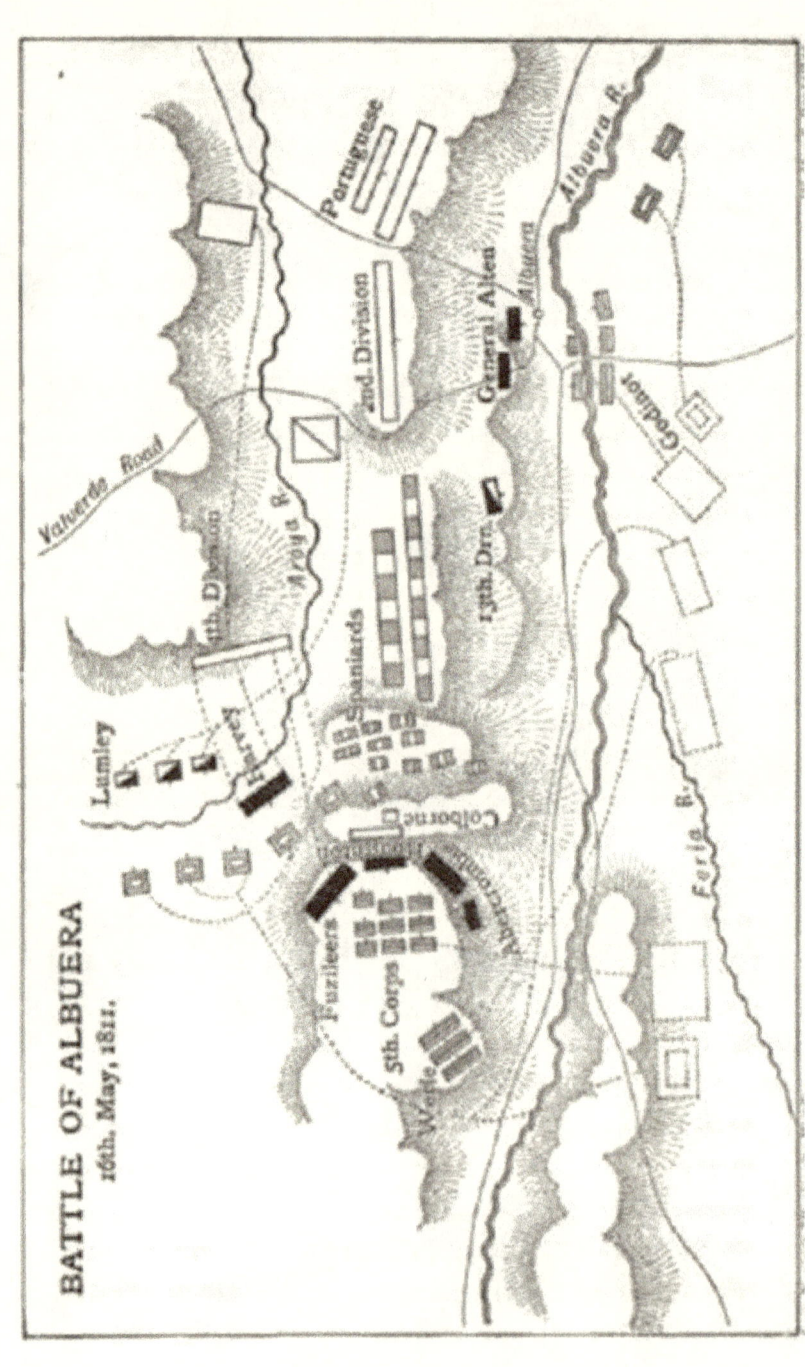

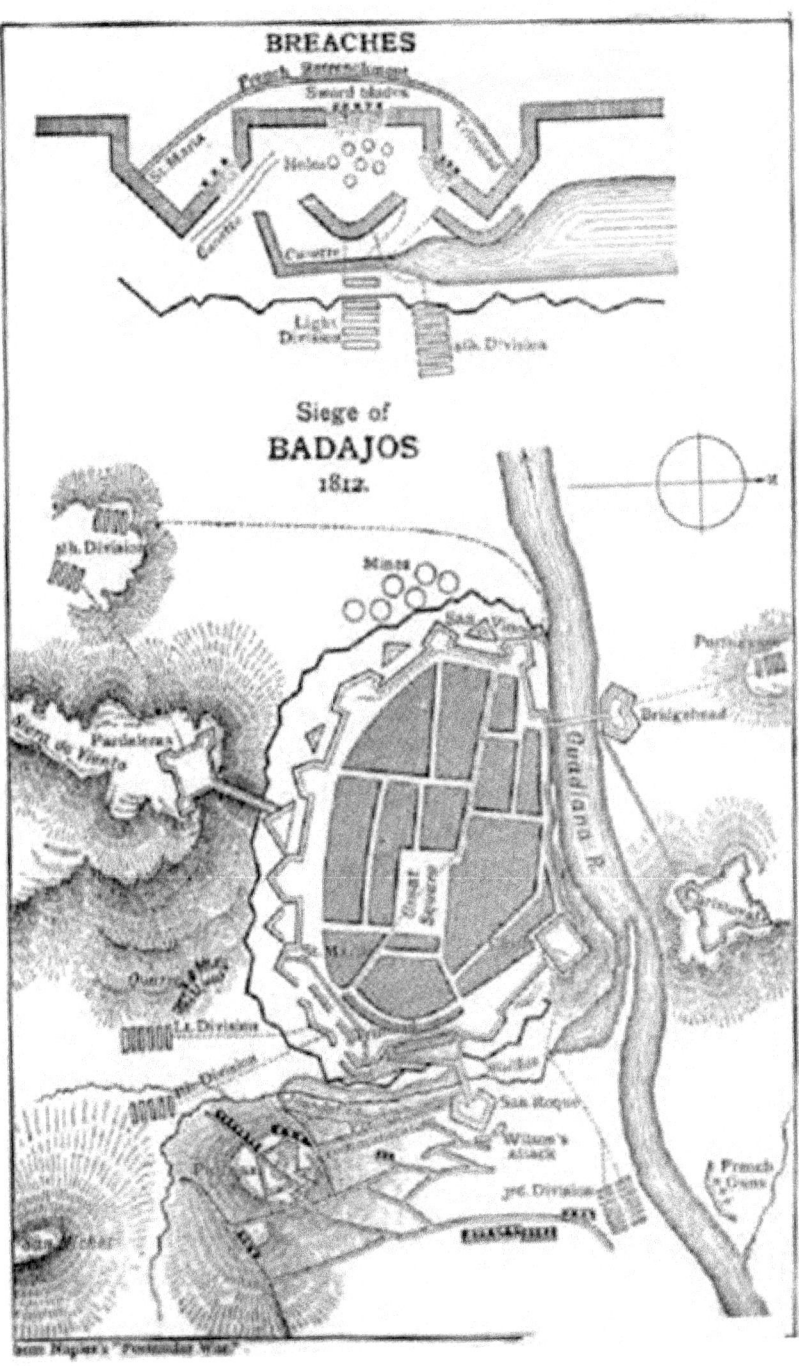

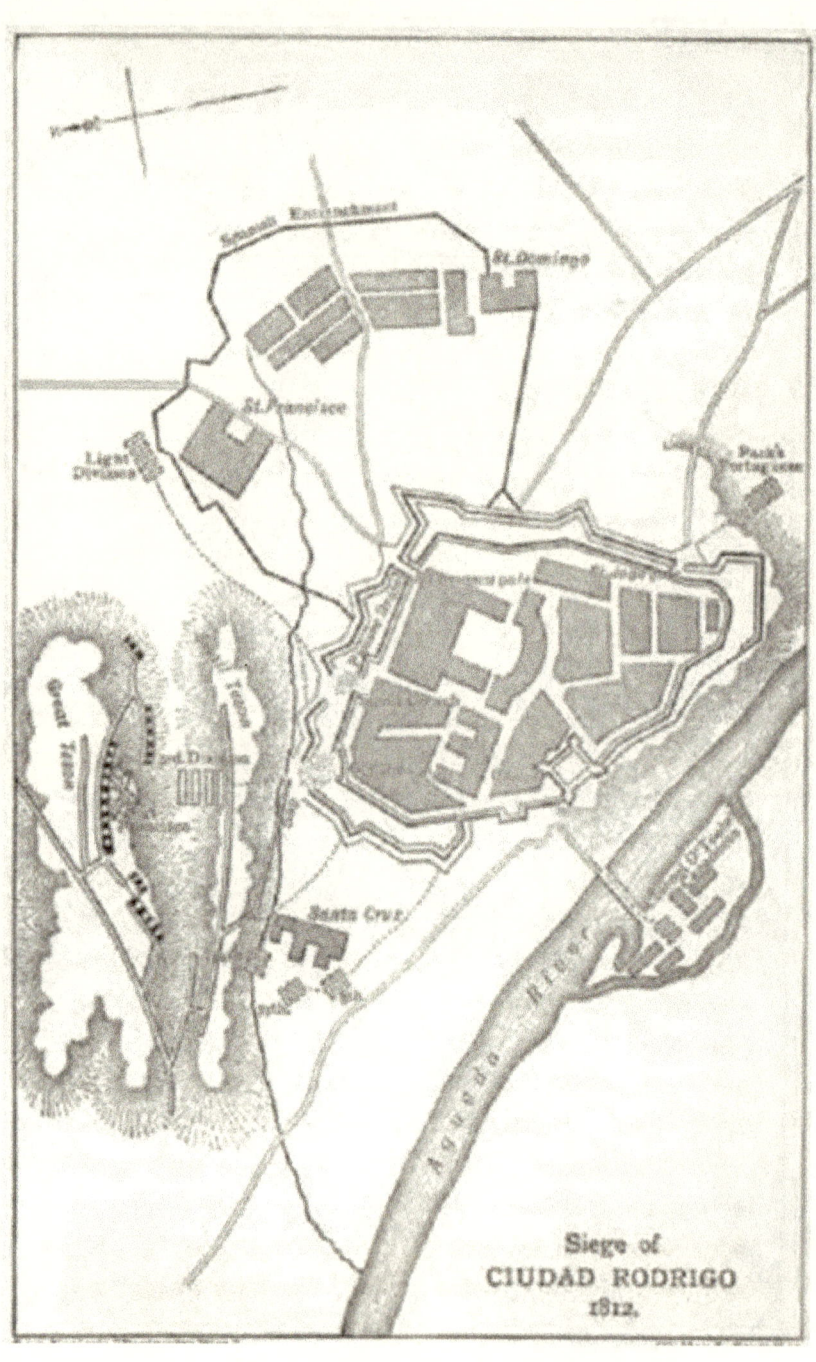

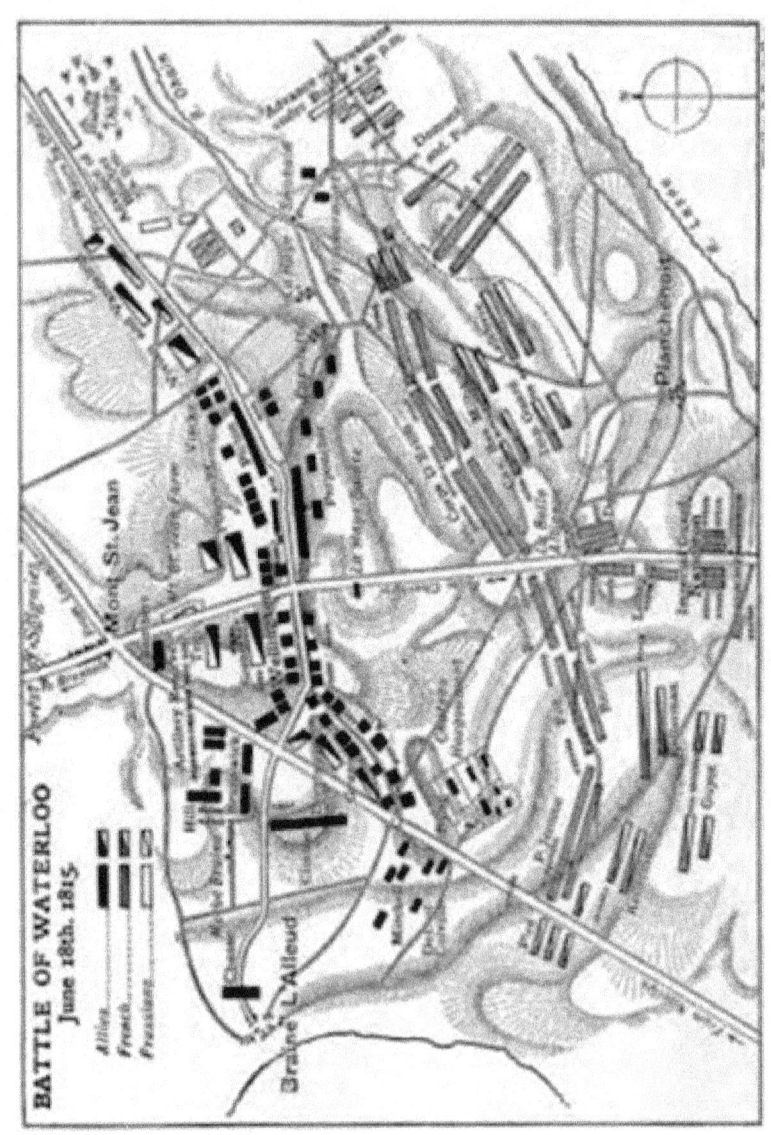

www.ingramcontent.com/pod-product-compliance
Lightning Source LLC
Chambersburg PA
CBHW031618160426
43196CB00006B/184